Kate Colquhoun's previous non-fiction titles were shortlisted for the Duff Cooper Prize 2004 and longlisted for the Samuel Johnson Prize 2003. As well as writing for several newspapers and magazines, she appears regularly on national radio and television. She lives in London with her husband and two sons.

# MR BRIGGS' HAT

*A Sensational Account of Britain's First
Railway Murder*

## KATE COLQUHOUN

Little, Brown

LITTLE, BROWN

First published in Great Britain in 2011 by Little, Brown

Copyright © Kate Colquhoun, 2011

The moral right of the author has been asserted.

A CIP catalogue record for this book
is available from the British Library.

Hardback ISBN 978-1-84744-369-4
C-format ISBN 978-1-84744-370-0

Typeset in Sabon by M Rules
Printed and bound in Great Britain by
Clays Ltd, St Ives plc

Little, Brown
An imprint of
Little, Brown Book Group
100 Victoria Embankment
London EC4Y 0DY

An Hachette UK Company
www.hachette.co.uk

www.littlebrown.co.uk

Central London. Detail from the 1862 Weekly
Dispatches map of London.

# Contents

BOOK THREE: JUDGEMENTS

What began with shock quickly developed into nervousness, fear and then destabilising doubt. From a muggy July in 1864 to a freezing November, not only London – then the greatest city in the world – but much of Europe and even North America was galvanised by the events described by the newspapers of the time as a *terrible drama of real life*.

The details of this account are drawn from primary record.

# PROLOGUE

# An Empty Railway Carriage

On the evening of 9 July 1864, Benjamin Ames, a thirty-eight-year-old train guard, was on edge. The 9.45 p.m. from London's Fenchurch Street terminus to the suburb of Chalk Farm was already five minutes behind schedule and, in the rush, there was no time to relock the carriage doors between stops. The train's driver ran the engine hard, reaching speeds of 25 mph and, hopeful that they were clawing back precious minutes, guard Ames dutifully recorded the exact time they pulled out of each station – Stepney at 9.55 p.m., Bow at 10.01 p.m. and Hackney Wick (also known as Victoria Park) Station just four minutes later at 10.05 p.m.

At 10.10 p.m. they had arrived at Hackney Station – the midway point on the line – but as Ames hurried to slam the carriage doors he was irritated to hear a commotion coming from the front of the train, threatening to scupper all his attempts to get it back on time. Harry Vernez and Sydney Jones, both employees in the banking house of Robarts, Curtis & Co. in the City, were calling out that something was wrong. The young clerks had just installed themselves in an empty compartment of the furthest forward of the varnished teak first-class carriages when Jones discovered blood on his hands and on the seat of his trousers.

Like most English locomotives at that time, each varnished teak carriage of the North London Railway train was divided into several separate, isolated compartments. Doors on either side, usually locked before leaving each station, opened onto the platform or the tracks but there was no communication corridor or door between them. Once in motion, passengers were unable to call to the driver, the guard or to passengers travelling in adjoining sections of the carriage.

Each box-like 'room' had two pairs of seats on either side, divided by an armrest, and was so narrow that ladies sitting opposite each other found their voluminous skirts pressed together and fussed with the ends of their shawls to prevent them becoming entangled. The stuffed seat cushions were upholstered in buttoned blue cloth with tough American leather underneath. On the floor was a strip of rough cocoa matting and overhead swung luggage racks made of thickly meshed cord. Each of the side windows was barred with sturdy brass rods to prevent passengers leaning out and each had a leather strap for passengers to steady themselves against the jolting of the locomotive. A single, smoky gaslight hung in the centre of the wooden partition wall, casting an unnatural yellow glow.

Cursing the fuss being made by the clerks, guard Ames retreated to his brake van at the extreme end of the train to fetch a bright hand-lamp and returned to enter the clerks' compartment, raising it before him. The first thing he saw was an upturned cushion.

As the guard's eyes adjusted to the light he was dimly aware that the air of the compartment was sickly-sweet. Then it dawned on him that some kind of vicious struggle had taken place. On the left-hand side – nearest the engine – blood pooled in the buttoned indentations of the cushions. It was still wet. Another large red spatter about the size of a crown piece trickled down the glass pane of the quarter-light on the same side, skirting round a small piece of what looked, to him, like flesh.

On the platform behind him a group of ladies who had just got out of the next-door compartment were complaining that their dresses and capes had been stained by drops – they thought them blood – flying through the open window of their carriage while the train was still moving. Further along the platform, unaware of the dreadful scene revealing itself under the glare of the guard's lamp, departing passengers queued to relinquish their tickets at the narrow gate before passing out into the emptying streets of Hackney. Other travellers with tickets for stations further down the line were taking their seats and expecting the train to pull out at any minute. The driver was waiting for his signal to go.

Ames heard only the buzzing of a fly as he stepped further into the empty carriage. He saw that small drops of blood had sprayed out over the seats on the left-hand side, hitting the padded armrest. Dark marks along the edges of the cushions suggested that bloody hands had been wiped along them. Turning to his right, he noticed, too, that the cloth of the armrest on that side was also saturated.

From the quantity of liquid blood it was apparent that someone had been brutally beaten in the carriage. But Ames had seen no evidence of a wounded man or bloodied assailant when the train stopped at Stepney, Bow or Hackney Wick stations. He had received no reports of screams for help. Had there been no such bellows? It would have been impossible for anyone outside the compartment to have witnessed what had occurred but it seemed extraordinary that such an attack could have gone unheard by anyone in the adjoining compartments. In the stillness of the evening the silent carriage held, for Ames, a chilling echo of menace.

Taking in the fact that the floor matting had been shoved

aside, Ames stepped towards the far side of the compartment, his raised lamp revealing, bit by bit, that the walls and open windows were also sticky with blood. The handles of the off-side door (closed, but unlocked) also appeared to be covered in congealing blood, both inside and out. The engine of the train grumbled, vibrating through the carriages as they lingered at the station. Peering through the window onto the track side of the train Ames saw no sign of movement, nothing odd. Even the sky was peaceful – the birds now tucked in safely under the eaves of the platform roof.

Turning again, lamp in hand, Ames noticed for the first time that the carriage was not as empty as he had at first thought. On the furthest left-hand seat of the carriage was a discarded black leather bag, its brass lock open and marked with darkening red smears. Looking under the same seat, he found a black hat, squashed nearly flat, bearing a maker's name: T. H. Walker, Crawford Street, Marylebone. On the floor close to it lay a thick cane topped with a heavy ivory knob – a 'life preserver' as it was known. It too was marked with a few red spots.

Pulling himself together, Ames drew up the compartment windows, retreated, and locked the doors behind him. Determined to get the train back on schedule, he gave urgent instructions to the Hackney stationmaster to send a telegraph to the railway superintendent at Chalk Farm. Then, stepping up into his brake van, he signalled for the driver to continue.

Though, for the guard, time had appeared to stall, the train had halted at Hackney Station for a mere four minutes. By a quarter past ten it was ploughing on through the warm summer night, preparing to deliver its last few passengers to the handful of remaining stations along the line.

At the Chalk Farm terminus, Station Superintendent George Greenwood, alerted by the telegraph sent from Hackney, was waiting on the platform. Turning away from the last passengers who were leaving through the ticket gate, the sound of their voices dimming as they moved away, Greenwood returned with Ames to the blood-spattered compartment of carriage 69.

The two men removed the crumpled hat, the heavy knobbed stick and the black bag, checked that the windows were firmly closed, and relocked the doors. Then they took the clues to the Superintendent's office and secured them in a locked cupboard. George Greenwood sent for the police.

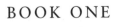

BOOK ONE

# CITY

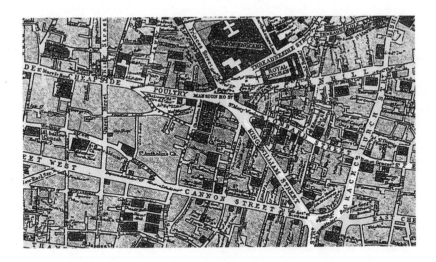

# CHAPTER 1

# *All Human Life*
# *is Here*

In 1864 more than ten thousand miles of railway track stretched across Britain, linking great cities, suburbs and remote country-side towns. Four decades earlier, sober-minded people thought the train, with its obstinate and erratic engine and its wobbling passenger trucks, was almost a madman's toy. Yet, trailing smoke and steam in its wake, the train had compressed the time it once took to journey in a horse-drawn coach from hours into minutes. It had broadened the horizons of every class of British citizen, redefining labour and the transport of goods, becoming vital to the pursuit both of business and recreation.

Since the days of railway madness in the late 1830s and mid-1840s, a wave of speculation and construction had caused a vast network of steel to transform the landscape. Tracks ran over rivers, spanned busy streets and shady lanes, cut swathes through fertile pastures, curved through lonely moorland and even crossed wide stretches of water by means of floating jetties or the iron span bridges constructed by the age's great engineers. In London, the first underground railway in the world opened in

1863. A year later, close to 250 million passenger journeys were taken across Britain, compared with 50 million during 1838 and 111 million in 1855.

Steam power dazzled, and mid-Victorians wondered and enthused at its vigour, energy and spirit. Emblematic of technocratic success, of enterprise, endurance, adventure and civilisation, trains delivered cotton to boats heading for China and India, they brought wool to Yorkshire and coal to the factories fuelling the industrial revolution. They took the post, delivered the exotic goods arriving in British docks from all over the world to shops in towns and villages, and enabled businesses to find new markets for their products. They spread the news of national and international events to the very edges of the country and they allowed Victorians to pursue their lives more quickly than ever had been imagined possible, encouraging leisure excursions among people who had, hitherto, rarely left the safety of their county boundaries.

Railway timetables forced the standardisation of time across the nation, enshrining speed as the new principle of public life: 'railway time' entered the lexicon, vast clocks adorned the façades of stations and it became a commonplace to assert that train journeys had 'annihilated time'. Certainly, although the Bible was the volume at the centre of Victorian society, *Bradshaw's Railway Timetables* – a brick-thick, monthly compendium covering an increasing number of lines with baffling complexity – was catching up. *Everybody grumbles at the railways*, wrote the celebrated railway historian John Pendleton during the 1890s; *they are the scorn of the punctual, the embarrassment of the tardy and the contempt of the irascible; but they have one great distinction – they have shaken us up.*

Trains, he wrote, had become the most *indispensable agent in national life*. Yet, to a society caught between conservatism and progress, the railways fostered ambiguous reactions. In the whistle and shriek of every approaching engine was evidence of rapid social and technological transformation. The stations, viaducts and embankments were conspicuously visible and new, signalling the investment of huge capital and the ascendancy of engineering achievement. They turned modest towns into sprawling cities and created startling new wealth. They were liberating, and they punctuated the map of Britain with possibilities, but they also devoured rural communities and displayed a perilous carelessness for human life – wheels ran off tracks, axles broke, boilers burst and there were countless collisions.

Woven into the excitement of railway travel, a corresponding nervousness had developed about the loss of individual control. The sense of being trapped in a box-like compartment, whirled along at speed and treated like just one in a stream of disposable, moveable goods was, at best, disorientating and, at worst, threatening. This vast force of industrial technology seeped into the language to spawn new metaphors – to 'run out of steam' or 'off the tracks' – and threw the fragility and helplessness of human life into relief. In 1862 the medical journal the *Lancet* published a paper noting that *uneasiness ... amounting to actual fear ... pervades the generality of travellers by rail*. It believed that, disasters aside, train journeys could easily make passengers very unwell: deafening noise confounded the ears, speed taxed the eyes and vibrations had an adverse effect both on the brain and the skeleton. The mental tension of being so transported could, the journal concluded, bring on total physical collapse.

By the 1860s novelists had been exploring the public's deepening apprehensions about the relentlessness of progress, technology and modernity for more than two decades, using the image of the speeding locomotive not just as a potent symbol of the advances of civilisation but of remorseless physical and moral destruction. Collapsing time with such ease, they questioned whether the railways might annihilate the human spirit with equal success. Dickens' Dombey, gripped by gnawing jealousies after the death of his son, is dizzied by *the very speed at which the train was whirled along ... The power that forced itself upon its iron way ... defiant of all paths and roads, piercing through the heart of every obstacle, and dragging living creatures of all classes, ages, and degrees behind it ... was a type of the triumphant monster, Death.*

Feeling vulnerable, rail users voiced their concerns. In the late 1850s, a Commons Select Committee had recommended the adoption by all railway companies of some means of communication between the train guard and his passengers but its suggestions had been ignored. In the first years of the new decade newspapers regularly focused on the plight of ticket-holders trapped in locked carriages with no means of summoning assistance should they need it. There were accusations that railway directors were neglectful and careless and that the government was apathetic and there were repeated demands that train companies should be made legally responsible for the safety of their passengers.

In reality, Victorian trains were fairly safe and reliable. Yet, unsettled by headlines recording 'frightful accidents', a subliminal fear about the pitilessness of their railways had lodged in the minds of second-generation Victorians. What had not yet occurred to anyone was that a passenger might be violently attacked while travelling. With the discovery of the sinister, empty, blood-drenched carriage at Hackney Station, it was becoming clear that something momentous might have occurred.

# CHAPTER 2

## Saturday 9 July 1864

That morning, at about eight o'clock, a substantial and influential banker – aged sixty-nine, standing five feet nine and weighing between eleven and twelve stone – left home for work wearing a shiny black silk 'chimneypot' top hat and carrying a walking cane. Tucked into a small black leather bag was a gift for his favourite niece. Nothing about him suggested that he was marked out for notoriety.

This man, Thomas Briggs, proved the Victorian rule that success repays steady diligence. Moving to London from Lancashire in his late teens, he had soon married Mary, three years his senior, who raised their four sons and two daughters while he toiled in the City of London, dedicating himself to the values most prized by this age: progress and respectability. Within a handful of years he had moved his young family northwards, away from the grime of the capital to the clearer air of the small suburban town of Hackney.

Briggs was now chief clerk at Robarts, Curtis Bank and was established in a fashionably large Regency townhouse at 5 Clapton Square. Boasting a pretty leaded fanlight over the front door, impressive cast-iron balconies and six-panelled doors, it was one of the best addresses in the neighbourhood, and he shared it with five women: Mary, his wife, her widowed sister Charlotte, an unmarried daughter also called Mary, a middle-aged cook and a young housemaid. The dark furniture gleamed, paintings hung in moulded frames and a prized collection of stuffed birds poised motionless under bright glass domes.

It promised to be a fine day as Thomas Briggs left home, turned right and quickly reached the end of the square. Crossing the main road, he strolled through the dappled shade of the churchyard of St John, skirted the medieval, white stone tower of St Augustine and, about six minutes after setting out, arrived at the modest timber structure of Hackney Station. Overhead, the arched, brick viaduct bore the clattering trains of the North London Railway. The station, the viaduct and the line were little more than a decade old and modest, recently built terraces stretched eastwards to meet the small-scale factories on the suburb's borders. In the space of a generation Hackney had grown from a remote neighbourhood of church spires and nursery gardens into an expanding town for the upwardly mobile. No longer reliant on horse-drawn cabs, it now took the inhabitants just twenty minutes to reach the City by train.

Hackney was situated at the halfway point on the North London Railway line from Chalk Farm to Fenchurch Street, a journey that described – roughly speaking – three sides of a square. Briggs took a first-class ticket and sat, as usual, with his back to the engine so that he could open the window without being choked by the smoke and soot that streamed from its chimneys. As the train pulled off towards the east, watercress fields receded and then the waterproofing and bone-crushing factories and the rope and chemical works of Hackney Wick. Then the line curved south, passing the construction site of the vast new Bryant & May match factory, skirting the eastern boundary of the grassy sweep of Victoria Park – London's first public park – before entering districts choked with cheaply built terraces for the working classes. Passing through these neighbourhoods, the train tipped due west again, rattling towards a fog of industrial smoke pierced in all directions by church steeples and factory chimneys.

The small terminus at Fenchurch Street was tucked into the south-eastern corner of the part of the capital known as the City, disgorging noisy hordes of passengers from its four platforms into the streets beyond. Jostled, clutching his cane as he descended the steep stairs to the entrance, Thomas Briggs emerged under a warming sky filled with clouds smudged by greasy smog. His habitual route to work took him along Fenchurch Street, past a labyrinth of multiplying lanes and crowded courts and then across the broad sweep of Gracechurch Street. Down to his left was the River Thames with its clattering harvest of steam and riverboats; straight ahead was Lombard Street, gateway to the stone maze of the mile-square City.

Briggs made his way along the narrow, curving thoroughfare of Lombard Street, past tall stone buildings that dwarfed the scuttling commuters and tradesmen jamming its pavements. On the façades of the stately financial offices hung ornate and gilded clocks; crammed between impressive edifices were chop houses, taverns, shirt-makers, hat shops and silversmiths, each vying for the custom of the black-suited men hurrying past their doors. Running either side to the north and south were similar broad streets, all linked by narrow alleyways housing second-hand clothes merchants, drapers and inns. These were the arteries of the City, each converging on its twin hearts: the dumpy, flat-roofed Bank of England and the grander Royal Exchange.

Fifteen minutes after leaving his train, Briggs reached No. 15 Lombard Street and his bank's imposing building. Every weekday between 9 a.m. and 7 p.m. he worked here, raising capital by issuing shares: money destined to fund new and developing industries, to build new bridges, factories and railway lines and to pump through the veins of the expanding British Empire. Today being Saturday, his working hours were shorter; by three o'clock, his work was done.

When he left work that July afternoon, Briggs turned left and was almost immediately at the end of Lombard Street. Ahead of him was Cheapside, one of the busiest streets in the capital, alive with an incessant stream of carts, cabs and drays, reaching way out to the west beyond the Central Criminal Court and the glowering mass of Newgate gaol, lined with elegant shops selling shawls, silver, feathers, scents and fancy goods from all corners of the world. As usual, hackney cabmen dodged gridlocks to escape into a web of narrow lanes; lawyers, merchants and stockbrokers hurried by under painted signs advertising boots, lace, plate glass or insurance. Men of leisure idled on the pavements, boys pushed handcarts, ragged children ran shouting into filthy courts and impoverished piece-work tailors carried their bundles to and from businesses in Threadneedle Street and St Swithin's Lane. Rising above it all in the near distance was the vast dome of St Paul's Cathedral, a soot-blackened edifice standing sentinel over the thundering tide of the City.

But Cheapside was not Briggs' destination. Instead, he turned left, heading for the stands for the brightly painted horse-drawn omnibuses that ranged along spacious King William Street, each heading out over London Bridge before diverging to follow separate routes. He paid sixpence and took his place on one of the five-a-side seats for the twenty-five-minute journey to the Lord Nelson pub in Peckham. From this stop it was just a short walk to the home of his niece Caroline Buchan, and he arrived there almost exactly at five o'clock.

Three hours later, after dinner, Briggs pulled on a chain attached to the buttonhole of his waistcoat. Fixed to it were a small swivel seal inset with a broken red stone, an old-fashioned key and a heavy gold watch. It was time to retrace his journey back to Hackney.

*

The sun was low and swallows wheeled in the sky as the banker alighted from his omnibus to walk back through the City's stone warrens. Above him, the thin sliver of a bright new moon pulsed from between the clouds. The sounds of the metropolis had thinned. Passing under the great clock on the façade of Fenchurch Street Station and into the station with its modern vaulted roof, he nodded to the newsvendor. Eating his supper on a stool near the booking office, the ticket collector Thomas Fishbourne looked up as Briggs touched him on the shoulder and said goodnight. Alone, the old man mounted the stairs to the platforms, his empty black bag in one hand and his ivory-knobbed cane in the other.

A dozen or so late-comers were still hurrying to join the 9.45 p.m. train which was running a few minutes behind time as Briggs settled himself in the furthest forward of the first-class carriages, in the near-side corner of the compartment with his back towards the engine and his cane and bag on the seat beside him. The doors were slamming.

At 9.50 p.m. the train pulled out of the station and began to pick up speed. As it headed east towards Stepney and then began its wide arc north to Bow, Thomas Briggs may have allowed his eyes to close.

# CHAPTER 3

## *The Duckett's Canal Bridge*

About a third of the way between Bow Station and Hackney Wick Station – also known as Victoria Park – the North London Railway track passed briefly through an undeveloped area bordered by marshes before the line turned west again into the City. On the edge of the over-populated, working-class neighbourhoods of Bow and Bethnal Green, this stretch of track was lonely, with no houses to overlook it – just an iron railway bridge that crossed over a sluggish ribbon of water known as Duckett's Canal.

At half-past ten on the night of Saturday 9 July, Guard Ames's train with its bloodied, locked compartment was still clattering west towards its final stop at Chalk Farm. Edward Dougan, Policeman 71 from the Bow Division of the Metropolitan Police, was on patrol in Wick Lane, a narrow, snaking roadway running north to south from Hackney Wick down to Old Ford. Hugging the eastern boundary of Victoria Park, the lane contained a few houses overlooking the park and an inn called the Mitford Castle.

It was dark and quiet, apart from the muted noises coming

from the tavern and the sound of a train running slowly along the embanked line behind it. Then PC Dougan heard someone call out. More shouts went up. Running towards the noise, the policeman reached a steep grassy slope behind the pub just in time to make out four or five men scrambling in the darkness down the incline. The group was cursing loudly that it had only just been missed by a passing down-train and several of the men were struggling to carry a heavy object between them.

Several minutes earlier, the driver of an empty train returning to Bow had noticed a dark shape between the 'up' and 'down' lines. Stopping the train just as it began to cross the canal bridge, he had reversed and waited while the stoker and the guard went to investigate.

The pale scythe of the moon was blurred by clouds as the two men climbed down from the engine and began to walk back along the tracks in the darkness. A warm breeze rustled the leaves of the trees and whispered through the briar and thorn bushes that spilled over the edges of the canal towpath. It rocked the surface of the streak of black water, feathering the scum that formed at its banks. The cooling air smelled of damp, green grass and of the remains of the smoke that funnelled during the day from the chimneys of the local factories. Small black shadows skittered before the men's footsteps, disappearing into the undergrowth and the brickwork of the viaduct.

The ground sloped sharply down on either side of the tracks as the two men continued along the ridge. The gravel crunched underfoot and a dim murmur of voices swelled from the pub down to their left. Nearing the object seen by their driver, the guard – William Timms – and his companion thought it probable that a large dog had been injured while crossing the line. As they drew closer they began to realise that they were wrong. A human form was lying on its back on the six-foot way – the space between the tracks – its head pointing northwards and its feet towards London. The dark-suited body was twisted, its right leg straight and the left drawn up, the right arm under the body and the left thrown across it. A dark thread of blood trickled freely from its head, soaking into the earth.

The Mitford Castle backed so closely onto the line where it met the canal that the glasses on the bar shivered with each passing locomotive. Inside, customers filled the large tap room with its bare board floors, wide windows, large empty fireplaces, smoky gaslights and an ill-assorted collection of tables and chairs. None of them had been aware of the discovery being made on the tracks behind until their conversations were interrupted by the urgency of William Timms' bellows for assistance.

Alerted by the shouting, the tavern landlord James Hudson and several of his customers had rushed towards the back door, groping blindly in the dark as they crossed the yard and climbed up the embankment towards the noise. PC Dougan had arrived just as they were coming back down again, hefting between them the black-clad body.

Learning that the railwaymen had found a man – insensible and bleeding – between the tracks, young Edward Dougan quickly took control. As the group entered the noisy pub, he directed them to place the limp body on a table in a small, dark-panelled room behind the public bar. Looking down at the man's ghastly-pale face, Dougan saw that blood from several head wounds was beginning to congeal over his forehead; the full, white beard was clotted with blood and wet with blood-flecked spume. The injured man's moans were unintelligible. He was barely alive.

Closing the door against the pub's rough crowd, Dougan sent immediately for a local surgeon and then, with train guard William Timms at his side, he began gently and patiently to search the body. First, he noted that the state of the man's clothes suggested a struggle rather than an accident. A single black stud was all that held his rumpled shirt together; the shirt collar was loose and the disarrayed clothes were spattered here and there with blood. Dougan removed some loose change from the injured man's pockets along with a bunch of keys and half a first-class return train ticket for that day. There was a diamond ring on his little finger, a silver snuffbox and a bundle of letters and papers in his coat pocket. Attached to the third buttonhole of his waistcoat was a single gold fastener for a watch chain, but the chain and its watch were missing.

Carefully, Constable Dougan removed all these belongings, though the watch fastener still attached to the waistcoat proved too complicated for him to undo. Turning his attention to the letters, the policeman found the address of a City bank and gave the order for a runner to go in search of someone who might identify the wounded man and alert his family.

At about eleven o'clock, Alfred Brereton, a recently qualified doctor from the crowded Old Ford area of the Bow neighbourhood, pushed his way into the back room of the tavern. On his orders, the injured man was moved to a more private room upstairs and laid on a mattress on top of a table. Then the doctor tried, but failed, to rouse him.

Taking stock, Dr Brereton's attention was caught by grazes on the skin of the man's forearm and bruises on his hands. Next he examined a jagged wound above and in front of his left ear, so deep that the cartilage was nearly severed from the head. Livid, bruised swellings stretched across the forehead and there were several more wounds to the crown of the head. Conjecturing that some of the lesions on the left side might have been caused by the fall from a moving train, Brereton advised PC Dougan that the more brutal lacerations on the vertex seemed to have been inflicted by a blunt instrument. The weapon had been used with such force that the skull had been crushed.

By midnight two more neighbourhood doctors had arrived at the pub. Both expressed surprise that a man with such extensive wounds was still alive but, like Brereton, they failed to revive him. As the three medics, the train guard and the young constable

waited in the first-floor room they heard, without realising its significance, the rattling wheels of an empty train making its way
back down the railway line to Bow Station. Passing behind the
pub, past the spot on which the injured man had been discovered,
carriage 69 – uncoupled from the rest of the train at Chalk Farm –
was being returned up the line to Bow, where it would be locked
in a shed for months.

*

To the north-west of the Mitford Castle, in Hackney, the elderly
wife of Thomas Briggs and her spinster daughter had expected
his return by half-past ten that evening. As each quarterly chime
from the bells of the nearby church of St John marked Briggs'
failure to arrive home, their anxiety had grown. Then, in the
small hours of Sunday 10 July, a knock was heard. Drawing back
its heavy bolts, the housekeeper opened the front door to a
stranger.

Mrs Briggs soon learnt that a dreadfully injured man believed
to be her husband had been discovered and she dispatched the
housekeeper to wake Thomas James, the second-eldest of her
sons, at his home nearby. At two o'clock, three and a half hours
after William Timms' discovery, this servant and Thomas James
(a marine insurance accountant) arrived at the Mitford Castle
and dashed upstairs. Apparently reacting to the sound of their
familiar voices and the clasp of the housekeeper's hand in his,
Thomas Briggs groaned pitiably. He seemed to be trying to
speak.

As news of the outrage spread, the inn had begun to fill with
locals eager for the latest intelligence, staying well past the time
that regulations forced the bar to close in the hope of hearing the
latest news. Slower to arrive was the Briggs' family doctor,
Francis Toulmin, who elbowed his way through the crowd to
join the huddle of doctors upstairs. Briggs was close to death. All
Toulmin could do was to make him as comfortable as possible

and make arrangements for his patient to be taken back home to Hackney in a litter.

*

By this time, Dr Alfred Brereton had been hanging around in the tavern for several hours and, leaving Toulmin in charge, he asked guard Timms to point out the exact spot where he had found the body. It was three o'clock in the morning as they left the busy upstairs room. Arming themselves with lanterns, they scrambled back up the embankment to the place where the tracks met the canal bridge. Crouching down at the spot pointed out to him by Timms, Brereton took a paper envelope from his pocket and rubbed it over a darkened patch of earth about a foot wide. The paper soaked up still-damp blood. Looking around, Brereton noticed a large, smooth stone close by. Stuck to the thickening smudges of blood on its surface were several grey and white hairs.

By the time Brereton returned to the tavern, the news that a blood-smeared railway carriage had been taken to the Bow sheds was exciting the crowd lingering there to discuss the night's events. The doctor determined to inspect it immediately. At the train depot he found the carriage, its cushions soiled with blood – some still liquid – and its windows streaked and spattered with gobbets of flesh and brain matter.

Brereton was systematic in his scrutiny. Turning his attention to the offside of the carriage – the side furthest from the platform and closest to the centre of the tracks as the train had travelled northwards – he discovered blood on the inside of the door. Climbing down from the compartment to examine its outside, he found more blood on the footboard, the iron step, the rear wheel and on the lower panels of the carriage. It seemed clear to him that Thomas Briggs had fallen head-first, his skull hitting the footboard and glancing off the wheel closest to the door before his body slumped onto the space between the tracks.

Re-entering the compartment, the doctor was struck by a glint in the fibres of the near-side mat and, bending down, he discovered a gold 'jump' link – designed to attach a clasp to a chain and to be its weak point in case of damage – trodden into the flooring. Pocketing it, he left Bow Works, walked directly to the police station in nearby Bromley and delivered the link to the duty sergeant.

*

As it dawned on the police that something unprecedented had occurred, Bow Division's senior officer, Inspector Walter Kerressey, took charge. A burly Irish ex-soldier, Kerressey had been in the force for twenty-five of his forty-five years and he supervised eleven first-class sergeants and over three hundred police constables in his division. By ten o'clock that Sunday morning he was following on the heels of Brereton, minutely examining carriage 69. He had already sent PC Dougan, weary from lack of sleep, to measure the exact distances between the spot at which the body was discovered and the stations on either side of it at Hackney Wick and at Bow. Other constables were walking over the tracks and scouring the banks by the Duckett's Canal bridge for a weapon, a footprint or anything else that might have been overlooked. The normally deserted spot was now swarming with local police.

Taking in the details of the blood-smeared compartment, Inspector Kerressey conjectured that the dark patches visible on the right-hand armrest had been made as a bleeding body was dragged over it, towards the opposite door. Then he travelled on from the Bow sheds to 5 Clapton Square in Hackney, arriving at eleven o'clock. Taken to see the unconscious man, he noted that there was no blood on Briggs' bruised hands, suggesting that the old man had not been the one to open the compartment door. Closely questioning the family, Kerressey then took detailed descriptions of the missing gold chain (a short heavy chain in the

Albert style, attached to a swivel seal and large gold key with the figure of an animal on top) and the clothes Briggs had been wearing when he left for work.

Kerressey then visited Thomas Briggs' Hackney watchmaker, who provided a precise description of the timepiece from his records: a heavy, old-fashioned chronometer with an open face, the workings numbered 1487 and the gold case separately identified by the number 2974. The inspector was beginning to marshal the basic facts of the case. From statements given the previous evening by the stationmaster at Chalk Farm, he knew that three items had been removed from the carriage and another member of his team – Police Constable Lewis Lambert – was sent to retrieve them. Lambert was to take the bag, the walking stick and the crumpled hat to Clapton Square to be identified by the family, before bringing them on to Kerressey at the Bow police station.

*

The house at 5 Clapton Square was filled with stunned family and visitors when, at about two o'clock on Sunday afternoon, the second policeman of the day arrived. Ushered into the parlour, PC Lambert expected the identification of the articles to be a simple but necessary routine. He was wrong. Though the family recognised both the bag and the stick, none of them had seen the flattened hat before. They each swore that it bore no resemblance to Thomas Briggs' hat – a black topper made of best-quality silk Paris nap, lined in white silk and made by his regular hatter, Daniel Digance & Co., 18 Royal Exchange. There was no question about it: the hat found on the train did not belong to the man lying upstairs.

*

At a quarter to midnight – little more than twenty-four hours after boarding the train at Fenchurch Street Station – Thomas Briggs died. He had never regained consciousness.

# CHAPTER 4

## *Ferreting for Detail*

Thomas Briggs' death meant that, for the first time since the invention of the railway, a murder had occurred on a British train. As the news reached his office across London at 4 Whitehall Place, the Police Commissioner Sir Richard Mayne recognised that his force would be expected to move swiftly and decisively or face the public's wrath. He believed that he had just the man for the job.

In 1842 – only thirteen years after the establishment of the first five divisions of the Metropolitan Police by Sir Robert Peel – Mayne and his co-chief Charles Rowan had obtained government sanction to create a new species of police inspector. No longer primarily concerned with the *prevention* of crime and without the visible authority of a uniform, these were the first detectives: eight conscientious men were selected, including Stephen Thornton and Jack Whicher. Encouraged by the adulation of writers like Dickens, Britain had broadly allowed itself to be seduced into a belief in the brilliance of these perspicacious, dogged, plain-clothed detectives. Scepticism, though, was growing, and admiration was balanced by distrust as delays and

irresolution from the elite investigators emphasised their fallibility. With this railway murder to solve, their reputation, once
again, was on the line.

Commissioner Mayne was now in his late sixties but the running of the Metropolitan Police remained his vocation. Lean and
distinguished with sharp cheekbones, a tightly compressed mouth
and hawkish eyes, he was dictatorial, averse to delegation and
prone to abrasiveness. With a single-focus determination that
awed his department, Mayne spent his days barking directives:
from dictates on expenses and the policing of coffee stalls to
instructions on how to wear the new 'Roman' helmets and chin
straps. Managing resignations, promotions, fines, dismissals and
rewards, he was also fanatical about minutiae, including the
proper management of race meetings, public houses and hackney
cabs; every day his spiky scrawl covered multiple pages of internal memoranda designed to keep his force on its toes.

Mayne chose a man he considered 'brilliant' to lead the investigation into Thomas Briggs' death: Detective Inspector Richard
Tanner. Like the best in the force, Tanner relied less on superior
intellect than on experience, tip-offs and the flat-footed errors of
judgement of most of his quarry. Five foot seven, with brown
hair, piercing blue eyes, a fair complexion and an open face, he
had joined the metropolitan force from his home in rural Surrey
as a constable in March 1851, aged just nineteen. Within three
years he had transferred to the Chief Office of the Metropolitan
Police in Whitehall Place, backing onto Scotland Yard, and was
soon busily nabbing pickpockets, counterfeiters, fraudsters and
'roughs'.

Tanner – known to his friends and colleagues as Dick – had
learned to rely on nods and winks from unlikely quarters, to
evaluate tips quickly and to separate malicious gossip from useful
information. He had watched the methods of the men in charge,
learning how to gather the reports and depositions needed to 'get
up' cases and make them stick. He gained experience in giving

evidence at trial and stored in his memory a cast-list of receivers, inciters and criminals along with their regular haunts, associates and aliases. As each investigation was completed, his income was supplemented by rewards from the Police Fund and by gifts and gratuities from grateful victims or their families – it was not uncommon to receive an extra five pounds or even twenty (six months' salary for an ordinary artisan) for a job well done.

Four years before the attack on Thomas Briggs, Richard Tanner had been a junior member of Detective Inspector Stephen Thornton's team, investigating the notorious Stepney killing of Mary Emsley. The young policeman had been cautious when their suspect – James Mullins – called at his home with 'information' about another man. Afterwards, he had also noticed that parcel tape on the suspect's mantelpiece matched that used on a suspicious package and, by having a bloody footprint cut from the boards of Emsley's wooden floor, Tanner had amassed crucial evidence that eventually sealed the man's fate in court. Walter Kerressey had also been a member of that investigative team and the case had given the two men their first in-depth experience of a widely publicised murder.

Tanner was now thirty-one, fresh from promotion to Inspector in the detective branch at Scotland Yard that spring. Married to Emma, he lived in nearby Westminster with her and their two small children. He was energetic and thorough, but the killing of Thomas Briggs was an unusually important case: it could make or break him.

*

Tanner took stock, knowing that progress in the first few days was crucial for morale, momentum and public confidence. At the Bow Division his old friend Inspector Kerressey, along with Superintendent Daniel Howie and PCs Lewis Lambert and Edward Dougan, had already ferreted for detail in the obvious places. Now Tanner pondered the bare facts already known, looking for clues.

First he considered the time of the attack. Dougan had measured the railway line. From Bow Station to the point at which the body was found totalled 1434 yards. From that spot to the next station at Hackney Wick or Victoria Park was 740 yards. Thomas Briggs had fallen from the train approximately two-thirds of the way between the two stations and, since train guard Ames reported that they had covered that distance on Saturday night in four to five minutes, Tanner could estimate that the assault took place in the three and a half minutes from 10.01 p.m. when the train pulled out of Bow Station.

Second, Tanner considered motive. The disappearance of Briggs' gold watch and chain suggested theft, but the victim's diamond ring and silver snuffbox had been left untouched and the loose change in his various pockets added up to almost five pounds – equivalent to a month's wages for a skilled labourer. This indicated that the assailant was working alone and in a hurry. But that supposition did not account for how the crime had been committed with such speed and without attracting notice. Despite the valuables left behind, the detective had to accept the idea that perhaps more than one man had been involved.

Tanner then went over the reports of the discovery of the injured victim. Briggs had lain unnoticed between the 'up' and 'down' tracks for only twenty minutes. Had his assailant meant to throw him from the train into the dark canal as it passed over the bridge, where his body might have eluded notice for hours? If so, had he simply mistaken the correct door? Or had he *meant* for his body to land on the line in the hope that the next passing train would cut it to pieces leading, perhaps, to a supposition of suicide?

The young detective wondered whether there was an obvious suspect. The ticket collector working at Hackney Wick Station on Saturday night had reported a rush among the rowdy crowd of passengers leaving the train at that stop. He described one –

a tall, dark-coated man who appeared to be in a hurry – kicking up a fuss about the delay at the ticket gate. This man's behaviour might be suspicious. Alternatively, as the engine waited at the Hackney Wick platform for its signal, the state of the empty compartment had gone unnoticed. No one appeared to have seen a bloodied man, or men, but it would have been possible to scramble down the embankment by the station rather than use the stairs, or to jump out of the unlocked carriage from the wrong side, land on the six-foot way and from there cross to the opposite track. It was also possible that the attacker – or attackers – had leapt from the moving train between stations, sliding down the steep ridge running to Duckett's Canal to disappear into the marshes or the crowded slums of Old Ford.

There was one certainty: the crushed hat left in the carriage did not belong to Thomas Briggs. Had it been innocently forgotten by a previous passenger? Tanner believed not. He thought it more likely that the hat belonged to the murderer who, in his keenness to escape, had mistaken Briggs' hat for his own. If he could track down the person who had worn this hat on Saturday night, Tanner was convinced that he would have the murderer. The question was, how to set about finding the owner among the millions of men in England's teeming capital city?

His first act was to circulate descriptions of Thomas Briggs' missing watch and chain to police stations, pawnbrokers and jewellers across London. Meanwhile, Inspector Kerressey's men were attempting to piece together the banker's movements during the previous day by interviewing the Briggs family and their associates. Statements had already been taken from Thomas Fishbourne (the ticket collector from Fenchurch Street Station) and from David Buchan, the husband of Briggs' niece.

Next, Tanner began to draft posters including details of the murder and descriptions of the stolen watch, chain and mistaken hats. Earlier that afternoon, Henry Lubbock, senior partner of Robarts, Curtis & Co., had visited the Home Secretary to pledge one hundred pounds in return for information leading to an arrest and conviction. The government had matched the offer so that Tanner was able to offer £200 for information received. Two thousand posters were rushed to print and dispatched to police stations across the capital and throughout the country. By Monday morning they would be hanging on placards and stuck to the walls outside police station houses, omnibus and news-stands and railway termini. The reward – four or five times what a working-class man might expect to earn in a year – was just what Tanner needed to flush out the murderer.

# CHAPTER 5

## *Morbid, Hideous and Delicious*

The new week opened to strident newspaper headlines broadcasting an *Atrocious Murder on the North London Railway*. Every known fact was reported: the contents of Briggs' pockets, the hat, stick and bag now in police custody, the broken link still attached to the waistcoat buttonhole, the distances and times taken to travel between stations, the serial number of the watch, a description of the missing chain and the names of all attending surgeons at the Mitford Castle tavern. Thomas Briggs was described as a *gentleman*. The *outrageous* act, readers were reminded, had been perpetrated in a *first-class carriage*.

The newspaper reports contained the usual mix of prurience and moral indignation, lingering on macabre descriptions of the pools and spurts of blood and the respectability of the victim. The lightning speed of the attack seemed astonishing. The fact that no one could have come to save him, had they heard Briggs cry out for help, provoked alarm. Each of the reports noted the disappearance of the banker's watch and chain but, in the welter of detail, there was misreporting too: both *The Times* and the *Daily News* wrote that Briggs' head had been battered with a sharp instrument, that his glasses were missing and that his left ear had been severed from his head; it was also suggested that he had been bundled out of the window of the train.

There was conjecture about the number of attackers and whether the murder was in fact a suicide. Doctors, swift to take up their pens to write to the papers, posited that the blood that spurted through the windows of neighbouring compartments was the result of an artery rupturing as the victim was being forced from the train. Some wondered whether, as Briggs went to the window to call for help, the door had flown open, precipitating him onto the line. Others suggested that Briggs had opened the train door himself and jumped out in order to escape robbery – a surmise deftly countered by another correspondent who pointed out that *someone* had closed the door behind him.

Most newspapers were quick to remind their readers of a robbery on the same spot some years earlier after which the thief had jumped from the train with the intention of escaping through the marshes – only to be captured and sentenced to penal servitude. The coincidence seemed extraordinary. Further, it appeared at least *curious* that the men claiming to have discovered the bloody compartment were fellow clerks in Briggs' own bank. Whatever their speculations, these reports were printed before Inspector Tanner's leadership of the investigation had been announced, and they all laid particular emphasis on their belief that the Bow police team headed by Inspector Kerressey were *instituting every possible inquiry with a view of detecting the guilty parties.* Failing, perhaps, to appreciate its significance, the intriguing intelligence that a broken hat had been found in the carriage and that it was assumed to belong to the murderer, *he having taken Mr Briggs' hat in mistake*, came almost as an afterthought.

If some from the middle classes felt a frisson of fear as they read their papers that day then it would not have been an entirely unfamiliar feeling. A new genre of extraordinarily popular literature had begun to appear during the early 1860s, swiftly

characterised as 'sensational'. Among these novels were Mary
Elizabeth Braddon's infamous *Lady Audley's Secret* (1862) and
Wilkie Collins' *The Woman in White* (1860) and all of them
were typically designed to unsettle readers with complex plots
that revolved around stolen inheritances, poisonings, imprison-
ments, adulteries, illegitimacies and night-shrouded skulduggery.
'Sensation novels' took as their settings not the urban criminal
underworld favoured by Dickens but the apparently safe domes-
ticity of rural country houses, and they caught the public
imagination, dominating the literary scene with their tales of
mystery, suspense and danger.

Sometimes called 'newspaper novels', the plots of these books
might have been taken straight from the Newgate Calendar – an
annual compendium of violent crime – and they mirrored the
emotive press coverage of extreme offences, feeding the Victorian
appetite for reading about transgression and brutality. Designed
to electrify the nerves, they proclaimed themselves to be (as Mrs
Braddon put it) *morbid, hideous and delicious*. In other words,
fear was part of their appeal.

But while it was titillating to read about murder from the comfort of an over-stuffed armchair, sensation novels – because they
located crime right at the heart of bourgeois homes – also hinted
uncomfortably at cracks within the Victorian ideal, insinuating
that even respectable society concealed a dark, criminal underside.
Critics were alarmed both by their lack of restraint and by their
tendency *to drug our thought and reason*; they considered them
to be an 'inferior' form of fiction and derided them as the *abominations of the age*. Despite the fact that they were dubbed
*dangerous and foolish*, the books were vigorously promoted by
the new bookstalls established by W. H. Smith on station con-
courses in the wake of the railway revolution, and they were
phenomenally successful, selling in their tens of thousands.

The murder of Thomas Briggs in a first-class railway carriage
so close to the centre of the metropolis, with its attendant air of

impenetrable mystery, was supra-sensational. It suggested an implicit threat to the day-to-day safety of society as a whole, as if the plot of a novel were spilling over into reality. The critic Richard Holt Hutton had written in 1861 that *every year* [sensation novels] *wander further afield in search of novelty, and glance more and more wistfully at the unexhausted store of the horrible, exceptional or morbid incident.* This murder, committed in a public – but effectively locked – space, broke all known rules. It pricked at the horrible fear that, beyond the pages of a novel, one's own ordinary existence could also be plunged into a chaotic hell. And, whereas sensation novels concluded with the discovery of wicked secrets and the restoration of order, the murderer (or murderers) of Thomas Briggs were unidentified and at large. It was a reality that unsettled every member of the public who travelled by train, shattering confidence in the security of their established routines.

The crime played, too, on an undefined but pervading sense of latent danger that had begun to develop during the 1860s. Second-generation Victorians were finding themselves increasingly anxious as they struggled to make sense of the rapidity of change in the world around them. It turned out that all that much-admired and ever-accelerating progress was also destabilising many of the orthodoxies that once sustained society. New and controversial theories propounded by men like Charles Darwin – *On the Origin of Species* had been published only five years earlier, in 1859 – confirmed that people could no longer rely on centuries-old geological, Biblical and scientific certainties. New wealth destabilised old hierarchies and class structures. Modernity changed everything and its benefits and drawbacks were vigorously debated. Lurking beneath it all was a growing uncertainty about where the individual fitted into this new moral and physical universe.

The railways more than anything else – both tyrannical industrial monsters and engines of progress – seemed to crystallise

# CHAPTER 6

## The Smiling Face of a Murderer

Letters from a public agitated by the news of the train murder were arriving at newspaper-editors' desks and at police stations all over the capital. One delivered to Scotland Yard suggested that tickets collected on the night of 9 July should be inspected for obvious signs of blood in order to surmise at which station the murderer had left the train and therefore where he had embarked. Another wrote that two frustrated bank clerks *known to be guilty of the darkest deeds* were seen entering the City at about eight o'clock on Saturday evening. The anonymous correspondent contended that a third man had been seen hanging around suspiciously with *a wach and chane* [sic] *and . . . a ring which I have never seen before.*

One of these notes stood out. It was delivered to Kerressey at the Bow police station at ten-thirty on Monday morning, sent by John Death (pronounced *Deeth*), the owner of a prosperous jewellery business in a district close to Thomas Briggs' bank. Death claimed that a gold Albert chain very like the one described in the morning papers, with its hook missing, had been exchanged at his shop earlier that very morning. Kerressey hailed a cab and travelled south-west to No. 55 Cheapside, right in the centre of the busiest thoroughfare in the City.

Death had worked in the same business for more than thirty of his fifty-one years. In his early days as a shop-man, employed by a person with an equally memorable name – Mr Greedy Mott – the jeweller had been woken one night by the sound of shattering glass and had chased a young thief through the gloomy neighbouring churchyard of St Mary-le-Bow. Called to give evidence in court, he had watched from the witness benches as the arrested youth was found guilty and sentenced to hang.

John Death now owned and ran the shop with the assistance of his brother Robert. He explained to Kerressey that, at about ten o'clock that morning, a stranger came to exchange an old-fashioned gold chain for something more modern. Using a pair of scales, John had weighed the stranger's chain and valued it at three pounds ten shillings – a shop-man's monthly wage; then he had offered the customer an alternative chain worth five shillings more.

The man had demurred, making it clear that he preferred to make a straight swap. Consequently, Death showed him several slightly cheaper chains from which the man selected a square-oval, secret-link Albert chain with a knot-pattern twisted key and a swivel seal. This one was worth five shillings less than the chain he had brought with him and, to make up the difference, the stranger chose a second-hand signet ring set with a white cornelian stone engraved with the figure of a head. He put the ring on his finger and took away the replacement chain packed in a small cardboard box bearing the name and address of the shop. The transaction had taken no longer than ten minutes.

At the time, nothing about the deal had struck Death as out of the ordinary; it was only later, as he caught up with the newspaper reports and read the description of Thomas Briggs' stolen chain with its missing jump link, that his suspicions had been aroused. In retrospect, John Death thought that this customer had been at pains to stand away from the showcases, as if nervous that he might be suspected of something underhand. He seemed shifty, avoiding the light from the windows and turning his face so that it was always partly concealed. Both brothers were adamant that they had never seen him before but they were able to give a detailed description of a fellow around thirty years old with a pale, almost sallow face, clean-shaven and without beard or side-whiskers. He wore a black frock coat and waistcoat, dark trousers and a black hat and he spoke good English with a foreign accent – possibly German or Swiss.

Examining the chain with a magnifying glass, Inspector Kerressey could find on it no traces of blood. Dirt, though, was visible on the inside of the links, suggesting that it had not been cleaned before it was brought to the shop. If this *was* Briggs' chain – and it matched the description – then it must have been wrenched from his waistcoat before the murderous blows had sent blood flying. Pocketing the chain, Kerressey left Cheapside and travelled north to 5 Clapton Square. It took only seconds for Briggs' daughter to identify it as her late father's property.

\*

Together with Superintendent Daniel Howie from Bow Division, Richard Tanner was also bound for Hackney, heading for the Prince of Wales tavern in Dalston Lane where Mr John Humphreys, the coroner for East Middlesex, was due to open the inquest into Thomas Briggs' death. The inquest's function, unaltered for centuries, was to establish both the fact of any suspicious death and, if possible, its cause. The coroner and his jury would consider whether enough evidence existed to prove that a crime had been committed – the *corpus delicti*; if there was a clear suspect, they would also have the power of formal accusation, effectively recommending legal action. In the crowded tavern that was just minutes away from his home at Clapton Square, the banker's body was laid out for inspection. Despite the horrific injuries to the side and top of his head, his face was calm. It appeared even to be smiling.

Things got underway as thirteen local men, all of them petty tradesmen, shop workers or junior clerks, were sworn to the jury. Then, Thomas James Briggs confirmed that the dead man was his father and identified the diamond ring and the walking stick as well as a pair of spectacles and a pocket book found in the pockets of his coat. The black bag, he said, had been borrowed from his younger brother, Netterville. Edward Dougan (the policeman in Wick Lane when the shout went up on the line) and Lewis Lambert (sent to retrieve the hat, stick and bag from Chalk Farm Station) also gave their version of events. Since it was impossible to continue without a known cause of death, these testimonies simply marked the formal commencement of the coroner's task. Little more than an hour after taking his seat, Mr Humphreys adjourned the proceedings for a week pending results of the post-mortem scheduled to take place the following day. There had been no mention of Inspector Kerressey's interview with John Death but Inspector Tanner knew it and was pleased: the swift recovery of Briggs' chain would give his investigation an early boost, suggesting that whoever was behind the attack on Thomas Briggs was making mistakes. The police had the hat left behind in carriage 69; now they could focus their attention on Death's young foreigner.

The following day – Tuesday 12 July – the story of *The London Murder* circulated through British households, giving voice to a burgeoning middle-class nervousness. *The Times* observed that *great surprise has been expressed that so fearful a murder should have been committed merely for the sake of an old fashioned watch and chain ... and many persons are of the opinion that the object of the murder was not merely robbery.* Had the perpetrator been mistaken in supposing that Briggs' black bag – *of the type generally used by bankers' clerks in removing bullion* – contained a heavy quantity of coin? Had the victim been observed for some time; in which case, had the violent attack been planned? Did this explain the unaccountable ease of the murderer's escape?

Reports fussed over the peculiar coincidence that two of Briggs' colleagues, Harry Vernez and Sydney Jones, had been the first to discover the bloody carriage. Curiously, even before the news of John Death's revelation had been announced, there were those who believed that the shape of the buckled hat supposedly belonging to the murderer was *something like those worn by foreigners*.

Shock and anger began to give way to fear. What disturbed the public mind above all was the notion that, since the murderer had so successfully managed both to enter a first-class carriage and to remain unremarked in his flight from the bloody compartment, he – or they – did not *look* like killers. They might have recalled the words of Robert Audley, hero of one of those recent sensational novels, who believed *that we may walk unconsciously in an atmosphere of crime, and breathe none the less freely. I believe that we may look into the smiling face of a murderer and admire its tranquil beauty.* Playing on that fear, the *Daily Telegraph* thought it *impossible to imagine circumstances of greater apparent security than those which seemed to surround Mr Briggs ... travelling first-class for a mere step of a journey, on a line where stations occur every mile or so ... If we can be murdered thus* – it wrote – *we may be slain in our pew at church or assassinated at our dinner table.*

\*

Five doctors were charged with conducting Thomas Briggs' postmortem that morning, including Brereton and the family doctor Toulmin. First they catalogued the bruises and scratches on Briggs' hands, knuckles and left forearm – wounds that appeared to have been made as he defended himself against blows from his assailant. Then the body itself was scrutinised. There were no extreme injuries: as each organ was removed, it was pronounced intact.

Focusing on his head, the doctors noted the deep, jagged wound that had severed the cartilage of the left ear. Anterior to that another wound extended to the bone and appeared to have been caused by something sharp. A further blow had fractured the whole of the upper portion of the temporal bone with such force that it was driven in, dividing and crushing the ear itself.

On the crown of the head were three incised wounds, each about three-quarters of an inch in length, and a fourth that measured three inches across. All of them appeared to have been made by blows directed from front to back and all extended through the scalp, cutting down into the pericranium (the skull membrane). Peeling back Briggs' grazed scalp to expose the cranium, the doctors found *a great quantity of effused blood* and a skull so extensively fractured that fissures in the bone radiated much like the damage inflicted on a sheet of plate glass by a stone. A small triangular portion of the parietal bone fell away from the rest of the skull. Blood was found between the scalp and the calvarium (or skull-cap) and there was more between the dura mater (or brain's membrane) and the brain itself. In other words, the fracture of Thomas Briggs' skull had produced a substantial and fatal sub-cranial haemorrhage.

*Fracture of the skull and compression of the brain* were recorded as the official causes of death. The doctors judged that some of these injuries, including the deep incision over the ear, could have been caused by the fall from the train as Briggs' head struck the stones between the tracks. The wounds over the crown, though, were consistent with powerful blows from a dull instrument. These strikes were all from above and they looked as though they were aimed first at the victim's left temple, consistent with the theory that Briggs had dozed off, resting his head against the side of the carriage as he journeyed home. It appeared that his assailant had then struck him repeatedly on the top of his head as he struggled to defend himself. Any one of the blows would have been sufficient to kill.

During the few violent seconds of the attack, Thomas Briggs had stood little chance. As his blood spattered over the windows, sides and cushions of carriage 69, he may not even have cried out. Yet it was difficult to credit the possibility that the train door had been opened and slammed again behind Briggs' falling body without drawing the slightest attention. Why had no one yet come forward to help the police?

# CHAPTER 7

## *Something to Astonish the Public*

Across London in the Palace of Westminster, black-suited gentlemen were raising angry questions in Parliament. Just days after the Board of Trade's letter to railway companies asking them to consider the introduction of an effective method of communication between passengers and their train guard, Thomas Briggs had become the victim of *one of the foulest murders committed in our time.* Alexander Baillie Cochrane – the fiery MP for Honiton – now demanded to know when the Board would compel railway directors to take action, but Milner Gibson – the President of the Board of Trade – was impatient with such questions. He believed that governmental interference would diminish the responsibility of the companies to act and, further, that alteration to existing carriages would be so costly that it would render any innovation financially impractical. Gibson's blunt refusal to consider the introduction of a new bill to force action from the railway companies garnered boos and groans from a substantial portion of the House.

It also galled newspaper editors. *The Times* accused the Board of Trade of having committed murder through neglect. It considered railway directors despotic and the government careless of public safety, recalling examples of carriages on fire and desperate passengers unable to alert the driver or guard. It also highlighted the plight of an eighteen-year-old called Mary Anne Moody, indecently assaulted by a fellow second-class passenger only a fortnight earlier. So terrified was Moody that she had tried to escape through the door, tottering on the primitive footboard as the train steamed along at 40 mph. Had a gentleman in a neighbouring compartment not leaned through the bars of his window and gripped her round the waist until the train pulled to a halt more than five miles later, she would most certainly have perished.

The murder was focusing attention on the closed, separate compartments endured by railway travellers and calls for government intervention grew louder by the hour. Many remembered the murder of an eminent French magistrate in December 1860. Judge Poinsot had been shot and robbed as he travelled in a first-class railway carriage through France, and his audacious murder had set writers thinking. In 1862 William Makepeace Thackeray wondered: *have you ever entered a first-class railway carriage, where an old gentleman sat alone in sweet sleep, daintily murdered him, taken his pocket book, and got out at the next station?* The following year a story in the *Globe* magazine described *the loudest screams ... swallowed up by the roar of the rapidly revolving wheels, and murder – or violence worse than murder –* [going] *on to the accompaniment of a train flying along at 60 mph.*

Within three decades railway carriages would irrevocably enter the public imagination as crime scenes in Zola's novel *La Bête Humaine* (1890). Taking the murder of Poinsot as its inspiration, the novel's plot would centre on the traumatic image of a deadly struggle in a gas-lit carriage witnessed by a passenger on a train passing in the opposite direction, impotent to assist. It would end with a runaway train plunging towards disaster, symbol of a society hell-bent on its own destruction.

The murderer of Judge Poinsot – supposedly a scarred, broken-toothed criminal called Charles Judd – had never been caught. *The Times* now believed that *it is plain that no man is safe from assassination, no woman from rape, as long as people are left, sometimes for more than an hour, with the impossibility of making known their situation*. Death, the paper suggested, was lurking in every traveller's shadow. For the privileged few, first-class travel had hitherto appeared to promise the safety of segregation, keeping the rough and the smooth comfortably apart. Now the isolation that had been so pleasurable was becoming unnerving and a feverish idea was taking hold: that the closed compartment was a provocation to murder, and that the multiple colliding worlds of the railway traveller represented unmanageable danger.

Fear radiated along the length of every train: anyone might be doubted, especially if he had the look of a foreigner. *Worst of all*, wrote the *London Review*, *is the horrid consciousness, not merely that you are uneasy, but that you are making the traveller in the opposite corner uneasy too ... Both parties simultaneously feel that it is possible Mr Briggs' murderer was affable in his manners. You know, as the train rolls on, that though he may pretend to be looking out of the window, your vis-à-vis is keeping half an eye upon your movements, and that you are keeping half an eye on his.* Some considered arming themselves. Others wondered if they should make out their wills before embarking on a train journey.

As the reaction of the public grew more febrile, the police worked under the pressure of constant scrutiny and were besieged with advice from the public in letters that told of shifty men in pawnbrokers' shops, dodgy characters on trains in Nottingham, Italian refugees of *desperate character* and murderous forgers and fraudsters. One correspondent hinted that employees of lunatic asylums who were not on duty on that day should be questioned, because *the fact of the body being thrown out in some short time proves it to have been someone in the daily practice of overcoming resistance and in ready knowledge of disposing of their victims.* Someone else suggested that drawings should be made of the wounds to Briggs' head. Then, using men of different heights, he posited, the police should reconstruct the battering to determine the height of the assassin, because *experiments will show that a man 6 feet high and a man 5 foot cannot make the same line or cut.* It was a theory startlingly ahead of its time: almost a century would pass before the police began to adopt this kind of mathematical analysis and, perhaps for that very reason, the letter was ignored. Prefiguring the later novels of Sir Arthur Conan Doyle, a lady in Islington wondered whether anyone had thought of using a bloodhound? Fearing it was already too late, she counselled the police of the advisability of having one or two of these *remarkable creatures* always on hand.

Forensic science in Britain was in its infancy and – anyway – the legal establishment was sceptical of allowing the laboratory to play too great a part in the detection of crime. Consequently the country lagged behind its European neighbours and though dactyloscopy – or fingerprinting – was pioneered in Britain and might have given Tanner's investigation proof beyond doubt, its acceptance as a standard police tool lay in the future. Similarly, the precipitin test to differentiate between human and animal blood would not be invented by the German scientist Paul Uhlenhuth until 1901. In 1864, all a chemist was able to do was examine spots under a microscope to divine first whether they were indeed blood, and then to make a guess as to their origin by comparing the shape of the cells to a rough chart of different animal types. It was not accepted police practice to collect hairs from crime scenes and nobody scrutinised either the bloodied stone lying close to where Briggs' body was discovered or the battered hat found on the train for such details. Microscopic evidence would not be springing to Inspector Tanner's aid. The only clues he had so far were the crumpled hat, descriptions of the stolen watch and chain and a possible description of the murderer.

Forsaken or lost hats began to take on a whole new significance. The Bow police station was already inundated with hats of all shapes and sizes recovered from park benches and dustcarts across the city, reports of suspicious hats being cleaned and information on those who had returned home hatless or with black eyes on the night of Saturday 9 July. Elsewhere, divisional police stations across London were being kept busy by a steady stream of eager citizens queuing to have their say. As each potentially fruitful lead was pursued locally, copies of the reports were sent to the Commissioner and to Tanner who was, in effect, sitting at the narrow end of a mighty funnel into which the public were pouring their insinuations, suspicions and fears.

There were allegations about ruptures within the extended Briggs family and at Islington police station a neighbour of Thomas Briggs at Clapton Square stated that he had travelled in the same train as Briggs on Saturday night. He claimed that a man between forty and fifty, slightly taller than average with a thick red face, side whiskers and moustache, had rushed into his second-class carriage before the train set off and had stared closely at each of the passengers. The guard had closed the door but the stranger had reopened it, jumped down onto the platform and rushed towards the front of the train in the direction of the first-class compartments.

Facing a welter of proliferating reports, Inspector Tanner was keen to focus on solid leads and his own instinct. Superintendent Howie had already questioned the hatmaker Walker at his shop in Marylebone but had drawn an exasperating blank. Inspector Kerressey had asked Briggs' son Thomas James to return to Clapton Square to remove the hook left dangling from the buttonhole of his father's waistcoat. Along with the jump link found in the carriage and the chain recovered from Death's shop, the

separate parts that held the chain to the stolen watch
attached it to his clothing were now reunited in police han

The banking district was awash with the rumour that Br
had been assaulted by a clerk holding a grudge and Tanner had
his suspicions about the two young clerks who had raised the
alarm on the night of the murder. During that morning the
Exchange had been feverish with reports that the police had
arrested a City man and it had taken a public refutation to
restore calm. In chop houses and taverns, on street corners and
in dealing rooms, fingers were being pointed at the men who
discovered the bloody carriage – Harry Vernez and Sydney
Jones.

The detective was also collecting information about the assault
and robbery on a train in the same spot back in October 1857.
The thief had been caught as he fled to the marshes and had been
tried and sentenced to four years' hard labour. That man – five
feet seven inches tall with a sallow complexion and thin features – had since been released, and those who remembered the
circumstances of his trial recalled that he was said to have threatened to *do something to astonish the public when he came out.*
Additionally, the description given by John Death matched that
of a known associate of this offender. If the clerks were as innocent as they claimed, was it possible that this ex-convict was their
man? The inspector deputed Superintendent Daniel Howie to
track him down.

Tanner's third line of investigation concerned Charles Judd –
the criminal assumed responsible for shooting Judge Poinsot in
France. Had Judd returned to England? Tanner asked the
Préfecture de Police in Paris to send him a photograph, a description of the man and copies of the case papers. All efforts must be
made to establish what had become of Judd. Playing a waiting
game, the detective ordered police divisions nationwide to keep a
watch over districts with foreign lodging-houses. Railway stations
and the London docks were put under surveillance and police at

Folkestone, Dover, Southampton, Harwich, Hull and Liverpool were ordered to stop and search any dubious-looking Germans seeking passage on boats leaving England.

*

On the morning of Tuesday 12 July the directors of the North London Railway added a further hundred pounds to the reward fund. Tanner redrafted the police posters, including John Death's description of their suspect. Each printed sheet would be some three feet long by two feet wide, printed with heavy black type.

The next morning these huge new posters screamed horrid murder across the capital and to the four corners of the country, broadcasting a reward equivalent to several years' pay for a metropolitan craftsman. Tanner's experience encouraged him to believe that, sooner or later, someone would come forward with evidence that would unlock the mystery.

# £300 REWARD
# MURDER

WHEREAS MR THOMAS BRIGGS chief Clerk to Messrs Robarts, Curtis and Co., bankers, Lombard-street, was Violently Assaulted in a First Class Railway carriage, and found on the Line of the North London Railway between Old Ford Bridge and Hackney Wick Station, on Saturday, the 9th instant, about 10pm, and has since died from the effects of the injuries he received

## £100 REWARD

paid by her Majesty's Government
PARDON to any accomplice not being the actual
murderer who shall give such information as shall
lead to the same result.

## A FURTHER REWARD OF £100

Will be paid by Messrs Robarts, Lubbock and Co.,
Bankers, 15 Lombard Street

## A FURTHER REWARD OF £100

will be paid by the North London Railway Company to any
person who will give information as above

A large old fashioned plain gold lever watch, open face, white dial, seconds hand, number 1487 and number inside 2974 maker 'Samuel William Archer, Hackney' and a best Paris nap hat, white lining, maker's name 'Digance Royal Exchange' inside were stolen from the murdered man.

A gold Albert curb chain, large gold key and swivel seal, stolen from the murdered man, has been found exchanged at a Watchmaker's shop yesterday for a square oval secret link gold Albert Chain, with knot-pattern twisted key, swivel seal, and a plain gold finger ring, white Cornelian stone, oblong shape, engraved head, by a man of the following description: Age 30, height 5 feet 6 or 7 inches, complexion sallow thin features, a foreigner – supposed German – speaks good English; dress black frock coat and vest, dark trousers, black hat.

A BLACK HAT Maker, T Walker, 49 Crawford Street, Marylebone, was left in the Railway Carriage by the Murderer.

Information to be given to Inspector Tanner, Detective Police, Great Scotland Yard: Superintendent Howie, K Division, Police Station, Arbour Square, Stepney, or at any Metropolitan Police Station.

# CHAPTER 8

## *Improbable Hypotheses*

On Wednesday 13 July, the fourth day of the investigation, Inspector Tanner and Superintendent Daniel Howie were in Somer's Town, a dilapidated district running between Camden, King's Cross and St Pancras that contained a largely impoverished and reputedly truculent foreign community. That morning a young German suspect had been apprehended there by the local police. John Death was summoned but, when Tanner showed him the prisoner, the silversmith was clear that this was not the customer he had served on Monday morning. Someone else fitting the description of the suspect had also been spotted behaving oddly on the 7.45 p.m. North Kent train at New Cross on the previous evening, but that trail had already gone cold.

*The London detectives are ... upon their trial*, contended the *Daily Telegraph* that morning. *It cannot be forgotten that they have to make up for arrears; that during 1863 ... murder after murder was committed with impunity. Our police have a character to keep, but they also have a reputation to regain ... they will be wrong to reject any hypothesis because it is improbable.* The press were also quick to focus on John Death's story and, in

the absence of other clues, the transaction in Cheapside came
under scrutiny. It seemed particularly noteworthy that the gold
chain had been exchanged rather than sold, and by someone who
behaved well enough in an upmarket establishment not to make
the Death brothers overly suspicious at the time. As jumpy commuters discussed the case, what afforded the most relief was the
fact that the suspect was supposed not to be an *Englishman*. One
might, perhaps, be less concerned about the predatory motives of
one's fellow passengers so long as their accent was unbroken.

But London was full of foreigners, a crucible bigger and more
complex than any other city in the world – a city thrumming to
*the eternal tread of feet upon the pavement*, as Dickens wrote in
*David Copperfield*. The immigration of poor workers had
brought problems of overcrowding in the rotting courts and
rookeries and the overpopulated neighbourhoods that made up
much of the turbulent 'East End' – a term first coined by
Dickens' friend, the journalist Henry Mayhew, in the 1850s. An
extreme away from the genteel squares, the vibrant shops and
the glittering lights of the new West End, these sunless slums and
blind alleys contained a grinding maelstrom of poverty. There
were the Irish, broadly considered disruptive; the politically
skittish French; the Jewish ghettos with their money lenders,
importers and wholesale dealers; the Italian vendors of macaroni
and ice creams; and, along the riverside by the Port of London,
the 'blacks', 'Johnny Chinamen' and 'lascars' working as sailors
or ships' servants. Recent European revolutions lived in the
memory and the middle classes feared the growing power of the
brooding, multi-ethnic mob packed into the eastern reaches of
the city.

Among the foreign communities, Germans did enjoy a better
reputation than most. Not only did the widowed Queen's origins
suggest kinship, but the English also admired German philosophy,
literature and music, and envied them their landscape and edu-
cational system. Wealthy Germans – bankers like the Rothschilds

and industrialists like Siemens – dominated both business and finance and glittered in society. Then there were refugees from the European revolutions – most famously Karl Marx, who arrived in 1849 – and a substantial colony of working-class Germans employed as clerks, watchmakers, sugar-bakers and tailors. Many had come to London either as part of a custom of *Wanderschaft* – broadening their horizons by seeking apprenticeship in the capitals of Europe – or as economic migrants fleeing the low wages, unemployment and agricultural failures of their own country. London could be brutally unyielding, but its booming economy also held the promise of freedom and opportunity and half of all Germans in the country lived in the capital, making their sixteen-thousand-strong community the largest of all the immigrant groups. Most had settled at London's eastern edge, particularly in the Leman Street area of Whitechapel – through which the North London Railway line passed – spreading out through Shoreditch to St George's-in-the-East and north-eastwards to Bow, Bethnal Green and Stepney.

On the whole, this working-class German community was considered productive despite their proclivity for heavy drinking, uncouth eating and the sort of loud street bands that drove the peace-loving crazy. Among the poorest were artisans employed in sugar refineries, confectioneries or tailors' workshops, who lodged in bulging tenement houses or rented rooms from working-class Londoners, segregated by their class but embedded enough to have established their own places of worship, newspapers and clubs. In the support system of 'Little Germany' there were numerous *Vereine*, including a German Gymnastic Society, a German Athenæum and clubs for theatricals, concerts, cards and songs. There was a German Mission, a German YMCA, a Society of Benevolence, a Legal Protection Society, German workhouses, orphanages, schools, restaurants and – at the edge of Hackney – a much-admired German Hospital.

The German husband of the Queen, Prince Albert, had exerted

a strong influence on his adopted country. Alive, public criticism
had centred on his poverty and the burden he laid on the public
purse; recently deceased, he had left the widowed Queen in a
paralysis of grief. Feelings were further complicated by the
Prussian invasion of Denmark in February 1864. Partly in consequence of the recent marriage of Edward, Prince of Wales to
the Danish Princess Alexandra, English sympathy was focused on
the Danes and only five days before Thomas Briggs was attacked
Disraeli had tabled a vote of no confidence in the British government for its failure to defend Denmark against the growing
belligerence of the Austro-Prussian forces as they fought for control of the duchies of Holstein and Lauenburg.

Now that a potentially German murderer was at large,
German immigrants – especially those that hovered on the edge
of poverty – found themselves increasingly unpopular. Any who
had taken temporary lodgings, who carried heavy walking sticks
topped with ivory knobs, or who had hurriedly left town with
their portmanteaus, fell under suspicion.

*

By Friday 15 July, almost a week since Briggs had left home for
the last time, Tanner had nothing new to feed to the pressmen
crowding around the entrances to Scotland Yard. He was still
waiting for a description of Judd to arrive from the Paris authorities, still searching for the man found guilty of the attack on the
line some years ago, and still wondering about the whiskered
man who had attracted attention to himself by entering and leaving carriages on Briggs' Saturday-night train. Several other
witnesses had seen the big, agitated fellow as he dashed along the
platform. No one could remember seeing him leave any of the
stations on the line. Who was he, what was he up to and why
could he not be traced?

Enquiries had been made in districts along the route of the
North London Railway, particularly at Bow, in the warrens of

East End neighbourhoods, across Hackney and throughout the City. Small mountains of reports covered Tanner's desk, the post brought new information each day and the heap of suspicious black hats at Bow station continued to rise while the squashed black hat found on the night of the murder – locked in a cupboard in Tanner's office – mocked the lack of results and yielded no further clues. The newspapers were making things harder, questioning police efficiency, demanding rapid results yet confusing things by repeating rumours that raised hopes that an arrest was only days away. For a while it was believed that Inspector Kerressey, in a post and chaise, was pursuing a suspect across the highlands of Scotland.

In Hackney, Thomas Briggs' cortège was leaving 5 Clapton Square. The blinds of the house had been drawn since his death on the previous Sunday evening and the family had exchanged their usual clothes for deepest black mourning. It is not clear whether Thomas' widow Mary or either of his daughters attended the funeral: Queen Victoria was not at Prince Albert's in 1861 and etiquette manuals were divided on the issue of whether women were sufficiently able to contain their emotions. It is possible that they watched from the upstairs windows of the house as the procession left the square, heading towards the New Gravel Pit Unitarian Chapel.

The shops on Hackney's main street were closed for the hour as a mark of respect, the pavements lined with mourners. The coffin's solemn route led past the Town Hall, leaving the station to the left as it passed under the railway viaduct towards 'Paradise Fields' burial ground – land that was once part of Loddiges' famous plant nursery. Briggs' body was interred in a small green meadow, among the graves of his wife's extended family. Nearby, trains running to and from the City clattered intermittently over their tracks.

His will instructed as little fuss and as little expense as possible. The family pictures and Bible were bequeathed to his son

Edwin; some silver went to Thomas James; George was given his diamond pin, gold ring and portrait in oils; his daughter Mary was left some remaining pictures. The stuffed birds and the gold watch (if it was ever retrieved) were allotted to his youngest son, Netterville, and each child, as well as his niece Caroline Buchan, received nineteen guineas. His widow Mary would keep the house and what was left of his furniture and investments.

The funeral was barely over when the police station at Bow received a telegraph from Camden train station claiming that a man wearing Briggs' hat had been arrested up the line in Hackney. Inspector Kerressey dashed over to Clapton Square, collected Thomas James Briggs and proceeded to visit each of the two Hackney police stations, but no one at either of them knew anything about the message. Telegraphs were sent back and forth and the two men travelled up and down the line several times, but to no avail. The affair turned out to be a hoax. Several men in different parts of town were also detained and questioned that day but all were eventually released. Long after sunset, officers from the Borough Division south of the river sent word that they had arrested a foreigner answering the description given by Death. The man was brought to Scotland Yard and Tanner sent an officer to rouse the jeweller. Hopes were running high as he arrived shortly before midnight, but the silversmith took one look at the stranger before shaking his head. As Friday came to an end, Tanner's investigation was struggling.

Over the weekend, the cheap papers gnawed avidly at the story and the unsparing nature of the attack excited general expressions of horror and indignation. This *foul and brutal crime, committed in the very centre and heart of our civilisation* – wrote one paper – was *the most horrible ... ever to disgrace this country*. Newspaper readership had grown fast during the nineteenth century, revolutionised by the new steam presses, cheaper paper, mass distribution through the rail network and the abolition of the newspaper tax in 1855 that caused their prices to fall.

The broadsheet newspapers catering to the middle classes had a combined daily circulation of almost half a million copies, while the weekend penny press – such as the *Penny Illustrated Paper*, *Lloyd's Weekly Newspaper* and *Reynolds's Weekly Newspaper* – sold perhaps three million copies a week. Since the first 'trial by newspaper' of the murderer John Thurtell in the early 1820s, newspapers had long discovered that printing the details of scandal or violent crime and its investigation could make them fortunes. Alongside speculation, they habitually printed all the salient details of ongoing inquiries, reporting on evidence given at preliminary examinations and inquests in coverage so fulsome that when the Home Office instructed barristers to take on the prosecution of a capital case they often referred their lawyers to the newspapers for details of the brief. Thus, the penny press fuelled an appetite for the minutiae of murder quite out of proportion to its incidence, profiting from a hunger for the sensational, while they also played an important role in driving the general increase of literacy, spreading the reading habit of the age to a working class previously deterred by the high price of books.

On Saturday, Thomas Briggs' local newspaper, the *Shoreditch Advertiser*, carried reports of the discovery of the body of a partly buried and decapitated child, deaths from fire and an attempted poisoning in Clerkenwell. Briggs' murder was not the only suspicious or criminal death, but what made it different was his stolid middle-class respectability and the mysterious disappearance of his assailant. In each of these other cases, a suspect had been taken into custody within days or even hours. By comparison, the railway murder was glaringly unresolved.

On Sunday, *Lloyd's Weekly Newspaper* used the murder to revisit the ongoing debate about capital punishment. If Briggs' murderer was caught, tried and found guilty then the punishment would be death by hanging and the paper was strident in its anti-hanging stance. *The public mind*, it wrote, *is, unhappily, seldom left at rest free from the horror created by the record of some foul and brutal crime, committed in the very centre and heart of our civilisation. No sensation novelist has yet invented a scene half so thrilling by its brutality and its blood as that which was enacted last Saturday night ... Society's sense of security is utterly shaken.* Lloyd's maintained that this crime was a proof that hanging did not deter the robber from adding bloodshed to the list of his transgressions, arguing that murder was often the only means by which thieves could hope to escape. *The great safe-guard society has against the increase of such miscreants is the efficiency of the police, not the severities of* [London's public hangman] *Calcraft*, it averred. *Certainty of punishment is the most efficient suppressor of crime, not severity of punishment.*

The papers lapped up the story but Tanner's investigation was losing momentum. Late on Saturday evening he pressed the Police Commissioner to order a careful scrutiny of all hospitals, surgeries, workhouses and prisons in the search for a man with fresh injuries. He organised new handbills to be printed containing a further description of Thomas Briggs' missing hat in a desperate effort to elicit more information and he pressed his men to speed up their investigation of other fragile leads. One was particularly striking. A man called Tomkins had visited Bow police station to report that a friend of his claimed to have passed Briggs' carriage on Saturday 9 July and to have spoken with him through the window. Tomkins reported that his 'friend' – a man called Thomas Lee – was certain that two other men had been in the compartment and that he could describe them.

The police generally distrusted anyone unwilling to present himself in person, but Inspector Kerressey dispatched one of his constables to interview Mr Lee at his comfortable villa on King Edward's Road, South Hackney. When that constable returned to the police station, he repeated to Superintendent Daniel Howie a story that had about it something of the ring of truth. Thomas Lee admitted that the reason he had not come forward was because he had been visiting a lady in Bow on the evening of 9 July and, since he was married, he feared drawing his family into a scandal. It appeared that he and Briggs had become acquainted while commuting from the City and had frequently shared a compartment as far as Hackney. On the night of the attack Lee said that he had seen Briggs in a carriage at Bow Station at about ten o'clock. Stopping at the window to wish him goodnight, he noticed that the banker was *sitting with his back to the engine. By his side was a man apparently tall and thin and opposite him a thick set man with lightish sandy whiskers with his hand in the loop of the carriage, and the hand seemed to be a large one. I saw this man particularly, as the light from one of the gas lamps on the platform was full upon his face.* He had not seen Thomas Briggs again. After conversing for a couple of minutes, Lee had entered a second-class carriage for the journey home.

Tanner had to consider whether this statement was important. It made sense to assume that such a fast and brutal act had involved more than one person. Possibly, it backed up the police suspicion that their prime suspect was the man convicted of theft a handful of years before on that same part of the railway line, since one of that convict's known accomplices fitted the description of the customer at John Death's shop on 11 July. Lee's statement also correlated with separate sightings of a tall, angry man leaving the station at Hackney Wick and with reports of a red-faced, whiskered fellow hurriedly examining the faces of passengers at Bow.

As dusk fell on Sunday evening news came that the criminal they'd been attempting to find had been traced: but he had died several months previously, putting him squarely out of the picture. Tanner was left with the description of two menacing men in the company of Thomas Briggs on the night he was murdered, and the diminishing chance that he would be able to track them down.

# CHAPTER 9

## *Something to Tell*

As the police investigation entered its second week it was getting warm, the second day of a heatwave that would last a fortnight. Untreated waste from neighbourhoods not yet connected to Bazalgette's new sewerage system flowed freely into the River Thames or festered in domestic cellars. The capital was enfolded in fetid stink. Costermongers struggled to keep the fish on their barrows fresh enough to sell; flowers, fruit and watercress wilted on the market stalls and milk was quickly turning sour. A haze of dust and grime hung over the sweating city.

At Scotland Yard there was a long list of unanswered questions. Was the blood on the clerks' hands and trousers an indication of their innocence or complicity? To whom did the crushed hat belong? What had become of Thomas Briggs' hat and watch? Would the murderer or murderers strike again? What real chance did they have of finding new suspects in the jungle of the capital now that more than a week had passed? Inspector Tanner was unsettled by the dawning possibility that the man who had exchanged Briggs' chain at John Death's shop had falsified his accent in order to throw them off course. Perhaps he was not a foreigner after all. Could the police afford to change direction? Their lack of progress was dispiriting, but the detective held firm to his belief in patience.

All across London, police divisions followed up fantasy sightings, tip-offs and distractions. Police in Westminster checked out a suspicious Swiss who had been seen by his landlady making himself a new set of clothes. In Peckham they were on the heels of a man who had boasted of having a fifty-pound watch and who had offered to bet anyone in the tavern that the murderer would not be caught. In Clerkenwell a man of about thirty, five feet eight inches, with carroty whiskers, a long black coat, black hat and white walking stick was the subject of police enquiries. In Clapham, a hansom-cab driver reported driving a customer wearing dark clothes and a hat, carrying a large cane and wearing an apparently false moustache. As the passenger struck a light during his journey, the gleam revealed a double-barrelled pistol tucked into his coat pocket. The news put the local police on high alert.

On Monday morning – 18 July – a boy called at the Bow police station asking to see Inspector Kerressey. He, too, claimed to have travelled on the same train as Thomas Briggs. When it arrived at Stepney the lad had noticed a tall, dark man getting in and out of carriages as if he was looking for someone, and the boy was certain that he got into a carriage where an old gentleman was seated. It was the third reported sighting of a tall, dark, agitated fellow on the train that night, but all efforts to trace him had been fruitless. The man had simply vanished.

*

Tanner and Superintendent Daniel Howie shouldered their way through the crowds outside the Prince of Wales tavern in Hackney for the reopening of the inquest. Within moments of their arrival, the coroner had them all on the move again as his clerks herded the jurymen and witnesses across the road to the more commodious space of the parish vestry hall. Even here, a disconsolate gaggle was left at the door as all the available public seats were swiftly filled.

The jury was re-sworn. First, Dr Toulmin, Briggs' relative and doctor, presented the post-mortem results, pointing to diagrams and holding up a human skull while describing the triangular cranial fractures and severe haemorrhaging within the brain. Attributing the fracture and depression of the left temple bone to the effects of the fall from the train, Toulmin repeated his conclusion that the fracture near the ear and the wounds on the vertex of the skull had been inflicted by a blunt instrument.

Little was expected of Briggs' niece Caroline Buchan, and spectators shuffled in their seats waiting for someone more interesting. She confirmed that her uncle had been sober when he left Peckham. Then she began to describe threats she thought her uncle had received from a man to whom he had refused a loan. A thrill ran through the assembly at the unexpected revelation. Swiftly, the coroner ordered Caroline to withhold the man's name.

Before the next witness could be called, the jurymen were herded back outside by a clerk and the public were left to stew as the thirteen men followed the coroner along busy Mere Street, processing towards the nearby railway station where they climbed the steps to the platform. There, in the rising heat, the blood-drenched carriage in which Thomas Briggs had been attacked stood waiting for their inspection. Brought up from Bow that morning, it was surrounded by police guards.

Inside, the carriage was hot and airless, the stale air rancid. The upturned cushions, the floor matting kicked to one side, the many splashes of dried and darkened blood both inside and out were just as Ames had previously described. The group waited as, one by one, each juror entered, took in the detail of what lay before him and then descended again from the carriage. The dismal scene presented powerful evidence of struggle and brutality, erasing any suspicion that Thomas Briggs' death could have been suicide. What it could not tell them was what exactly had occurred, nor how a man with murderous intent had been able to take his place in the first-class compartment without drawing attention to himself.

Leaving the train carriage to its frustrating silence, the jurymen retraced their steps back to the vestry hall. Eager attention was focused on the next two witnesses, Harry Vernez and Sydney Jones. Public speculation about the two bank clerks' involvement in the crime was rife but, as they gave their version of events for the first time in public, both men adhered to the story that they had been returning home from a boat trip on the River Lea on Saturday 9 July when they discovered blood in the compartment. Following their testimonies, a railway official at Hackney Station was sworn and corroborated their tale: he had seen the two arrive at the station only minutes before the train drew up at the platform. The clerks were off the hook.

Only one other new fact slipped out, almost in passing. The victim's son, Thomas James, told the coroner and jury that two IOUs, signed by David Buchan, had been found in his father's pocket book. Thomas Lee's new evidence would have thrown suspicion elsewhere but, in spite of the fact that his statement supported others taken by the police, Lee had not been called.

*

As the ninth day of the police investigation drew to a close, near the lowering bulk of the Great Western Railway terminus in Paddington a hackney carriage driver stopped to water his horse at the stand outside the Great Western Hotel. One of about five thousand metropolitan drivers of four-seater hackney 'cabs' licensed to take private passengers for fixed fares, this cabman was poor – he rented rather than owned his horse and its four-wheeled, bright-red-painted carriage.

The driver had been out on the roads for twelve hours and was aiming to call it a day within the half hour. As he climbed down from the box at the front of the cab, his eyes fell on a police notice and he read – he would later say that it was for the first time – the descriptions of a hat bought from Walker's in Marylebone, of the chain exchanged at Death's in Cheapside and of the suspect with his German accent. Turning to the police waterman – whose job it was to limit twenty cabs to a stand – he asked what height the waterman thought him to be. Fixing his attention again on the handbill stuck on the wall and rechecking the description of the suspect, he turned over in his mind a recent conversation with his wife. Spurred by the offer of the three hundred pounds' reward, the cabman then hauled the horse's head out of its bucket and whipped the animal into action, heading for Earl Street East on the district's shady border. Rushing inside number 68, he asked his wife if she knew what had become of the small cardboard box he had seen his young daughter playing with. Pulling it from the corner of a table-drawer, he then marched back out to his cab.

By quarter past eleven, Jonathan Matthews was pushing through the door of the Hermitage police station, part of the Marylebone division of the force. Telling the duty sergeant that he had something to tell about the murder of the man on the North London train, he waited. In common with the police across London, Inspector Thomas Steer had been bothered constantly by people who thought they were on to something, bringing all kinds of reports and surmises about the murder of Thomas Briggs. Wearily, he picked up his notebook and prepared to take down one more extraordinary account.

The first thing that struck Steer as unusual was that Matthews, whose job took him all over town, swore that he had known nothing of the highly publicised murder until an hour or so earlier. It seemed very unlikely. The rough-spoken, Wellington-booted cabman sat with his hat on his knees, leaning across the table with excitement. Steer watched the weather-coarsened face and the flushed cheeks, waiting for the cabman's tale to unfold.

Jonathan Matthews spoke of a young German tailor from Chemnitz in Saxony who was called Francis – or Franz – Müller who had, for a short while, been engaged to Matthews' sister-in-law. Then he drew from his coat pocket something that made Steer begin to pay closer attention: a cardboard box with the name and address of John Death printed on the top. The cab driver contended that the box had been given to his daughter to play with on Monday 11 July by Müller, who had come to tell his wife that he was leaving the country. The jeweller's box and its link to a young German marked Jonathan Matthews' story as different from the vague sightings and suspicions that had made up the greater part of the public's response to the Briggs murder. Urged to continue, Matthews related that Müller worked for a City tailoring business called Hodgkinson's in Threadneedle Street and that he had been lodging in the Old Ford area of Bow. There was also a peculiar story about a hat. Several months ago, said Matthews, Müller had admired one of his own new black beaver hats and tried it on. It was too tight, but he liked it, and Matthews had agreed to get him one a little bigger in return for a waistcoat Müller promised to make. Matthews had ordered the hat from the same shop – Walker, of Crawford Street, Marylebone – and collected it ready for Müller when he visited the following weekend.

Now Steer was alert. Matthews' statement linked the information gathered from the Death brothers not simply to a specific German tailor but to one who apparently owned a hat manufactured by the same hatters as the one found in the bloody carriage. Believing that Matthews had brought them something precise, Steer pulled on his overcoat and told the cabman to drive them both to the man's home. Clattering through darkened streets, they made for the rundown neighbourhood of Lisson Grove on the borders of Paddington where Jonathan, his wife Eliza, and their four young children lived in cramped rented rooms in a small house shared with two other working-class families.

Steer wanted to go back over Matthews' story. Speaking in turns, Jonathan and Eliza complied, telling him that they had known Müller for about two years. The German had once worked for a relation and, as they became more friendly, he began to eat with them most weekends and was soon courting Matthews' sister-in-law. The two had become engaged until the girl broke it off, alarmed by what she called her fiancé's petty jealousies. On the whole, Eliza said, Müller was an inoffensive, trustworthy sort of fellow and good company. He was a little prone to boasting, but she liked him.

Steer pressed them about the hat. Out in all weathers, Matthews grumbled that he got through nine or ten new hats a year. He said that during the previous November Müller had admired his latest purchase and asked for a duplicate for himself. The hat Matthews ordered for him cost ten shillings sixpence and, like his own, had a merino strip on the underside of the brim – *because*, said the cabman, *of its not wearing so greasy as the nap*. He asked for the brim to be turned up a little extra on each side since that was what Müller had most liked about his own. The new hat was kept in its box until Müller collected it, leaving a new black waistcoat in exchange as promised. Matthews mentioned to Steer that the last time he had seen Müller – a couple of weeks before the murder – he had remarked how well the hat suited the German and had noticed that there was a mark on the inside brim where the young man pressed his thumb to remove it. A slight additional curl had also developed along its edge. Matthews had made a point of asking if Müller had done it on purpose.

Unfortunately, Jonathan Matthews was unable to show Inspector Steer his own original Walker-made hat. He had replaced it in June, he told the inspector, with a cheaper hat from Down's shop in Long Acre.

Eliza filled in the background about the box. A week earlier, on Monday 11 July – two days after the attack – she told Steer that Müller had called between two and four in the afternoon to tell her he was leaving for New York. He stayed about three hours, boasting that the City tailors for whom he worked were sending him abroad to work on the impressive salary of £150 a year. Knowing that jobbing tailors of Müller's type generally received about twenty-five shillings a week and that £150 represented three times his current annual wage – knowing, too, that Müller was prone to spinning yarns – Eliza had been inclined to take what he told her with a pinch of salt.

*He was limping*, she told the inspector, and he had explained this by telling her that a letter cart ran over his foot on London Bridge the previous Thursday. She recalled, too, that the German had shown her a gold chain, detaching it from his waistcoat buttonhole and dropping it into her hand – a light gold chain that she thought rather inferior to the one she was used to seeing him with. He also showed her a ring on his little finger with a cornelian face that he said was a present from his father in Germany. Before he left, the tailor had given her ten-year-old daughter the small cardboard box to play with.

As she drew to the end of her tale Eliza added that, as he was leaving, Müller had collected his hat from her dresser and that she had complimented him on how well it had worn. *Oh, this is a different hat*, he replied. Then he left. Neither she nor her husband had much idea how to find Müller now but they did have a photograph he had once given Matthews' sister-in-law, and a piece of paper with the address of his lodgings in Bow. Casting about in the same drawer in which she had stored the small cardboard jewellery box, Eliza handed them both over to Inspector Steer.

The policeman had heard enough. Summoning a fast, two-wheeled hansom and bundling Matthews quickly into it, he set out for the home of his superintendent in nearby Marylebone. So far as Steer was concerned, they had made a breakthrough.

# CHAPTER 10

## *The Wind Blows Fair*

The hansom carrying Inspector Steer, Superintendent William Tiddey and Matthews rattled over the cobbles into Scotland Yard, pulling up smartly at the rear entrance of the Chief Office. Inspector Tanner was not far behind and, after listening to Matthews' story, he knew that there was an obvious way to test it out. Rising to unlock a cupboard, the investigation's lead detective reached for the crumpled hat retrieved from the North London Railway carriage on the night of 9 July and passed it to the cabman. Matthews did not pause. This was, he was certain, the same hat he had bought for Müller: it had the same easily identifiable striped lining, the same merino underband, a curled brim and a distinguishing mark which he had already described to Inspector Steer – the imprint of a right-hand thumbmark.

Once Jonathan Matthews had convinced Inspector Tanner that the broken hat belonged to Franz Müller, the inspector split his men into two groups. Steer was ordered to Bow to trace the tailor while Tanner and Tiddey set off for the City. It was already past eleven. A hansom on 'special arrangement' was engaged to convey the two men through the night and across the metropolis.

Whipped through darkened streets brightened by flaring gaslights, it travelled eastwards along the Strand and into Aldwych, passing grand houses, vibrant theatres and the coloured lights and impromptu performances of the 'penny-gaffs'. Along Fleet Street and up deserted Ludgate Hill it continued, veering north and turning its back on the thick, snaking Thames. Passing the Old Bailey Sessions House and the grim, dark walls of Newgate gaol, the ancient tower of St Sepulchre's church appeared in front of them as they swung hard right into Newgate Street.

By comparison to the still-busy West End, the City roads were deserted. The inns, taverns and chop houses were closed; the costermongers' barrows had been covered and abandoned until the next day's business. Occasionally they passed dustmen, cross-ing-sweepers, lamplighters or men with watering-carts dampening the dust on the widest streets. Scavengers and cloth-pickers idled through rubbish discarded during the day, sending odd bits of paper flapping across the pavements in the breeze. Bill-stickers and boardmen fixed advertisements to the walls of busy street corners. Except for these night-workers it was quiet and the air was still thick from the warm day. Where Newgate Street became Cheapside, the dome of Sir Christopher Wren's enormous cathedral filled the night sky. Hard by the church of St Mary-le-Bow, whose bells declared anyone born within their hearing a cockney, the cab pulled up with a lurch.

Tanner descended, hammered on the door of number 55 and entered the night-gloomy jeweller's shop. Since his interview with Inspector Kerressey a week earlier, John Death's days had been endlessly interrupted as he was summoned from his business to station houses across London, but none of the suspects he was shown was ever identifiable as the man with whom he had exchanged chains. Tanner now showed him the box handed to the police by Jonathan Matthews and Death confirmed that it was similar to the one in which he had packed the chain for the suspicious foreigner. But he was equally clear that he and his brother used dozens of similar boxes each week.

Then the detective passed the photograph of Müller to John Death. *Yes*, he said, this was the man he had previously described – the customer who had offered Thomas Briggs' watch chain for exchange on Monday 11 July. After all the false leads and diversions, Detective Inspector Tanner's investigation was making headway.

*

By the time the hansom drew up outside the house at 16 Park Terrace, Old Ford, on the margin of Bow and Bethnal Green, it was one o'clock in the morning on Tuesday 19 July. According to Matthews and his wife, this was the address of the German, Müller. The windows of the house were dark and there was no sign of movement from within. Tanner decided to wait until first light.

For centuries, these eastern margins of the capital had housed large groups of French Huguenot, Irish, Jewish, European and African immigrants in tradesmen's terraces thrown up since the 1840s by speculative builders. The growth of the London docks, the development of the North London Railway and increasing industrial sprawl along the River Lea had all combined to turn Old Ford from a quiet hamlet with small silk mills in the 1820s into a congested neighbourhood of water, gas and chemical works, breweries and brick-fields. Old Ford also gave its name to a road running east–west on the southern side of the three hundred green acres of Victoria Park. At its western extremity stood Park Terrace – a line of two-storey working-class houses made of yellowish brick already begrimed by smoke and smog. Number 16 was just minutes' walk from one of the park entrances and no more than ten from the Duckett's Canal bridge to the east and the railway tracks on which Thomas Briggs was found insensible. Tanner weighed it up. On the one hand, this was a likely neighbourhood for the murderer. On the other, he knew that each of the railway stations at Bow and Hackney Wick were a mile distant, whereas an omnibus passing the end of Park Terrace ran directly to the City. Was it plausible that the German tailor used the North London Railway line to and from his work, rather than catching the more convenient 'bus?

The Square Mile and the districts to its east were the centre of the London garment industry, a nexus for thousands of labourers stitching shirts, ties, collars, suits and waistcoats. Some were salaried journeymen in upmarket tailors like Hodgkinson's of Threadneedle Street, crafting hand-stitched clothing for the well-to-do; others did piecework for Jewish and German contractors, turning out cheaper, machined coats and trousers by the score. Many of these tailors barely scratched a living. Since the introduction of the Singer sewing machine from America at the Great Exhibition of 1851 the number of workers – mostly women – toiling for a pittance in squalid back rooms on rented machines had grown quickly, reacting to a growing demand for stylish clothing at low prices. From the English tailoring industry of the 1860s came the first coinage of the term 'sweated labour'.

City streets were pitted with small workshops competing to fulfill demand for fancy shirting and coats but even in decent shops the pay was low and the hours either irregular or tediously long. Seventy-two-hour working weeks were common. Eyes were strained in the dim lights, fingers were roughened by needles and bodies ached as they bent over the twenty thousand stitches needed for every handmade shirt. It was an insecure, shifting, seasonal profession and it fed on a floating population of workers. If Franz Müller had planned to travel to America, his decision was probably determined by the season. Parliament would soon end for the summer and the wealthy were already streaming from the capital: summer business was always slack.

As he waited, Tanner considered the fact that a gold chain worth three pounds represented between three weeks' and one month's wages for even a thriving journeyman tailor. The cost of the cheap beaver hat bought by Matthews for Müller added up to several days' pay while the guinea-each silk toppers favoured by bankers were more than a week's salary – well beyond his normal reach. The tailor sought by Inspector Tanner was clearly worldly enough to walk into Death's shop without drawing undue attention to himself and yet canny enough to dodge and survive in the underbelly of the city.

In Park Terrace, the two-storey, narrow terraced houses were still and the street was deserted for the five long hours of the detective's vigil. In the dawn chill a low mist hung over the grass in nearby Victoria Park. Signs of life began: doors slammed behind porters leaving for work at their docks warehouses and barrow-sellers setting out to restock their carts. At six o'clock Tanner saw movement at the windows of the dingy cottage at number 16.

Interrupting Ellen Blyth and her husband George, a messenger in the City, in the scramble to get seven children ready for the new day, Tanner entered the narrow hallway of the house. Unused to police visits, the family was startled.

Mrs Blyth answered his questions unhesitatingly. She confirmed that their two small upstairs rooms were generally let in order to supplement the tight family income. A young tailor, about twenty-three or twenty-four years old, known to them by the name of Franz Müller, had lodged in the first-floor back room since late May, paying four shillings a week. Currently, the room was empty. Müller had given proper notice and left for America on the previous Thursday – 14 July – five days after the attack.

Tanner's volley of questions came fast. Mrs Blyth answered that she was fond of Müller; she had known him a good year before he came to lodge with them and had *always known him to be a quiet, inoffensive, well-behaved young man. I had plenty of opportunity of judging of his temper in every respect, he used to take his meals with us – he did so on the Sunday – he was of a very kind and humane disposition.* Müller had, she said, left home on Saturday 9 July at about eleven in the morning. When she and her husband went to bed twelve hours later *he had not come home then, he had a latch-key. I did not hear him come in that night.* The next morning – Sunday – she saw him *between 8 and 9 o'clock – he breakfasted with us. He stopped at home during the day, and in the evening he went out with me and my husband, and came back with us.* Yes, she repeated, *he spent the day with us on Sunday.*

It was crucial to Inspector Tanner to discover exactly what Müller had been wearing on both Saturday the 9th and Sunday 10 July. *I am sure of the trousers he wore on the Sunday,* said Ellen. *They were the same as those on the Saturday.* Her husband, George, added that *it was about the 7th that he hurt his foot. It was hurt by a cart running up against it and from that time he wore a slipper, up to the Sunday. He wore a slipper on the Sunday morning and I went out with him on the Sunday for a walk in Victoria Park, and my wife went with us.* Limping around the park that Sunday, Müller might have passed just yards from the place where Briggs' body had been found on the line by the Duckett's Canal bridge. Tanner also noted that the German's foot had not been so badly hurt that he had been forced to rest on a bench.

Handing the detective a single slipper that had been left behind in his room, Mrs Ellen Blyth said she had noticed nothing out of sorts with her lodger on Sunday: he was *in his usual cheerful spirits* all day. She had not heard of the murder for several days and then it had never crossed her mind to link it with Müller. Asked whether the German owned a chain, she told Tanner that on the evening of Monday 11 July Müller had come in with a friend of his called John Hoffa. In the course of their conversation Müller had shown her a new gold watch chain. He seemed pleased with it, though she confessed that she had not taken any particular notice.

The two young tailors, she said, were very often together – in fact, during the week following the murder Hoffa had shared Müller's room between Monday and Wednesday, not having rent for his own lodgings. As far as she knew, Müller had left London for New York on a ship called the *Victoria*. He had sent her a letter, dated Saturday 16 July, posted by the ship's pilot when he had left the ship at Worthing on the south coast. Taking the letter down from the mantelpiece, she passed it to Tanner. He read: *On the Sea, July 16, in the morning. Dear Friends, I am glad to confess that I cannot have a better time as I have; if the sun shines nice and the wind blows fair, as it is at the present moment, everything will go well. I cannot write any more, only I have no postage. You will be so kind to take that letter in.*

Mrs Blyth now remembered that when Müller first arrived to live with them he had brought a long black box containing his clothes and another, cardboard, hat box. The hat box was still in his old room. Tanner followed Ellen upstairs. There was the box, bearing the name of a maker: Walker of 49 Crawford Street, Marylebone. In every other respect Müller's room was stripped and empty. They were several days too late.

# CHAPTER 11

## Tuesday 19 July 1864

Six days after the attack on Thomas Briggs, Müller's ship had sailed with the tide, passing through the East Dock into the Shadwell Basin and out to the Thames. Following the curve of the river to its estuary it had turned south, skirting the coast; by the time he wrote to the Blyths on Saturday, the *Victoria* had cleared the shoulders of the Downs.

Was it possible that a guilty man would make no attempt to cover his tracks? Was his carelessness with the hat and jewellery box, his parading of the new chain and ring and his openness about his plans a sign of his innocence or his stupidity? Was his foot really injured days before the murder as he had told Eliza Matthews and the Blyths, or had it been hurt as he leapt from a moving train?

Half an hour after leaving Park Terrace, Tanner arrived at the lodgings of Müller's friend, twenty-seven-year-old journeyman tailor John (or Johan) Hoffa, who confirmed that he had worked with Müller at Samuel Hodgkinson's business in Threadneedle Street and that Müller had worn a slipper on his injured right foot between Thursday 7 July (two days before the attack on

Thomas Briggs) and the middle of the following week. Hoffa was insistent that Müller's departure had been planned rather than precipitate. Anyone who knew his friend, he said, had been told about his plans to leave for America for at least a fortnight before he boarded ship.

When Tanner asked about Müller's finances, Hoffa said that his friend had been working at Hodgkinson's for about six weeks up to 2 July and that he had seen him several times with enough money to pay for his ticket to America. During the week before he left, Müller had stitched some new shirts for his planned voyage and earned a little extra money by helping Hoffa with some contract work. On Saturday 9 July both he and Müller had worked at the house of Godfrey Repsch, a German contract-work tailor at 12½ Jewry Street, Aldgate, a narrow court in the labyrinthine streets near the eastern edge of the City. When Müller arrived mid-morning, he had changed into a pair of old trousers and slippers and worked on his shirts until the light grew too dim to continue. At about a quarter to eight he put back on the trousers he had arrived in – Hoffa was not able to describe them – pulled on a dark frock coat and left. Wearing a boot on his left and a slipper on his injured right foot he told Hoffa that he was heading to Camberwell to visit his sweetheart. Hoffa imagined that he had taken an omnibus over London Bridge from one of the stands either on Gracechurch Street or on King William Street, right by the bridge.

Inspector Tanner had already noted the proximity of Müller's workplace in Threadneedle Street to Briggs' bank in Lombard Street: the two grand thoroughfares were linked by numerous alleyways and lanes that cut through behind the Exchange. Müller's lodgings in Old Ford also put him within a short walk of the Duckett's Canal bridge where Briggs' body was found. This new piece of information – that Müller had journeyed south by omnibus on the night of Saturday 9 July – reinforced the detective's sense of the odd congruence of the two men's

movements. Camberwell in the south adjoined the neighbourhood of Peckham, where Briggs had travelled that same evening
to dine with his niece. The omnibus routes to each destination
differed but they also intersected: on their return to the City
both bus routes converged at Borough High Street and both
crossed London Bridge.

Müller was not destitute. He had relatively stable work and
good lodgings. But while Thomas Briggs had devoted his working life to Robarts, Curtis and worn the uniform of the British
banking elite, Müller seemed to have drifted between employers
and displayed a vanity that encouraged tastes well beyond his
means. Inspector Tanner had to consider whether the tailor's
aspiration might also have bred resentment. Had Briggs' black
bankers' bag and gold watch chain caught the poor tailor's eye?
Had the attack, as some papers surmised, been premeditated?

According to Hoffa, Müller had been to the London docks on
the morning of Monday 11 July. Dodging out of the City past the
Tower of London, the sail-makers' shops, rope suppliers and
tinned-food grocers, slipping through the main entrance to the
western docks with its fortress-like brick walls twenty feet high,
Müller would have joined teeming crowds of seamen, labourers
and job-seekers. The docks were a world of noise, moored with
more than three hundred vessels and filled with the clatter of
cranks and hydraulic lifts, the creaking of the rigging, jabbering
warehousemen and touting porters. Assailed by the fumes of rum,
then the sick stench of hides and the thick fragrances of coffee,
tobacco and spice, Müller had – according to Hoffa – searched
the North Quay and found the office of Grinnell & Co. who were
offering cheap passage to America on an old-fashioned sailing
ship called the *Victoria*, due to leave for New York at the end of
the week. Four pounds was more than he earned in a month and
Hoffa told Tanner that Müller returned from the docks claiming
that he did not have enough money for a ticket and asking his
friends for loans. He assumed that Müller had spent all the money

he had seen him with the new chain and ring his friend was now wearing and, when he asked him about it, Müller said that he had just bought them from a man at the docks. Knowing that Müller owned an old watch given to him by his father, Hoffa wondered why his friend did not pawn that for the fare.

By midweek Müller was still trying to raise enough money for his ticket and, on Wednesday the 13th, he sent Mrs Repsch to Hoffa's work to ask for help. Hoffa gave her a spare set of his own clothes to pawn for twelve shillings and received in return two separate pawn tickets. These were for goods she had already pawned for Müller at Mr Annis' shop in the Minories: a dark frock coat for six shillings and a chain for more than a pound. To Hoffa it had seemed like a good deal.

Pawnbrokers were normally the haunts of the desperate and tailors like Müller, surrounded by affluent City men who represented unattainable financial freedom, were fodder for their business. Close to seven hundred pawn shops were established within a radius of ten miles from the Royal Exchange, each of them averaging five thousand pledges a month for bundles of clothes, tarnished jewellery, furniture, linen, plate or anything that might raise enough to bring temporary relief in hard times. Announcing themselves with three brass balls above the door (popularly known as 'swinging dumplings') or a painted sign with three red balls on a blue background, some brokers were respectable; more often they were dirty money-lending shops in shadowy side streets. Their stock hung in the rafters or was heaped in ramshackle cases: silver teaspoons, watches, doubtful rings, prayer books, neckerchiefs, strings of coral or remnants of silk or satin – even children's shoes.

Pawnbroker business was conducted quickly. Bundles were received over the wooden counters in return for the short-term loan of cash representing perhaps half the value of the item. Two tickets were made out by hand, each with a description of the goods and the (often false) name of the customer. One was attached to the articles which were wrapped in brown paper and stored and the other was given to the seller until payday or a windfall allowed for it to be redeemed. Anything left unclaimed beyond its due date was sold.

For the inspectors of the Metropolitan Police, these shops were part of the common round of detective work and Tanner was determined that all Müller's recent transactions must be investigated. He wanted to find Thomas Briggs' missing gold watch and to trace it back to his suspect, and he wanted the coat pawned by Mrs Repsch. Whoever murdered Thomas Briggs would have had blood on his clothes. Had Müller worn that coat on the night of the attack? The Blyths were certain that he had worn the same clothes on Saturday and on Sunday, a suit with no obvious sign of having been recently and rapidly cleaned. But if the black coat turned out to have bloodstains overlooked by the Blyths it would link Müller to the assault on Thomas Briggs.

Inspector Tanner returned to Scotland Yard. He had narrowed his focus to one individual but time was against them. If Müller really was on his way to America then he had a five-day head start and could easily put himself beyond their reach, vanishing into a country steeped in the chaos of a civil war. Someone would have to give chase and, if Müller was caught in New York, then formal papers would be needed in order to request his extradition. Consequently, a flurry of hansom cabs was dispatched across the city by officers at Scotland Yard and, at the Bow Street Police Court in Covent Garden, a magistrate stood ready to hear witness depositions at a private sitting. While Superintendent William Tiddey played puppetmaster, choreographing the arrival of the various witnesses at Bow Street that Tuesday afternoon, Tanner arranged for new bills carrying descriptions of Müller to be printed and sent to all ports. Telegraphic messages were sent to Liverpool with instructions for all departing vessels to be searched, just in case he had not sailed with the *Victoria* after all.

Out beyond the City, amid the wheeling seagulls and shrill crowds of the docks, Tanner then sought the porter for the Grinnell Line who confirmed, after being shown the photograph, that Müller had been there several times from Monday the 11th looking for passage. In his office on the North Quay, James Gifford – shipping agent for Grinnell and their vessel the *Victoria* – also told Tanner that the German had been at the quay three times on Wednesday the 13th, first to ask the fare, then to pay and collect a ticket (without bothering to give a false name), and finally to store some parcels wrapped in canvas. Tanner wondered about these parcels. Did they contain the usual items, like soap and bacon, that poor emigrants took along to see them through the voyage? Or might they have concealed a blood-spattered coat and trousers? Tanner also needed to find out whether Müller had actually embarked. The agent was fairly certain: the last time he had seen Müller was on board the *Victoria* just before the ship sailed early in the morning of Friday 15 July.

Hurrying from the docks to nearby Aldgate, Tanner set course for Jewry Street, a dingy alley where several rickety timber-framed houses had survived the Great Fire of 1666 and where thin sunshine lost out to soot and dust from the nearby railway viaduct. He found both Elizabeth Repsch and her German husband Godfrey at home at number 12½

Unlike Hoffa, Elizabeth was able to remember precisely what Müller had been wearing on Saturday 9 July: dark green and black trousers and a dark frock coat. She was sure that on Monday the 11th he had worn the same coat but a different, paler pair of trousers. That day, he had shown her a chain he said he had just bought at the docks for three pounds fifteen shillings, and a ring reported to have cost another seven shillings and six-pence. When Elizabeth admired his new hat, Müller told her that the old one was broken and that he had thrown it into the dust-hole at the Blyths'.

Elizabeth Repsch was most detailed in her statement about

Müller's new hat. It was of such good quality that even her husband had remarked that it looked like a guinea topper – a hat, in
other words, worth an entire week's wages. Müller denied it,
telling them that he paid just fourteen shillings for it a couple of
months earlier, but that he had only worn it on a couple of
Sundays. Then, when Tanner pressed her about Müller's old hat,
Elizabeth had excellent recall: it was *a plain black beaver with a
merino rim inside and striped lining, broad brown stripes and
broad blue stripes edged with black and white*. The lining was so
unusual, she told him, that she would recognise it anywhere. Her
description exactly matched the crushed hat locked away in
Tanner's office at Scotland Yard.

Mrs Repsch seemed not to be particularly fond of Müller,
admitting that she had known him for about two years and that
she thought him a bit of a show-off. He had boasted to her (here
Tanner heard the echo of Eliza Matthews' story) that
Hodgkinson was sending him to America on an inflated wage,
though she said she had not believed it. Did they know Jonathan
Matthews? Godfrey Repsch said he had known the cab driver for
about eight years but that they rarely saw each other. Tanner did
not pursue the connection. The black morning coat that Mrs
Repsch had pawned in nearby Minories was preying on his mind.
Hoffa now had that ticket and Tanner had already sent a police
constable to retrieve it and bring it along to Scotland Yard.

Did the Repschs know what had become of Müller? Godfrey
did, since he had seen him off: *I went on board the* Victoria *with
him. Everybody that knew him knew where he was going.*

*

As Tanner continued his enquiries during the afternoon of
Tuesday 19 July hackney cabs hired by the police were convey-
ing the six central witnesses from Bow, Aldgate, Cheapside,
Peckham, Hackney and Paddington to the Magistrates' Court at
4 Bow Street. By mid-afternoon, Jonathan and Eliza Matthews,

John Hoffa, the silversmith John Death, Thomas James Briggs and the train guard Benjamin Ames were gathered with Sergeant George Clarke of the detective police and Inspector Steer from Paddington, waiting to appear before the Chief Magistrate.

Inspector Tanner arrived with the walking stick, black bag and crushed hat discovered in carriage 69, the cardboard box given up by Matthews and Thomas Briggs' broken chain which had been surrendered by John Death. He had one new exhibit. The second ticket held by Hoffa in return for his spare suit of clothes had indeed turned out to be for a gold chain also pledged at Mr Annis' shop in Minories. When this chain was shown to John Death, the silversmith was ready to swear that it was the very one that the stranger took away from his shop on the morning after the murder.

Despite its lofty reputation, Bow Street Magistrates' Court was rather squalid, described by the *Illustrated London News* several years before as made up of *dingy, fetid, close smelling rooms . . . the walls greased and stained by the ceaseless friction of the forlorn and ragged groups of witnesses and prosecutors who . . . lounge about in every avenue.* Established in 1740 on the site of the capital's first police office and designated its superior magistrates' court, it had been the locus for committal proceedings of dozens of the most infamous criminal cases in the land, and it handled up to three hundred cases each day. Legions of police and black-gowned lawyers jostled in the hot corridors among swarms of poor men and women either summoned to give statements or arriving with complaints or to make enquiries about missing friends or strayed children. Reporters swarmed around the entrance.

Tanner, his colleagues and the witnesses were soon hustled into a narrow chamber where the Chief Magistrate Mr Thomas Henry would preside over the taking of depositions designed to form the skeleton of the case against Müller. The witnesses' stories were all repeated. The hat, stick, bag and chains were each identified and entered as evidence. Each short statement was copied in a court clerk's bold copperplate, signed by the witness and certified by the magistrate. At six o'clock, several hours after they had begun, Tanner held a warrant for Franz Müller's arrest and the formal depositions. All that was now needed in order for the documents to be admissible in a United States courtroom was the signature of the envoy extraordinary to the United States and the embellished seal of the legation in London.

Worn out by almost thirty-six sleepless hours, Inspector Richard Tanner finally called in at Chester Square to discuss progress in the case. The Commissioner was waiting – already dressed for the evening's performance of Gounod's opera *Faust e Margherita* at Covent Garden. Tanner had already visited the Foreign Office that afternoon to collect government dispatches for the acting British consul in New York and passports for two witnesses and two members of the police force. Despite the recent success of sub-sea cables in Europe, the Atlantic continued to defy attempts to create a line of communication between the two continents. Within the year an effective cable would be in place but, for now, there was no way of contacting the captain of the *Victoria* to confirm her position or whether Müller was still on board, and it was impossible to request the New York authorities to take action on their behalf.

He was aware there was a chance that the Commissioner might depute him to chase Müller across the Atlantic, organise his arrest and bring the suspect home for trial. But Tanner was caught off guard by Sir Richard Mayne's order that he leave within the hour, accompanied by Sergeant George Clarke and the two men still waiting in the cab outside – John Death and Jonathan Matthews. The first ship bound for New York was scheduled to depart the following morning – Wednesday 20 July – from Liverpool. If they failed to catch the express train north that evening, the next boat did not leave until Saturday.

The inspector would be leaving behind several loose threads:

they had still not succeeded in ruling out the involvement of Charles Judd – suspected murderer of Judge Poinsot – nor had they managed to untangle the information given to them by Thomas Lee about the two men sharing the same compartment as Thomas Briggs when his train pulled out from Bow. The responsibility for straightening these worrying uncertainties would not be his; the investigation would go on without him and he knew that it might be months before he would be back home.

By ten to nine Tanner, Clarke, Death and Matthews were hurrying under the massive arch at the entrance to Euston Square Station. Dodging into the Great Hall and swerving through crowds of passengers and piles of luggage, they skirted porters and trolleys to reach the down platform, sweating in the furnace-like heat that thickened under the great iron and glass roof. With a burst of steam, the nine o'clock night express bound for Liverpool shuddered away, gaining speed as it passed slum, factory and suburb. Smoke billowed over its spine and lingered in its wake as the train hurtled into the night, whirling the four men away from London.

BOOK TWO

# VOYAGE

# CHAPTER 12

# *Flying from Justice*

Müller's four-pound ticket on the *Victoria* was one of the cheapest available for a cross-Atlantic voyage. For an estimated nineteen days he would be cut off from the rest of the world, crammed into primitive, overcrowded steerage accommodation. Basic weekly provisions would be supplied to each of the sixty or so passengers, including a pound each of salt pork and beef, the same amount of flour, oatmeal and peas and two pounds of potatoes and bread or biscuits, but the passengers would have to feed themselves, preparing their own meals by boiling the dried peas for three or four hours before adding a little meat to form a watery stew. Sometimes the meat would fall apart and disappear; at others, some rough character would take a fancy to the porridge and purloin it all. The 'fresh' water was barely potable; fruit and fresh meat were out of the question.

Müller would have to stand up for himself in the scramble to eat and decency and comfort would be almost impossible: there were few lavatories and hand-basins provided the only means to wash. The shared, windowless cabins were airless and cramped with just enough room for a narrow bunk bed with space underneath to store travelling trunks which would slide across the floor in heavy weather, crashing against anything in their path. Sickness could spread rampantly – typhus, cholera and dysentery often posed as great a threat to emigrants as shipwrecks – and, as the days passed, it was likely that vomit and unemptied chamber pots would make the stench in passengers' quarters overwhelming.

With little privacy, lice proliferated, quarrels could flare and the cramped conditions could only be temporarily escaped by remaining on deck. There Müller might shiver in the salt spray as the boat rolled through the swells. If the weather was bad and the boat was caught in storms, he would be forced back inside to suffer the interminable tedium of entrapment alongside his fellow passengers as they contemplated their futures in the New World.

The German had a good lead on Inspector Tanner, but the *Victoria* was an old-fashioned wooden sail packet and it was still possible that her scheduled nineteen-day voyage could stretch to several weeks. Tanner's vessel, the Inman Line's *City of Manchester*, was twice as big – a modern, iron-hulled screw steamer with three mighty boilers powering engines of 400 horsepower. She was expected to cross the ocean in under a fortnight, promising the detective a sliver of advantage. It all depended on the weather. With a fair wind it was possible that Müller could disembark a day before Tanner arrived. If so, the detective's chase was in vain.

Tanner took spacious second-class cabins which cost seventeen guineas a head, four times more than the price of a ticket on the *Victoria*. With a dining room and a separate deck on which to stroll, he and his companions would have a far more comfortable time of it than their quarry. Even the steerage passengers on the *Manchester* would be better off than Müller on the *Victoria*. She was among the first steamers fitted out to carry them in an acceptable level of comfort, providing warm, well-lit and venti-lated rooms, three hot meals a day and washrooms with soap, towels, mirrors and running water, all for a fare of six guineas a head. It was such a successful innovation that Inman vessels gained a reputation for their size, comfort and speed and, despite the American Civil War, steerage tickets to New York were snapped up weeks ahead of sailing. Some 132,000 emigrants had arrived in New York in the first six months of that year, thirty thousand more than the year before, many of them lured by the new ease of passage as well as the promise of a thousand dollars for enlisting in the Yankee army. Arriving from all over Europe, Germans represented the largest group of foreigners setting foot on American soil.

*

As the two ships ploughed towards America the mood at Scotland Yard was buoyant and, in Tanner's absence, his co-chief – Detective Inspector Frederick Adolphus Williamson – assumed control. Jonathan Matthews' revelation on Monday evening had injected new life into the flailing police investigation and there was plenty more legwork for the police to complete, but Tanner knew that the case was in good hands: fondly known to his men as 'Dolly', Williamson was a man of dry good humour and shrewd common sense.

In case the *Victoria* should dock in Ireland, Williamson asked the constabulary office at Dublin Castle to instruct all ports to conduct searches. Next, dispatches were sent to all Crown representatives in Germany requesting information on Müller's background. Once he had briefed the press on Wednesday morning, Inspector Williamson travelled to Clapton Square to urge one of Thomas Briggs' sons to go to New York in case their father's hat or watch should be discovered on the suspect. Leaving the family undecided, he then turned towards the station at Hackney Wick, hoping that Townsend, the ticket collector on duty on 9 July, would be able to identify the impatient, black-coated man at the ticket gate that night as Müller, which would fix their suspect at the scene of the crime. But Williamson was disappointed. When Townsend saw Müller's photograph, he denied ever having seen him before.

Müller's former lodgings were now the focus of intense police scrutiny. As the witnesses were engaged at the Bow Street court on Tuesday, Inspector Steer and Superintendent Tiddey had been at 16 Park Terrace. Outside, the dust-hole was emptied bucket by bucket and its contents sifted for evidence. Inside, they scoured the first-floor back room in which Müller had lodged. On the face of it there was little sign that Müller had left anything behind apart from the Walker hat box and the slipper already in their possession. Nothing on the shelves, on the small mantel over the empty hearth, or under the lumpy mattress; no discarded papers and no discernible signs of blood on the tatty strip of carpet or on the boards.

The small fireplace had evidently not been used for some time. Inspector Steer knelt in front of it. Leaning sideways and twisting his head in order to push his arm right up to the shoulder into the chimney, his hand brushed against something soft. Casting around, he caught hold of a piece of material and withdrew it. Stiff with large spots of what looked like dried blood and dirt, the material appeared to be the torn sleeve lining of a man's coat and seemed to have been used to clean a pair of shoes before being shoved up the chimney. Steer sent the material straight to Professor Alfred Swaine Taylor at Guy's Hospital for analysis. Taylor, sometimes called the 'father of British forensic medicine', was a chemist and toxicologist at the forefront of an emerging science; his opinion was increasingly sought by the police in the investigation of bloody crimes, and Steer knew he would set to work fast.

Meanwhile, Superintendent William Tiddey set out to piece together the complicated jigsaw of the pawnshop transactions made by Müller in the days before the *Victoria* sailed. John Hoffa had told Tanner that although Müller had seemed to have had enough money for his passage during the week of 4 July, his last few days in London were spent in a desperate scramble for cash. By working out how Müller had come up with the money for his fare, Inspector Williamson hoped to uncover more clothing or jewellery to link him to the crime.

Hoffa had given Mrs Repsch a suit of clothes to pawn for Müller, and received two pawn tickets issued by Mr Annis in Minories. One was for a black coat, already retrieved but bearing no marks of blood, or indeed any signs of having been involved in a struggle; both sleeve linings were intact. The second ticket was for the gold chain also retrieved by the police and identified by John Death as the one he had given in exchange for Mr Briggs' on Monday the 11th.

Tiddey discovered that another of Müller's co-workers at Hodgkinson's tailors, John Henry Glass, had also helped Müller. Unlike Hoffa, Glass said that he was unaware that Müller had money prior to 9 July but he did have some idea of how Müller had raised cash during the week before he sailed. Glass told Tiddey that *on Tuesday, 12th July last, he came to me in Mr. Hodgkinson's shop about 4 o'clock in the afternoon. He offered me a gold watch. He said if I would not buy it he had not money enough to go to America.* The watch was one Müller had worn for months, but Glass could not afford it. Suggesting that Müller come back the next day, Glass told Tiddey that *he did come about 9 o'clock … and he and I went together to a pawnbroker's, named Barker. I forget the name of the street.*

Barker's was in Houndsditch, an extension of the Minories bordering the eastern edge of the City. Here, Glass paid one pound to redeem a gold chain that Müller had pledged weeks earlier. Jumping on an omnibus, the two then travelled several miles west to Cox's, a broker in seedy Prince's Street off Leicester Square, where they *pawned the watch that he had offered me the day before, and the chain that I had just got out of pawn, for £4. Müller took the money.*

Glass gave his friend five shillings for the ticket. Both caught a 'bus back as far as Bank where Glass went back to work and Müller headed directly to the London docks. In total, Glass had outlaid one pound, five shillings, but he was now in possession of goods worth more than the four pounds. Even if he could not come up with the money to redeem the items himself, he could always sell on the ticket at a profit. It was a good deal for both men.

It was disappointing for Tiddey that his enquiries had failed to turn up any new items of clothing – a frustration compounded by the fact that when he went to recover the pawned watch from Cox's it turned out not to be Thomas Briggs' old-fashioned chronometer. Nevertheless, the policeman's piecing together of Müller's various deals had not been profitless. The police had now recovered three gold watch chains: Thomas Briggs', the chain given in exchange for it by John Death, and Müller's own cheaper chain, worth a fraction of the others.

It was also striking that, like his silk hat, the dead man's watch remained unaccounted for. Without a chain with which to attach it to a waistcoat, was it likely that Müller would have kept hold of it?

On Tuesday morning, *The Times* had alarmed its readers with reports that the police investigation was at a standstill. Twenty-four hours later, following Inspector Williamson's briefing, their tone had changed and the front pages of the dailies broadcast with confidence *The Discovery of the Murderer. London and all the world*, wrote *The Times*, *will be thankful that such a clue has at last been found to the track of the murderer of the late Mr Briggs as to leave no doubt that the miscreant will be brought to justice.* With a great surge of relief, the long, narrow columns of all the broadsheets were again full of the unfolding story, picking over the details of the previous day's police activity.

## CHAPTER 13

# A Fabric Built of Straws

So far as the papers were concerned, Francis (as the papers called him) Müller was *the actual murderer*. The story was already dramatic but the police chase promised to be intoxicating. Müller might temporarily have escaped, but the detectives and leading players in his proposed downfall were pursuing him at full tilt on a steamer which, wrote *The Times, barring accidents, will reach America at least four days before the sailing vessel that conveys the villain*.

International affairs had also moved forward. Those same Wednesday papers covered details of a truce between Denmark and her German aggressors in anticipation of the opening of peace discussions in Vienna. But the German name on everyone's lips was not Otto von Bismarck – the militaristic Prussian 'Iron Chancellor' proposing to redefine the power balance of Europe – but Müller, a twenty-four-year-old, thought to be from a Cologne family of gun-makers.

Müller was variously said to have been indignant at losing his own watch and chain in a brawl with a woman and to have arrived back at his lodgings on the night of 9 July *much confused* and speaking of an accident in the City in which his ankle was injured. *According to the representations of Matthews' friends*, wrote the *Daily Telegraph*, the man was morose and fond of drink. Some reported that he had been violent and savage towards his fiancée – Matthews' sister-in-law – others that she had branded him *a murderer in intention*. Hitherto, the nameless suspect described by the Death brothers had seemed innocuous with his slim build and his pale, whiskerless face. Now it seemed that he was *a man of great resolution and singular energy* [with] ... *a character for extreme violence which caused him to be disliked by his friends. His forehead was low, his cheek-bones prominent and his general expression of face somewhat forbidding.*

The gold watch chains, the crumpled hat, the thoughtlessly discarded cardboard jewellery box, the injured ankle and Müller's flight on the *Victoria* added up, according to the *Daily News*, to sturdy links *in the chain of circumstantial evidence* pointing to Müller's guilt. That these 'facts' might also be coincidences, and that none of them provided direct proof of the actual crime, seemed unimportant. In the eyes of police and press, the accumulation of so much detail against the German simply cornered him.

Nowhere was the power of circumstantial evidence put more succinctly than by the barrister Robert Audley – hero of Mary Elizabeth Braddon's recent novel *Lady Audley's Secret* – as he confronted his guilty aunt. It was, he told her, *that wonderful fabric which is built of straws collected at every point of the compass ... infinitessimal trifles* [on which] *may sometimes hang the whole secret of some wicked mystery ... a scrap of paper; a shred of some torn garment; the button off a coat; a word dropped incautiously ... A thousand circumstances so slight as to be forgotten by the criminal, but links of steel in the wonderful chain forged by the science of the detective officer.* But there were also those who were uncomfortable with the fallibility of this kind of evidence. While the majority of newspaper readers were already swayed by the strength of the details so far known about Müller, others took note of small inconsistencies and alternative suspicions that allowed room for doubt. One or two reporters reminded their readers of the inquest's finding that threats had been made against Thomas Briggs over his refusal to sanction a loan. Though they also wrote that *the individual alluded to is a man in a respectable position, and his threat is believed to be simply one of those idle menaces in which disappointed people sometimes indulge without any intention to carry them into execution*, the implication remained that no one could be quite sure.

Almost hidden among the columns devoted to Müller's supposedly proven menace was another worrying detail about the boy who, on Saturday 9 July, had seen a flustered man at Stepney Station entering the carriage in which an old gentleman sat, supposed to be Thomas Briggs. The boy's account touched on a confusion that none of the detectives had solved. What readers did not yet know – because the police had not revealed it – was that there were several others telling the same story.

*

Inspector Williamson was beginning to be unsettled by other people's doubts. Tanner had interviewed James Gifford – the agent of the American New York Packet Company – at the docks and, when the agent had seen the photograph of Müller, he had been certain that this was the man to whom he had sold a ticket for the *Victoria*. Now, though, Gifford was not so sure. A couple of Germans called Phillip Wetzell and Wilhelm Müller had recently wanted tickets for New York on the *Cornelius Grinnell*, due to sail on Thursday, and Gifford now thought that one of them bore a strong resemblance to the photograph shown to him by Tanner. The men had refused to give their addresses, but had let slip that they lived in the neighbourhood of Victoria Park.

If Gifford had made a mistake, then it was probable that Inspector Tanner and his witnesses were in pursuit of the wrong man. Could they have been mistaken? Franz Müller's name was on the passenger lists for the *Victoria* and Godfrey Repsch said that he had gone on board. Exasperated, Inspector Williamson put Superintendent Daniel Howie on the track of the two new German suspects.

Williamson was also alarmed by a report from the chief constable of the central police station in Sunderland, Colonel Hogg. On Tuesday the 19th a nervous young man calling himself Franz Müller – described as about twenty years of age, five foot five, fair and with no moustache or whiskers – had asked a local shipping agent for a three-pound ticket on the *Charmer*, bound for Singapore. When the agent later read the name and description of the suspected murderer in the shipping gazette he had called the police. Colonel Hogg had subsequently uncovered evidence that this suspect had behaved oddly during the previous handful of days, refusing to leave his lodgings, and Hogg had become alarmed. The *Charmer* had already left port. Hogg asked Williamson for advice on how to proceed.

The Police Commissioner Sir Richard Mayne had also received a recent visit that raised questions about the direction in which the investigation was moving. Colonel Reade Revell said that an acquaintance – another man keen to keep the police out of his affairs and his name out of the papers – claimed to have spoken to Thomas Briggs on the Fenchurch Street platform on the 9th. While at Bow Station, this friend had received a telegraphic message summoning him back to the City. Quitting the train and catching sight of Thomas Briggs, he had asked the old man to relay a message to his family that he would be late home. During that brief conversation this man had also noted that two other men shared Briggs' compartment.

The story corroborated Thomas Lee's evidence and fitted with several other sightings which suggested that two men – neither of them similar in description to Franz Müller – were seen in the murdered man's compartment before the attack. None of these statements had been made public. Had Briggs found himself confronted by two other well-dressed villains in the inescapable confinement of his compartment? Mayne had also received a letter, from Mr Knox of Camberwell, relating a similar tale: that the cousin of a boy at the local school had been on the train and was sure that he had also seen two men alongside Briggs that night. The Police Commissioner scrawled a note to Inspector Williamson about his interview with Colonel Revell but this, and the letter from Mr Knox, may simply have foundered in the piles of letters and statements from hoaxers and timewasters still littering police desks at Scotland Yard. No further statements were taken and it appears that neither report was followed up.

A new rumour began to circulate, suggesting that the pilot boat leaving the *Victoria* at Worthing had taken on a passenger who had changed his mind and asked to disembark. Ordered to investigate, Daniel Howie found that the pilot, William Atkinson, was already away with another ship but his daughter was able to confirm three things that set the policeman's mind at rest. She said that the pilot boat habitually collected several pilots before heading for land which might account for the rumour. She also thought it impossible that a passenger would have been allowed to join the pilot boat; and she confirmed that her father often carried letters ashore on behalf of passengers. As he left her, Howie thought it was likely that Müller had asked Atkinson to post the note addressed to his landlady Ellen Blyth and he was satisfied that Müller was unlikely to have escaped with the pilot as feared.

There were other small satisfactions for the police. Inspector Williamson was gratified to learn that Professor Taylor's scrutiny of the material found in Müller's fireplace had allowed him to conclude that the blood was human. Additionally, the identity of the cab passenger whose flaring match had revealed a concealed pistol turned out to be a respected warder from a nearby house of correction, closing the loop on an unresolved suspicion.

# CHAPTER 14

## *Ninety in the Shade*

The Commissioner wrote personally to Thomas James Briggs to request the victim's second-eldest son to re-attend Bow Street later that week, on Friday 22 July. It would mark almost a fortnight since his father was attacked in carriage 69.

As they worked to construct a case against the German tailor, both Inspector Frederick Williamson and Sir Richard Mayne concluded that the papers taken to America by Inspector Tanner might not be quite as watertight as they had hoped. Although the extradition treaty between England and America was generally honoured, there had been several instances of oneupmanship and intransigence between the two nations during which prisoner surrender had been denied. With hindsight, both Williamson and the Police Commissioner considered that the depositions taken at Bow Street Magistrates' Court on Tuesday the 19th had been rushed. It troubled both men that the American authorities might rule them insufficient either to arrest or to extradite Müller.

New statements – more of them and all containing finer detail – would have to be swiftly prepared. If this could be concluded at Bow Street on Friday, then they could be taken to New

York by Inspector Kerressey on the Inman Line's *City of Cork* which was due to leave Liverpool on Saturday morning.

As the witnesses were rounded up for another day at the magistrates' court, the press got wind of the plans. Aware now of the direction of the police investigation and of Inspector Tanner's pursuit, groups of sightseers began to amass around the entrance from the early hours of Friday, straining for a glimpse of the characters whose stories filled their daily papers. Outside, it was another splendid day and the temperature was already ninety degrees in the shade. Inside, newspaper reporters jostled for position amid the airless crush of the close little courtroom, notebooks poised.

The session began mid-morning and Chief Magistrate Thomas Henry once again presided. Thomas James Briggs repeated his identification of the chain and walking stick that had belonged to his father. The train guard Benjamin Ames reprised his evidence, as did John Hoffa, and Robert Death stood in for his absent brother to describe their suspicious customer and identify the various chains.

Attention turned to the eight witnesses whose official statements were to be taken in public for the first time. Elizabeth Repsch agreed with Jonathan Matthews' earlier deposition that the crumpled hat definitely belonged to the German suspect. As Inspector Kerressey showed her the hat found on the train, she was adamant: *I know it from the peculiar colour of the lining. I have frequently observed the lining when he has come to our house wearing it.* Telling the court that Müller had boasted about his new gold chain and ring when he visited on Monday the 11th, she confirmed what she had already told Inspector Tanner, that on that visit Müller had been wearing a different hat, *which he put down and I observed it was nearly a new one with a white silk lining. I said to him 'why you extravagant man, another new hat?' He said he had had it a month and that he had smashed his old one and thrown it in the dust hole.*

As the day wore on, Dr Brereton recalled the blood-soaked earth on the site where the body was found. He also described his examination of the carriage on the following morning, his discovery of the broken link in its floor matting and the victim's wounds as catalogued in the post-mortem report. Next, the policeman Edward Dougan described the state of the victim when he was found and detailed the contents of Thomas Briggs' pockets: the quantity of money, a bunch of keys, half a first-class return train ticket, a silver snuffbox and a number of letters. He recalled the victim's rumpled shirt and its single remaining stud, his diamond ring, the gold fastener for a guard chain hanging in the buttonhole of his waistcoat and the fact that Briggs' watch and chain were missing. Following Dougan, train guard William Timms went over the details of the discovery of the body on the line, and then Briggs' nephew David Buchan confirmed that his uncle was sober when he left Nelson Square, being *a man of extremely temperate habits*.

It was the deposition of Thomas Lee that galvanised the reporters on the side benches, all of them alert for new information.

Lee was coy about his reasons for being at Bow Station on 9 July – he said he had *gone for a walk* – but he stuck determinedly to the story he had already told the police. Thomas Briggs and he were well acquainted, he said, and they had spoken for several minutes while the train waited at the platform. Briggs was then *quite well and in his usual spirits*. By his side was an apparently tall, thin man and opposite him sat *a thick set man with lightish sandy whiskers with his hand in the loop of the carriage, and the hand seemed to be a large one*.

Asked how it was that he could see so clearly on a dark night, Lee replied confidently that *the light from one of the gas lamps on the platform was full upon his face*.

In the muggy courtroom the reporters scratched down statements that would provide fodder for the weekend papers.

Thomas James' grief reminded them that a husband and father, violently murdered, was still mourned. The witnesses, by turns flustered, eager, nonplussed or reticent, provided a diverting cast. The exhibited hat, chains, cane, bag, cardboard box and pawn-brokers' tickets were all props worthy of the melodrama of the gaslit stage. Beyond these, Thomas Lee's evidence raised questions about Franz Müller's guilt. If there had been two men in the carriage at Bow with Thomas Briggs it seemed clear that neither corresponded with descriptions of Müller. Bare-faced and thin, he was said to be short. Might he have appeared taller than he actually was when seen by Thomas Lee? If he *was* one of the two men, then where was his accomplice? Unsure what to make of Lee's statement and of its refusal to coalesce with the evidence so far amassed against Müller, the press wondered whether this witness was to be trusted or whether the direction of the police investigation was flawed.

*

By just after six o'clock on Friday evening, Inspector Walter Kerressey was armed with a bundle of new documents certified by Chief Magistrate Henry and by the United States Minister Charles Adams, a dossier designed to withstand the most careful scrutiny of American law. He also carried a duplicate arrest warrant, fresh Home Office letters for the consul in New York, a brand new passport and a small parcel containing the three gold chains.

Accompanied by Superintendent William Tiddey, Kerressey made his way to Euston Square Station. By the next morning he would be on board the *City of Cork*, a ship capable of reaching ten knots, newer and faster even than the *City of Manchester*. It would easily outpace the *Victoria* and might even beat Inspector Tanner to New York.

There would be silence for at least a month while the investigation continued in London. That morning, as the witnesses were gathering in Bow Street, Inspector 'Dolly' Williamson had received a second, unwelcome intelligence from Colonel Hogg, announcing that they had a *man in custody whom we suspect to be Müller*. A foreigner had apparently been arrested for stealing two bags from a railway station and was found to have a duplicate ticket for a gold watch pawned in Shoreditch on 29 June, and a memo book containing the name Müller. Hogg was jumpy and Williamson had taken the next express for Stafford.

It turned out to be a fruitless journey. The arrested man bore no resemblance to Jonathan Matthews' photograph of Franz Müller, nor to either of the men described by Thomas Lee. Leaving him in custody, Williamson boarded the next train south, bringing with him a photograph of the prisoner, his notebook and the pawn ticket. He would soon find that none of it added up. Summoned by a concerned Mr Henry to Bow Street on Saturday morning, Inspector Williamson reported that the whole business had been a waste of time.

Still disquieted by shipping agent James Gifford's concern that he had given the wrong information to the police, Inspector Williamson left Bow Street for the docks, where Daniel Howie had brought together Robert Death, Ellen Blyth and Thomas Lee. Boarding the ship *Cornelius Grinnell*, Williamson took the German passengers Phillip Wetzell and Wilhelm Müller to one side and paraded them before the waiting group. No one recognised either of the men. Both were quickly released.

Williamson's confidence that Tanner had not embarked on a wild goose chase was further bolstered by the arrival of the much-anticipated documents from the Préfecture de Police in Paris. In response to their request for details of the murder of Judge Poinsot four years earlier, the French authorities had forwarded a careful description of their suspect, the escaped convict Charles Judd. He was, it turned out, *ferocious* in appearance: about five feet five inches tall with brown hair, grey eyes, a long face with a large chin, broken teeth, a black beard and a red scar

# CHAPTER 15

# Who but a Madman?

*The assassin – for it would be an affectation to scruple about disregarding in this instance the sound conventional rule that untried men are presumably innocent – has succeeded in temporarily escaping,* reported the *Liverpool Mercury. He doubtless hugs himself in the fond belief that the broad Atlantic will soon roll between him and the baffled avengers of blood … As this man's guilt is deeper and darker than the guilt of common murderers so it seems right and fitting that his punishment should include elements of mortal anguish beyond any penalties which the law can inflict … the concentrated agony … of the dock, the condemned cell and the scaffold.* The *Liverpool Mercury* was not alone in deciding that the German was guilty. Although the rule of innocent until proven guilty was enshrined in English law the Victorian press paid little heed to prohibitions against stirring up prejudice against suspects or prisoners awaiting trial. Yet the fact that every scrap and rumour – no matter how false or vitriolic – could be published in order to boost newspaper circulations did cause a frisson of unease in legal quarters.

The transatlantic chase of Inspector Tanner and his men

heightened the tension already generated by the murder, creating a circus-like atmosphere in which every piece of new information elicited dismay, amazement or horror. Anyone with an interest in the case – anyone who might later be called to give further evidence or to sit in judgement on a prisoner – was able to read the testimonies and even the addresses of every witness.

Reports about Müller's identity, character and background were typically immoderate. There was relish at the prospect of his capture and the retribution it would unleash. A fortnight had passed since the murder when the weekend papers pored over the evidence heard at Bow Street that Friday. Just one, the liberal-minded *Daily News,* refused to brand Müller as a monster. His conduct and manners while in England, it wrote, were ascertained to have been *good and even gentlemanly ... he was never known to be in liquor; he generally returned home straight from his work and it is said that he never frequented public houses.* Though these facts appeared broadly to fall on deaf ears, they signalled a preoccupation in middle-class society about what it meant to be British. As the empire grew, so did a conviction that a standard must be set for the world. 'Foreigners' might have their different ways but sobriety, reliability and frugality were the markers of a truly civilised Englishman and set above all these was the importance of self-control. If the *Daily News* was to be believed, the immigrant Müller's conduct was disconcertingly British.

Jonathan Matthews, on the other hand, was an enigma: discovering that he had recently been declared bankrupt and that his hackney cab was as yet uncertified, the papers began to wonder whether he was a noble wretch or an underhanded fraud. Despite his salacious reasons for being at Bow on the night of 9 July, Thomas Lee had adhered to his original story and he generally passed muster as a *gentleman*; since he knew Thomas Briggs' habits well enough to have been surprised to see him out so late, his story was convincing. Elizabeth Repsch was characterised by most as something of an oddity, prone to paying *particular notice of the hats men wear*, while gentler Ellen Blyth, who *had never taken any particular notice of his hat*, seemed to the newspaper men to be straightforward, honest and innocent.

The press expressed delight in the progress of the case and looked forward to what else might be revealed when the coroner reopened his inquest in Hackney on the following Monday. As for the police, some wrote that wonderful things were now said of them but the breakthrough in this investigation had sprung from accident. All the zeal and industry of the Metropolitan force and all their trained skill appeared to be hopelessly at fault until a little girl happened to show a pasteboard box to her father. Only then did suspicion centre on the German tailor. *We hear it complained*, wrote the *Liverpool Mercury*, *that our famous detectives are little better than bunglers, after all*. The detective force had been weighed in the balance of popular public opinion and found wanting. *Neither Sir Richard Mayne nor his men will be entitled to any praise for their behaviour in the matter*, wrote *Reynolds's Weekly Newspaper*. Did they not resemble a pack of bewildered foxhounds beaten by an ordinary, untrained dog? For a force reputed to cost the country half a million pounds a year, their *glaring incapacity*, their *clodhopping blundering* was indefensible.

The murder had occasioned a public clamour for detective success, for evil to be contained and order reimposed. What the country wanted was superhuman sagacity and ingenuity on the part of their police force, for heroism that would confirm that they were protected. It now appeared that they had something more rational and ordinary: sometime-skilful men who were not endowed with preternatural gifts but who relied on happy accident. Detectives might deal effectively with the delinquents and frauds, the thieves, sharps and pickpockets who operated in the underbelly of the city, but this murder was different. Violent crime was not supposed to happen in first-class carriages by unrecognisable men gliding away on noiseless feet. Had it not been for chance, the papers now suggested, this shadowy murder might have baffled them. It was a fact that did little to reassure the public that they were adequately protected.

If the railway murder recalled the plots of gripping contemporary novels then the papers added their own irresistibly lively coverage designed to boost their circulations by feeding on those widespread anxieties about the dangers of modernity. Despite the evidence of progress wherever one turned, they voiced fears that the beast lurked still at the heart of modern civilisation. While the nation waited to see if Müller would be caught, the perceived dangers of railway travel remained undiminished and passengers continued to wonder indignantly why those in charge were doing nothing about the risks associated with the *solitary-cell system of railway travelling*. Why, they asked, was the government not turning the excitement of the present moment to practical account? Suggestions for remedies came from every quarter. Murderous assault might be prevented by the introduction of sliding glass windows between the carriages – panes that could be curtained for privacy or drawn back to summon help from the passengers in neighbouring compartments. Alternatively, trellises might replace the panels between compartments, allowing a clear view along the length of the carriage. Evil-intentioned persons would be deterred and timid minds eased by the introduction of bells, whistles, signal-boards or speaking tubes, by external 'sidewalks' with handrails, or by the fitting of trapdoors into the roofs of the train. There might be travelling police and separate ladies' carriages; insurance policies against this new kind of liability might be sold at the ticket offices; it might be expedient to outlaw the barring of windows and the locking of compartment doors between stations.

In America, Confederate troops were being driven back from Washington after marching so close that *Mr Lincoln might hear the Southern cannon from the windows of the White House*, as the *New York Times* reported. On American battlefields an estimated ten thousand men were killed weekly, but against those anonymous deaths, the murder of one elderly gentleman on a suburban railway line dominated the British press.

*

Heading towards New York, Detective Inspector Tanner, Sergeant George Clarke and Detective Inspector Walter Kerressey were ignorant of the mounting criticisms of the London police and English government. They were equally unaware that small ripples of doubt about Müller's guilt were beginning to spread, fuelled by the announcement of Williamson's trip to Stafford, the searching of the *Cornelius Grinnell* and other rumours that included the sighting of an anxious, bloodied man at the railway station in Dundee. Even the letter sent to the Blyths from Worthing was now suspected in some quarters of being a ruse designed to throw detectives off the scent.

At the reopening of the inquest in Hackney on Monday morning, 25 July, it transpired that – almost a week after first searching Müller's lodgings – the police had found another potential murder weapon. Because of the small amount of blood found on Thomas Briggs' discarded cane, it was unclear whether it had been used as a bludgeon. Now another walking cane made of whalebone and India rubber and topped with a heavy, leaden finial had been discovered hanging by the bed of a fellow lodger at Müller's former home in Park Terrace. Conjecturing that Müller had borrowed and then replaced it surreptitiously, the cane had been sent to Professor Taylor to be tested for marks of human blood. It turned out that the Professor's findings were inconclusive.

The coroner also pressed Eliza Matthews over whether it was possible for her husband to have remained ignorant of the murder for a whole week. Had he really never discussed it? Could he have missed the police bills displayed conspicuously across the capital? Was he not, like most drivers, prone to read the papers left behind in his carriage? Eliza admitted that her husband could read and that they took *Lloyd's Weekly Newspaper* each weekend. On Saturday 16 July, though, she said that the paper was left unread since they had been visited by her sister's family. Nevertheless, it dawned on even casual spectators that, given his job, it was somewhat bizarre that it took Jonathan Matthews so long to bring his suspicions to the police.

The coroner was unwilling to hear the testimony of any more witnesses. The inquest jury, though, were interested in the evidence given to the magistrates on Friday by Thomas Lee and pressed for him to be sworn. Repeating his description of the two men he saw in the carriage with Thomas Briggs, Lee explained again that *it was the lamp outside which gave me the most distinct view. The compartment in which Mr Briggs was sitting had drawn up near a gas lamp on the platform.*

Was it possible, asked the coroner, that these two men might have left the compartment before the train moved off from Bow?

*Yes. There was time for either of them to have got out after I had got into my carriage.*

*Did you see any attempt to do so on the part of either of them, by their opening the door at all?*

*No, I did not.*

*They made no manifestation of their intention to get out?*

*I did not see any.*

If Lee was right, at least one – possibly two – crucial suspects remained unidentified. But his admission that either man might have left the train at Bow somewhat undermined the force of his statement.

*

Letters expressing misgivings continued to be addressed to the Police Commissioner. Correspondents found Matthews' story suspicious and thought it possible that he was motivated by the three-hundred-pound reward. One pointed out that *in our opinion it is very difficult to get fitted with a hat even by a professional hatter.* How likely, he wondered, was it that a hat would be purchased for another on the off-chance that it might fit?

Questions were also asked about the wisdom of showing John Death a single photograph of the suspect rather than several from which he might have taken his pick. One letter expressed disbelief at the silversmith's ability to identify so unhesitatingly one casual customer out of the hundreds he must serve, particularly as he had sworn under oath that the man who came to his shop on 11 July had been careful to keep to the shadowy parts of the room. Why, wrote others, had Matthews been shown the crumpled hat at Scotland Yard rather than asked to identify it from among a variety of different hats? Had he been asked to try on the hat to demonstrate that it was too large for him? Had anyone ever heard of a man asking a friend to buy him a hat and expecting it to fit? Was there a man who could identify the hat of his most intimate friend without being shown it first? What had become of Matthews' hat? Had the police behaved properly in expecting perfect honesty from this bluff cab driver?

Several of the Police Commissioner's correspondents wondered whether Thomas Lee's evidence was being taken seriously enough. Letters began to appear in the press, including one printed in the *Daily Telegraph*. Signed from 'Do Justice' and dated 25 July, it backed up Lee's story by claiming that an acquaintance *shook hands with Mr Briggs while he was sitting in a first-class carriage at Bow Station, and that there were then in the same carriage 'two ill-looking men'.*

Concern grew. What if all the circumstantial evidence was only that? What if the suspicions were a mere collection of crochets? Similar uncertainties kept the readers of those excitingly mysterious sensation novels on the edges of their seats and their authors often pointed out that *the species of argument which builds up any hypothesis out of a series of probabilities may, after all, lead very often to false conclusions.* If this murder turned out to be a ghastly enigma, if it threatened to remain unsolved, then life was imitating art.

Though *there are many circumstances of grave suspicion against Müller*, wrote 'A Barrister' from Lincoln's Inn to the editor of the *Telegraph, there are also facts strongly tending to induce a supposition of his innocence.* Matthews' evidence, for a start, was of so extraordinary a nature as to demand the strictest scrutiny. Was it possible that he had delayed making his statement in order to gain the money without sacrificing an innocent friend? So many aspects of this story, posited the 'Barrister', constituted prima facie evidence of Müller's innocence. He asked *who but a madman, knowing himself to have but just been guilty of an atrocious murder and not being in immediate want of money (as is proved by his exchanging not selling the chain) would have deliberately gone out of his way to connect himself with the crime?*

In an editorial on Monday 25 July, the *Daily Telegraph* agreed. *We know of certain events affecting Müller which occurred at the time of the murder of Mr Briggs, but we do not know directly that the one man was ever in the presence of the other; therefore, in order to convict Müller we have to invent a story which shall not only accord with all the known facts but which shall accord with them much more probably than any other story that could possibly be suggested.* The paper urged the country to regain perspective. Fact, rumour and surmise, it believed, had been mingled so confusedly in the various accounts presented to the public that it was difficult to know what constituted tangible evidence against the German.

The newspaper reminded its readers of the notorious frailty of circumstantial 'proofs', that Müller had worked for a reputable company, that the Blyths were a respectable married couple whose opinion of Müller's good character should not be ignored, that he gave more than a week's notice, and that some evidence suggested that he had injured his foot on Thursday 7 July and was wearing a slipper on the night of the murder. It questioned whether it was possible for a murderer to appear in good cheer at breakfast the next morning, wearing the same suit of clothes he had worn the night before without any signs of their being cleaned in a hurry. It seemed to the paper most unlikely that a guilty man would so conspicuously boast about his new chain and hat or that he would broadcast so freely the name of his escape vessel.

*If the evidence stopped here*, the editor continued, *we should have no hesitation in saying not merely that it is insufficient to convict Müller but that it renders his guilt extremely improbable.* As for Matthews' testimony about the hat, it remained to be seen whether it would stand up under cross-examination. For now, the paper considered that its truth had not been established. *We are particularly anxious to impress this observation on the public mind. He should be judged without prejudice ... No wise and cautious man will dare to say at present that Müller* cannot *be innocent.*

If this were true, where did it leave the London detectives?

# CHAPTER 16

## *City of Strangers*

Several drunks in different districts of the capital had begun to confess to the murder. Hauled up in front of magistrates, all of them were judged to be lunatics or serial fabricators. Letters about being imprisoned in railway carriages with the delirious, the threatening or the downright odd still filled the papers and there were reports that one of the City's most eminent young solicitors, Thomas Beard, boarding a train at Fenchurch Street, had been alarmed by a sinister co-passenger staring covetously at his watch and chain while quizzing him about the recent murder. The tall, black-clad man appeared to be concealing a leather-covered cosh. Sick with fear, Beard had leapt out at the next station and raised the alarm, *thoroughly convinced that a murderous outrage was purposed.*

Newspaper reporters speculated on the progress of the ships crossing the Atlantic, couching their conjecture in prose worthy of a suspense thriller. The London detectives and their two witnesses were heading towards a divided nation exhausted by three years of hard fighting, to a country in which casualties mounted in their tens of thousands, where the price of food, fuel, clothing and rent forced many into poverty and where the scent of war suffused the air. *The Times* reported that Müller's ship, the *Victoria*, was making little headway against strong headwinds and high seas. By the end of July, nearly a fortnight after leaving London, she had only just reached Cape Clear off the coast of southern Ireland.

In New York, sketchy details of the London railway murder began to trickle into the press. Confined to the earliest-known facts, they communicated simply that a gentleman in a first-class carriage had been severely beaten and flung, in a matter of minutes, onto the tracks by an assailant who left no material clue. What they did not yet know was that the suspected murderer was en route to their city, pursued by Metropolitan Police detectives in two separate ships. As new details of the Briggs case emerged, the story would grow from a small foreign news report into a New York City talking point.

*

Unlike the *Victoria*, Inspector Tanner's *City of Manchester* had powered across the ocean. Sixteen days after leaving Liverpool the vessel navigated the final stretches of New York's harbour. Slipping past Governor's Island on the morning of Friday 5 August, she edged through a forest of masts and a clamour of packet ships, clippers and ocean steamers to reach her dock on the south-western edge of Manhattan Island. Three days into the voyage, Tanner had fallen down a companionway ladder and was under the care of the ship's surgeon, in severe pain. Once in port he was assailed by the heat and the shouts of the stevedores, the crush of the passengers, porters and relatives who seethed between cargo hauls and luggage stacks. Only when he and his three companions had cleared quarantine and immigration did the London detective manage to establish that the *Victoria* had not yet been seen.

Passengers from the *Manchester* streamed through Castle

Clinton, the old stone fort on the water's edge in lower Manhattan used as an immigration station, registering their arrival while some changed their money, sought directions or prepared to sleep on the floor for a night or so until they got their bearings. His formalities completed, Tanner hailed a horse-drawn cab for the group including John Death, Jonathan Matthews and Sergeant Clarke. Quitting the riverside stink, the foundry stacks, the groaning wharves and packing sheds, they left the Hudson River docks in their wake, pushing through a snarl of laden wagons to gain the southern edge of Broadway. Here they headed north, rumbling past a confusion of narrow lanes and slums as they made their way towards the centre of the city.

As the warren of southern streets gave way to the twelve parallel avenues that stretched northwards as far as 44th Street, old timber villages were being replaced by distinct stone precincts. All that existed above 44th Street were surveyors' pegs stuck into the baked mud and taut lines of string that marked out the city's plans for expansion. Up at the line proposing 59th Street, a vast wilderness of 760 acres was earmarked as a park for a population that was growing so fast that it had quadrupled in the three decades since 1830. For now, though, everyone was packed into the southern reaches of the island; everything here, exclaimed the visitors' guides, was *din and excitement. Everything is done in a hurry ...* [and] *all is intense anxiety.*

Heading uptown, Tanner's cab passed the crowds of black-suited bankers and merchants in Wall Street. A little further along on their right they reached the eleven-acre triangle of an area known as The Park with a central fountain in the shape of an Egyptian lily throwing columns of water up into the dusty air. This was the civic centre, margined by imposing public buildings and dominated by the marble-columned façade and lofty clock tower of City Hall. To the left were the five-storey offices of the *New York Times* and, behind City Hall on Chambers Street, the United States District Court.

Union soldiers mingled with watermelon and pineapple vendors in the New York streets. After sixteen days at sea, Broadway was bewildering, alive with snapping reins and shying horses, fine shops, bright clothes, vagrant children, burly cops and advertisements for Phineas T. Barnum's American Museum with its giants, dwarves, Indian warriors and French automata. Small entrances to oyster cellars vied with the grander façades of glittering eating houses such as Taylor's and Maillard's Saloons and the renowned Delmonico's. Horse-drawn locomotives ran on tracks right down the middle of streets. Passing under humming telegraph wires, the cab pushed its way through an entanglement of carriage wheels and carts.

Tanner's destination was the Everett House Hotel at 17th Street on the north side of Union Square, a hotel that advertised itself as usefully positioned for the centre of town, the cars and the stage coaches – New York's equivalent of the London omnibuses. It would be their base for the foreseeable future. Transplanted into this crucible of half a million strangers, Tanner, Clarke, Death and Matthews were foreigners in a city of immigrants. It was late afternoon. Tomorrow, Tanner would begin his official calls.

He would find that fuller details of the Briggs murder had begun to appear in the New York press, the American papers explaining that *English railcars are very different from those to which we are accustomed in this country*, as journalists lingered over their comparative isolation. They emphasised the disappearance of Thomas Briggs' watch and sprang on the evidence both of the jeweller John Death and of the cabman Jonathan Matthews. It was now apparent that the suspected murderer was bound for their city and that witnesses were also expected imminently, in the company of at least one Scotland Yard detective.

The British murder story was manna for the fiercely competitive newspaper offices clustered along printing house row by The Park. With ten-cylinder power presses housed in gargantuan press rooms, their steam boilers and engines churning out news sheets as broad as one's arms could stretch, the fifteen daily papers in the city had a combined circulation of around 140,000 copies. The Briggs story provided a distraction from coverage of the battles between the north and south and from the remorseless lists of those killed in battle.

Leaving the Everett House Hotel on Saturday morning, 6 August, Inspector Tanner found New York stewing under hazy skies. The city was *en fête* as it celebrated Admiral Farragut's audacious victory at Mobile Bay the previous morning, and the establishment of a blockade that isolated much of the Confederate fleet in the south. Tanner learned from the American owners of the *Victoria* that their ship was freighted with a cargo of iron and was making slow progress. Incredibly, she was not expected for at least another two weeks. He had time to put himself in touch with all the chief agencies in the city, beginning with the acting British consul Pierrepont Edwards, a thirty-one-year-old New Yorker born of British parents. Edwards would give him all the support in his power, beginning with an introduction to the man acting as the solicitor to the English government, Francis Marbury.

Marbury was crucial to their success. If their arrest of Müller was successful, then Francis Marbury would plead the British case for extradition. One of the best-known lawyers in the city and at the height of his career, he had built his reputation by pursuing some of the most famous railroad suits of the previous decade and he was not to be underestimated. He now advised Tanner that they must be careful to adhere strictly to the letter of the American law. Since Britain had no extradition treaty with the state of New York, the arrest must be made under national law by an officer deputed by the United States Marshal. Following that arrest, Tanner would have to obtain from the New York Commissioner a warrant to detain the prisoner and only when that had been granted could their plea for extradition be lodged. Marbury would be there at each stage to advise

Inspector Tanner on the legal requirements to bring off his task successfully.

Tanner's next destination was in the lower reaches of the city, the New York Police Headquarters on the corner of Mulberry Street and Bleeker. Passing the two huge trees outside the entrance, mounting the grand steps and entering the raucous building, he was anxious to discover whether this department – already fighting fires on multiple fronts – would give him the assistance he needed. Though it had been established for sixteen years, with London's Metropolitan force as its model, the NYPD faced a climate of aggression exacerbated both by immigration and the American Civil War – only a year earlier, frenzied mobs of immigrants had rioted for three days against being drafted into the Northern army. Organised gangs driven by the lure of money and political power were growing in strength and the city inhabitants increasingly viewed their police as both inefficient and corrupt. Tanner had no idea what to expect.

In the event, his task proved surprisingly easy. By the time he left the building, the Chief of the New York Metropolitan Police, Superintendent John Kennedy, along with Inspector Daniel Carpenter, had proposed a plan. One of their best officers, John Tieman, would be placed at Tanner's disposal. Tieman spoke German and would be able to act as interpreter if Müller failed to understand their questions; he would also be authorised by Marshal Robert Murray to act on behalf of the federal authorities. It was suggested that this officer should station himself with Sergeant George Clarke about eight miles south on the eastern edge of Staten Island. Overlooking Lower New York Bay, they would wait with the medical officer whose duty it was to board every ship in order to impose quarantine restrictions when necessary. As soon as the *Victoria* was in sight, the police would accompany the medic on board, arrest Müller and hold him until he could be taken ashore.

On Sunday 7 August, two days after the arrival of Tanner on

the *Manchester*, Inspector Kerressey's ship docked in New York. The city newspapers were already reporting Tanner's meeting with the Police Department at Mulberry Street the day before and the English murder story that had seemed rather parochial only weeks before was escalating: readers were told that the *Victoria* with Franz Müller on board was so keenly anticipated that the harbour police boat had been placed at the detective's disposal. As each transatlantic ship brought more recent British papers, details of the London investigation were repeated. The American press expressed incredulity at the German's ostentatious exhibition of the prizes of his crime and derided him for failing so glaringly to cover his tracks. The transaction at John Death's shop, the various pawnbroker deals, the gifting of the cardboard box and the 'shallow' story about the injury to his ankle were, to them, mere *proofs of his stupidity*.

Set against the visceral terrors of the Civil War, the murder was unlikely to provoke the shock it had caused in England and, to American reporters, Müller's behaviour appeared to be dense rather than malevolent. Yet a notorious murderer was about to arrive on Manhattan's shores. Shouted by the newsboys on street corners, the promise of a dramatic denouement on America's doorstep rippled across the city.

# CHAPTER 17

## *The Last Person in the World*

A white glare bounced off the water in the harbour, blistered from the pavements and rebounded between the buildings. August in New York brought thick and heavy air and the heat leached energy.

The pain in Inspector Tanner's back was easing under the care of a New York doctor with the bizarre name of Quackembos, but his general discomfort only grew in the unrelenting swelter. Kerressey had gone south to join Clarke and Tieman at Quarantine Landing on Staten Island. Unused to inactivity, there was little left for the restless Tanner to do but write reports for the Commissioner in London to be dispatched with each departing ship.

Tanner judged that the American authorities would offer little resistance to giving up the prisoner should they apprehend him, but he worried that American newspaper attention was beginning to complicate things. *In consequence of the publication in the papers of all my movements there is a possibility of Müller escaping*, he wrote. He was concerned that a pilot boat might board the *Victoria* way out at sea and that indiscreet conversation or a recent newspaper taken on board might warn Müller of their presence and precipitate his escape or suicide. Aiming to limit this possibility, Tanner had asked the British consul to communicate with the telegraph station out at Sandy Hook, a thin spit of land projecting into the Atlantic that all ships had to pass on their approach into New York Harbor. As soon as the *Victoria* came into view it was agreed that the station would telegraph the news to the officers on Staten Island. The consul also circulated a letter to all known pilots working the Sandy Hook waters, impressing on them the importance of discretion, advising them to take no newspapers on board the *Victoria* and desiring them to request of her captain the imprisonment of any passenger called Müller. Leaving nothing to chance, Tanner added his own offer of a sixty-dollar – or five-pound – reward.

Tanner was also preoccupied by the rumour that a German recruiting agent for the army called Essinhen had hatched a plan to intercept the *Victoria* in open sea, persuade Müller to escape with him and then enrol him in the army in order to collect a thousand-dollar bounty. Reporting these fears to Richard Mayne in London, Tanner emphasised that he had made all practicable arrangements to defeat the plan, but admitted that it was an almost impossible task. Knowing that there was little possibility of Müller's ship landing much earlier than 20 August, he still went to meet the arrival of every large ship, battling through the crowds to quiz their captains. Had they seen or spoken with the *Victoria* during their voyage?

A week passed. On Friday 12 August the capture of the *Adriatic* by the Confederate steamboat the *Tallahassee* reminded Tanner of the perils faced by all transatlantic shipping. Widely feared, this pirate boat patrolled the waters of the north, capturing fishing and pilot boats, barques and passenger ships and looting their coal, provisions and money. The *Adriatic* had left London a week after her sister-ship, the *Victoria*. Caught and raided en route to New York, her 163 passengers were cast ashore with their *cracked vases, bird cages, cats, dogs and other pets brought with them from the Old World*: then the ship was burned. If the slow-going *Victoria* were to suffer a similar fate, then Müller would evade them all. The *Tallahassee* had also hijacked the *James Funk*, the pilot boat engaged by Tanner to attempt to intercept the *Victoria*. Try as he might to anticipate and stave off any possibility of the German's escape, the detective was impotent against the threats posed by the machinery of the Civil War.

Another week went by. On 19 August, Inspector Tanner at his post in the city and Inspector Kerressey and Sergeant Clarke at Quarantine Landing kept a strict watch, expecting the ship hourly. Down at Castle Clinton, through the mighty black gates of the immigration station, Tanner waited in the shade of its stone walls, commanding a view of the entire harbour, eager for the wavering speck of a mast to appear on the horizon.

The consul, Pierrepont Edwards, had alerted him to the fact that a gentleman in Manhattan was purporting to be an agent of the German Legal Protection Society in London. This agent had told Edwards that he was instructed to engage representation for Müller and had asked to be present at any arrest in order to caution the prisoner about his rights. He said that Müller's defence in England had been placed in the hands of the solicitor Thomas Beard who ran a thriving business in Basinghall Street in the City; he was clever, dedicated and, ironically, the man driven to such fear by a fellow passenger on a train a few weeks earlier. For four days Tanner had anticipated that the agent of the German Society would present himself at the Everett House Hotel, but he had not appeared.

*

In England, newspapers reporting the Vienna peace talks expressed growing alarm at the aggression of Prussia towards Denmark. In this hostile, anti-German climate, the German Legal Protection Society, or Deutscher Rechtsschutz Verein (based at 73

Moorgate Street in the City of London), provided free legal assistance to its nationals in Britain and was fixed on assisting their compatriot. Thomas Beard, the solicitor it had engaged, was noted for his thoroughness, but in the absence of his client there was little he could do but hope that someone would come forward.

On 9 August a paragraph appeared in *The Times* earnestly inviting *any person who can furnish information as to the movements of the accused Franz Müller on the day of the alleged murder (the 9th inst) and the three subsequent days to communicate same to the undersigned the solicitor, Thos. Beard, 10 Basinghall Street, City.* The next day another appeared in the *Morning Advertiser.* They were seeking information from all available quarters, aiming to provide Müller with a plausible defence by proving that he was not on the railway at the time of the murder. These advertisements, along with reports of the ongoing proceedings of the inquest in Hackney, kept the story alive.

On Tuesday 23 August, as Tanner embarked on the eighteenth day of his New York vigil, the Home Office in London learned a little more about Müller from the Royal Police Directory in Munich. The German authorities wrote that he was from Langendernbach in the Duchy of Saxe-Weimar, that he had arrived in their town in May 1859 as a journeyman tailor aged nineteen and had been employed by several successive businesses. His description fitted that supplied by London and it was known that he had left Munich in February 1861. Regarding his character, they announced that *nothing whatever has transpired to his disadvantage* – in fact, Müller had himself complained of being robbed by a fellow lodger while working in Munich. A second report from the President of Police at Cologne completed the picture. Müller had been registered there from July 1861: *he was an active, clever workman, however inconsiderate and not to be trusted, but endeavoured to make good ... by a cheerful obliging behaviour.* They confirmed that Müller had obtained a visa for London in March 1862 and that he had absconded from Cologne without repaying several small loans advanced by his colleagues.

*

The *Victoria* had been at sea for forty days. Through the interminable hours of Wednesday the 24th the southern horizon of the harbour remained clear. Only as the sun began to drop to the west did she appear off Sandy Hook and begin to make her way into the Lower Bay.

The pilot boarding the ship off Sandy Hook conveyed to her captain, Champion, the facts about his passenger Müller. Two armed crewmen were ordered to watch the suspect without alerting him to their surveillance. Meanwhile, the telegraph station sent a message to Quarantine Landing confirming that the vessel making its approach was the *Victoria*.

Instead of heading out towards the ship, Tanner turned away from the shore, forced back into the city to meet Francis Marbury. Their quarry was now in American waters and within Marshal Murray's federal jurisdiction and the Crown's solicitor could petition for a formal warrant to be issued for his arrest. Only when the paperwork had been finalised would the detective get the chance to confront the man he'd been chasing for weeks.

At Staten Island, George Clarke, NYPD Officer John Tieman and the medical officer Dr Swinbourne scrambled into a small boat and pushed away from the shore. Drawing up alongside the sail packet just before six o'clock, they boarded and made straight for Captain Champion's cabin.

An excursion boat had passed close to the ship earlier that evening as she began to negotiate the bay and its passengers had called loudly for 'the murderer Franz Müller'. It could have meant disaster for the London detectives, but their calls appeared not to have been heard or understood by those on deck. In the warmth of the summer's evening as the ship loomed towards it, landfall, more passengers emerged to stand talking and laughing in clusters, to lean over the sides or to squint at the Manhattan shore as the sun settled towards the horizon. It seems that none of them wondered at the thousands of people thronging the Staten Island shoreline in the hope of witnessing the arrival of Mr Briggs' murderer. On board the *Victoria* belongings had been packed away ready for disembarkation and the air buzzed with anticipation. Tense faces broke into smiles and relief sounded in bursts of laughter after long weeks at sea.

Emerging from his cabin, Captain Champion – followed by the medic and the two police officers – stepped out onto the deck and made his way through the huddles of passengers towards the stern of the ship. After a moment, he shouted for all steerage ticket holders to come forward in order to be checked by the quarantine doctor. Gradually, the milling passengers congregated, several names were called and men and women began to step up, answer questions, allow their eyes, mouths and foreheads to be examined and then retire again. When Franz Müller's name went up, a compact young man of about twenty-four, wearing neatly fitting but shabby clothing, came forward. Sergeant Clarke and Officer Tieman moved to stand one on either side of him. Waiting for questions from the doctor, Müller instead felt his arms grasped firmly by the two men as he was led forcibly to one side.

The German simply asked, *What is the matter?*

It was not the reaction that Clarke, the only British policeman on board, had expected. There was nothing starting or nervous about the young man's behaviour as Officer Tieman made his arrest for the murder of Thomas Briggs. Instead, Clarke watched the tailor's eyes widen in apparent bewilderment. There was a moment of silence before Clarke realised that Officer Tieman appeared to have forgotten the details of the charge. Then Clarke spoke for the first time: *Yes. On the North London Railway between Hackney Wick and Bow, on 9th July.*

Müller's response was straightforward: *I never was on the line.*

It was a calm process. As he escorted Müller downstairs to the empty saloon, Clarke explained who they were. Tieman then searched the prisoner, finding eleven shillings in his trouser pocket and a small key in his waistcoat.

*It is the key to my box*, Müller said.

Under instructions from the captain, a large black trunk ornamented with brass nails was retrieved from Müller's berth in cabin 9. When it was brought into the saloon, the prisoner confirmed that it belonged to him.

Bending to unlock it, Sergeant Clarke threw back the lid to reveal Müller's belongings: one or two dirty shirts and their separate collars, a spare pair of working trousers, a few scarves, a couple of brushes, a towel, an umbrella, a pair of gloves and a handkerchief. Packed on one side were the tools of the tailor's trade: a measure and a pair of scissors or shears. There was no spare waistcoat, coat or overcoat.

In the corner of the trunk George Clarke found a top hat made of fine black silk with a white silk lining, with the maker's name of Digance, Royal Exchange – but it was low-crowned rather than the tall style habitually worn by Thomas Briggs. There was also something sewn into a piece of cloth and tied with a ribbon. Weighing the pouch in the palm of his hand, Clarke's back straightened. Pulling open the ribbon, Clarke fixed his gaze on Müller as a heavy gold pocket watch, maker's mark Archer of Hackney, fell from the folds of the bag. The prisoner held Clarke's eye and answered all his questions without hesitation. He claimed that the watch – whose serial number corresponded to the watch stolen from Briggs – had been his for about two years, bought from a man at the London docks. He said he had owned the hat for twelve months. Forgetting, perhaps, what he was said to have told Mrs Repsch, he mentioned that he had bought it in the second-hand markets of Petticoat Lane.

Nothing in the tailor's demeanour indicated evasion. Under

Tieman's care, Müller was confined to his cabin and his clothes were minutely examined for traces of blood. The shipping agent Gifford had said that Müller took several parcels on board. Conjecturing that one of them might have contained clothes worn on the night of the attack, Clarke searched for it to no avail. The policeman also sought out a fellow passenger in order to repossess a waistcoat Müller said he had given away in exchange for a small leather reticule – it was newer than the tatty one currently worn by the German but it, too, appeared clean. There was nothing about any of Müller's clothing to indicate that it had been worn by the murderer, barring that Clarke noted that the cuff from one shirt sleeve was missing.

*

By the early hours of the following day, a crowd of thousands had once more gathered around Manhattan's Battery to witness the landing of the 'English Murderer'. Richard Tanner and John Death were already on board, conveyed by police harbour boat earlier that morning.

Tanner had had weeks to prepare for this meeting. He was purposeful and unhurried. Leaving John Death on deck, he disappeared below to place Müller in a group of male passengers corralled by a ship's officer and then summoned the jeweller. It took just moments for John Death to identify the prisoner as the man he served on 11 July at his Cheapside shop.

There was still the question of the ring. Asked by Tanner whether the box contained all his belongings, Müller complained that a piece of jewellery had been stolen from him while on board. Pressed to describe it (*was it a red stone?*) the German spoke of a gold ring with a white stone engraved with the figure of a head, the very ring Death had already described as a part of the transaction the morning after the murder.

Since the black silk hat found in Müller's box was reserved as evidence against him, he was lent a cap to wear before being escorted to a Custom House barge that steamed ashore to its dock, dwarfed by the hulking prows of moored transatlantic packets. Rushed through immigration, he can have caught only glimpses of the excited crowd. By ten o'clock he was at police headquarters at Mulberry Street where his arrest was formalised. Tanner offered him breakfast, urging him to take a mutton chop, and he spoke so kindly that Müller broke down for the first time, weeping for several minutes before gathering his wits and accepting tea, bread and butter. Then he was driven up to Broadway to Bleeker Street to be photographed for police files. Just before two o'clock, he was taken to the office of Marshal Robert Murray in the courthouses at Chambers Street – an appointment that would ratify his arrest and set the machinery of extradition grinding into gear.

Reporters and spectators jostled around the steps of the Marshal's office, anxious for the first sight of the murderer, yet, as the prisoner emerged from the police cab, they fell quiet. With his short stature, light hair and small, grey, inexpressive eyes, dressed in the only suit of clothes he possessed, Müller appeared to the reporter from the *New York Herald* to be less fierce villain than *cowering wretch who seemed more dead than alive.* Expecting, perhaps, a powerful presence equal to the publicity he had received, the crowd was confused by the mundane, flesh-and-blood reality.

*To look at him*, the *New York Times* reported the next day, *one would think he was about the last person in the world who could deliberately plan and successfully execute any very heinous crime.* Müller's face was unremarkable: skin pulled tightly over prominent cheekbones; rippling, dark blonde hair combed back carefully from a narrow forehead; a fine, small nose and eyebrows so pale they all but vanished. His grey eyes were so deeply set that from a distance only the shadows cast by his prominent brow bones were visible. In the pockets of soft flesh between his brows and over his thin upper lip, there was a slackness. Despite

# CHAPTER 18

## *No Slipshod Examination*

The extradition hearing opened on 26 August in the imposing United States Circuit Court building located behind City Hall at 39 Chambers Street. On one side of a large table in front of the presiding Commissioner Chas Newton sat Francis Marbury, the three English policemen and their two witnesses, John Death and Jonathan Matthews. On the other, the tailor sat alone, wearing a dark tweed coat, a dark waistcoat buttoned nearly up to his chin and a white necktie. The room was crammed with onlookers. As he waited for the man assigned by the authorities to defend him – ex-judge Beebe – Müller's lips remained tightly compressed, betraying no sign of emotion. He looked small and stupefied.

Since his arrest there had been a forbearance about the prisoner that some found disturbing. Even the police were struck by his lack of emotion. What the *New York Herald* had described as the *diabolical* locus of the murder and the thrilling transatlantic chase had put the story on the front pages of the newspapers, but the inscrutability of the supposed murderer was something of a disappointment. The previous afternoon, hustled before US Marshal Murray, he had remained implacable as he confirmed his name and explained to the Marshal that he had a sister in the city and expected her to come to his aid. Only once, when he caught sight of Matthews at the back of the room, did his face momentarily but visibly blanch.

The agent apparently employed by the German Legal Protection Society in London failed to appear at that preliminary hearing and Müller appeared to be helplessly alone. Under American law, had he been able to afford the two thousand dollars for bail, he would have been released and might have escaped into the battlefields. Instead, he was shuffled back into the police van and returned to the police cell at Mulberry Street.

Up at the Everett House Hotel that evening, Inspector Kerressey had sat down to write with breathless lack of punctuation to Daniel Howie at the Bow police station. He relayed the details of Sergeant Clarke's arrest, the discovery of the missing watch and hat and the disappearance of the ring. Müller, he wrote, was said to have been *one of the most agreeable passengers on board ... The murder of Mr Briggs was frequently a subject of conversations.* He told of the throngs along the shoreline at Castle Gardens and the pack of spectators lingering around police headquarters at Mulberry Street. He wrote of his surprise that Müller's co-passengers had suspected nothing, that they had thought the German's appearance rather more gentlemanly than most and his appetite more robust. Clarke was relieved and excited. He was enjoying the mood of satisfaction that had settled over his colleagues.

Richard Tanner had written too: a short, triumphant telegraph addressed to the Police Commissioner that would leave on the fast steamer, the *Baltimore*, on Saturday morning. As the boat passed between Ireland and the west coast of Scotland, his words would be telegraphed to Greenock, forwarded from there to Reuters in Fleet Street, and then rushed by messenger to Scotland Yard. On 6 September, nearly two weeks after Müller's arrest, Sir

Richard Mayne would read the news he had been waiting for: *the* Victoria *has arrived at New York and Müller has been arrested. The hat and watch of Mr Briggs were found in his possession. Müller protested his innocence and the legal proceedings in reference to his extradition are progressing.* Released to the press, the news would be shouted from newsstands and England would hold its breath for the outcome of the American hearing.

*

The United States Circuit Court house had been an opera house and a comedy theatre before being turned over to the federal government in 1856. The proceedings of Friday 26 and Saturday 27 August would be no less dramatic.

Commissioner Chas Newton entered the packed courtroom at eleven o'clock. Everyone waited for Müller's defence counsel ex-judge Beebe to arrive until, to their surprise, word came that he had defaulted on his responsibility, pleading a conflicting engagement. Turning to the prisoner, Newton asked if there was anyone in the city who might support him. Standing, holding a blue cotton handkerchief tightly in one hand, Müller's voice wavered, betraying a slightly foreign accent as he repeated quietly that he still expected his sister to appear in court in order to help him.

*Has your sister any friends here?* asked Newton.

*I do not know, sir, she came to this country by herself.*

He had her address in Nassau Street, only a few blocks south of the courtroom, but if she could not be found, and since he was a stranger here, Müller said he would be satisfied with the assistance of the court. Exasperated, Newton considered his options. Mr Chauncey Shaffer happened to be in the courthouse that day. He was swiftly assigned to Müller's defence.

This was a stroke of luck for the prisoner. Shaffer was an impressively canny criminal attorney, renowned for his eloquence and flair and admired for his successful defence at some of the most notorious murder trials in New York's Southern District

Court. As he agreed to go into battle for Müller, a whisper went round the room that this prominent lawyer rarely lost a case. Calling on the assistance of Mr Edmond Blankman to act as his junior, the formidable Chauncey Shaffer asked for, and was allowed, a short time to confer with Müller.

The British consul's legal representative, Francis Marbury, had advised Tanner that the purpose of the hearing was summarily to hear both the evidence accumulated against Müller and in his defence. Commissioner Newton's responsibility was simply to consider whether, had the offence happened on American soil, there would be sufficient evidence to commit the German for trial under American law. If so, under the terms of the British–American extradition treaty signed in August 1842, a certificate of criminality would be issued and permission granted for his release into the custody of the London detectives.

Silencing the shuffling of the courtroom spectators, Commissioner Newton signalled for Marbury to begin his case and the lawyer rose, recapitulated the main points of the case and then proposed to read out both sets of witness depositions taken at Bow Street Magistrates' Court on 19 and 22 July. Shaffer objected immediately on a point of law, declaring that since the majority of the witnesses were unavailable for cross-examination, their statements could not be heard. Marbury was ahead of him, countering that the Act of Congress provided for their reading. Shaffer tried again, submitting that there was no proof to show that the depositions were properly authenticated. Marbury returned that not only had they been certified by the American minister in London but that the London officers had witnessed the proceedings at Bow Street. Shaffer was overruled.

Müller's defence changed direction. Shaffer's junior, Edmond Blankman, waxed on the vulnerability of the prisoner, a stranger in a strange land, charged with a most heinous offence. *It is our duty*, he said, *to see that none of the rights and privileges of the accused are neglected. It is our duty to see that no slipshod examination* [takes] *place and that the forms of law are strictly complied with. These depositions* [are] *not legally and properly authenticated as required by the law.* Since they were not in the form that could be used in an English murder trial, Blankman contended that, under the Act of Congress, they were not admissible in New York. It was an audacious contention, though Newton disagreed, ruling that all the London depositions must be heard.

Over the next hour, Francis Marbury read aloud all the papers submitted by both Tanner and Kerressey. He gave particular emphasis to the statements demonstrating that Thomas J. Briggs had identified the chain exchanged at Death's and that John Death had subsequently confirmed that the prisoner was the man from whom it was received. Marbury laboured over each fact, uninterrupted, emphasising that collateral evidence had been accumulated from a great number of different sources. Then he turned to call his first witness.

Inspector Richard Tanner stood and took the oath, confirming that the Metropolitan Police Commissioner had directed him to lead the investigation. Asked about the battered hat found in carriage 69, he confirmed *I have kept that hat in my possession under lock and key. It is a black, ordinary man's hat ... bent – the name of T. H. Walker, maker, was in it, Number 49 Crawford Street. The hat appeared to have stains of blood on it. I exhibited it to Matthews who is here present.*

Marbury pressed Tanner to prove that the hat could not have been swapped or misidentified. *I had the hat in my possession before* [the coroner] *Mr Henry and on that occasion I showed* [it] *to Mr Ames and the witness examined it. It was the same hat I got from Kerressey.* Tanner also confirmed that he had been present during the witnesses' oaths on 19 July, that he was in the habit of seeing warrants issued and depositions taken and that they were all *in the usual form in which depositions are taken in London,* delivered into his hands directly by the magistrate. He asserted that he had seen the blood-spattered carriage and the dead body of Thomas Briggs, and he produced the pawn ticket received from Hoffa which related to the chain Müller was supposed to have carried away with him from Death's shop.

Marbury's questions over, Chauncey Shaffer pushed back his chair and rose purposefully to his feet.

*Were you acquainted with Mr Briggs during his lifetime?*

*Can you be sure that it was the body of Mr Briggs at the inquest?*

*Did you apply tests to determine whether the stains on the hat were stains of blood?*

*Surely it is a very ordinary hat?*

Tanner replied firmly in each case to questions designed to destabilise his testimony. He said that he had not known Thomas Briggs, that no tests had been applied to the hat which was, he accepted, a very ordinary one.

It was Marbury's turn again. He prompted Tanner to describe the production of the circulated handbills. He pressed him to explain that Briggs' own watchmaker had provided a detailed description of the missing watch, as well as the serial numbers on the case and the workings. The inspector confirmed that both those numbers corresponded with numbers on the watch found in Müller's box when he was arrested on board the *Victoria*.

Shaffer let it go. Could Tanner tell him *how many persons occupied the compartment of the car in which Mr Briggs had a seat from Bow to Hackney?*

*I do not know*, said Tanner.

*When was Mr Henry, the magistrate, appointed?*

*I do not know.*

When Shaffer suggested that the authenticity of the depositions was in doubt, the detective showed emotion for the first time, raising his voice to state *I have had many cases before the magistrate* and adding, emphatically, that *the depositions are similar to those I have seen in hundreds of cases.*

Walter Kerressey was the next to take the oath. He, too, was asked by Marbury to confirm that he had been present throughout the second Bow hearing and had watched each witness properly sworn and each statement duly signed, emphasising that there had been no room for official error. Once again, Marbury posed questions designed to leave no doubt that the crushed hat was genuine: Kerressey confirmed that the hat shown in court on 22 July was given to him by Tanner and separately identified by Elizabeth Repsch.

The only flaw in Kerressey's testimony was that he had not been present when the American minister in London signed the papers now in court and that, never having seen Mr Adams' signature, he was not personally able to verify it. Suggesting that these facts rendered the depositions invalid, Shaffer was again overruled by Commissioner Newton.

Edmond Blankman hoped to shake the certainty of the next witness, John Death, under cross-examination. But the jeweller stuck firm to his belief that he could identify the prisoner. He accepted that he served *maybe twenty people a day* and that with reference to Müller *there was no special mark about him by which I knew him.* Nevertheless, Death countered, he had found it easy to pick Müller out from *eight or nine persons all strangers to me* when he boarded the *Victoria*.

He was also resolute and convincing about his identification of the chains. *I never saw the same pattern of chain before*, he said of the one belonging to Thomas Briggs. *It has a certain peculiarity by which once seen I would recollect it again.* John Death was, demonstrably, a man trained to notice the detail of things and was so unruffled by the questions put to him by the defence that he even added weight to his testimony by criticising the police's description of the chain as partly inaccurate: *a chain somewhat like this is called the Clyde chain*, he said. *I would not call this an Albert chain. And this is a swivel seal. The description of this seal given in the proclamation does not properly describe it.* Death's confidence was unshakeable: Müller was the customer who came to barter with him on 11 July and Blankman could not rock his certainty.

Franz Müller watched impassively as Jonathan Matthews was asked to stand. *I have known him about two years,* said the cab driver. *I once bought a hat for him.* Matthews' testimony centred on the hat he claimed to have procured, the same hat he had seen Müller wear several weeks prior to the murder, the very one shown to him by Detective Tanner and exhibited at the Bow Street Court. *I could not well be mistaken about the hat,* he growled. Conceding under cross-examination by Chauncey Shaffer that *the accused was a steady man and I should have given him a good character but for this case,* Matthews remained unmoved by Shaffer's apparent preoccupation with their being two Walker hats, each identical to the other. On the contrary, he seemed to find the questions amusing. The hat he had bought for Müller was *a little easier* than his own, he replied. It crossed no one's mind to ask whether the cabman had been asked to try on the bent hat in London to see how well it fitted.

Marbury had only two more witnesses to call, George Clarke and John Tieman. Both described the arrest of Müller on the *Victoria* and repeated Müller's denial that he had ever travelled on the North London Railway line. Clarke identified the gold watch and the hat found in Müller's box. *He said he had the hat about a* year, Tieman said in response to Shaffer's questions, *and the watch two years.*

The British government's case for the prosecution was closed. Dusk was falling over the city and Commissioner Chas Newton adjourned the hearing until the following morning at eleven o'clock.

# CHAPTER 19

## *Gathering Clouds*

Wagons and carriages jostled against each other outside the Chambers Street court on Saturday morning as eager spectators hurried to arrive on time. The ladies' wide cotton crinolines filled the corridors as they pressed into the courtroom, their straw bonnets competing with the gentlemen's toppers. Along with the pack of newspapermen, they waited keenly for the arrival of the German prisoner, wondering aloud what Shaffer and Blankman might achieve in Müller's defence.

Blankman began by asking for a postponement, citing the *exceedingly intricate and voluminous* nature of the depositions and the fact that they had been given only ten minutes to confer with their client. As precedents, he cited two recent cases in which the British government had obfuscated over American demands for the extradition of two men accused of murder. The first concerned a negro slave called Anderson who had fled to Canada. The case had been delayed for months, said Blankman, before it was finally adjudicated in London and then Anderson had been released on the grounds that, as a slave, he had been justified in making his escape by any means. The second case centred on the murderous capture of an American vessel, the *Chesapeake*, by American men who had fled to Liverpool. Again, said Blankman, the British government had prevaricated for months before refusing American demands to return them for trial.

*I do not claim that because one nation refused to do right another should follow its example,* he averred, appealing to a latent American hostility to a perception that their former colonial masters had behaved with patrician arrogance. The court erupted into applause.

Further, contended Blankman, no finding from a coroner's inquest had been produced for the American court. Since the jury at the inquest in Hackney had not yet returned a verdict, the case for murder had not been made and, if the inquest's judgement were to be one of manslaughter, then there was no provision for prisoner extradition within the law. *Our client positively asserts his entire innocence of the charge,* concluded the lawyer. *The small delay we seek is as little as the court could grant.*

Francis Marbury, counsel for the British Crown, calmly countered that ex-judge Beebe had spent an evening with the prisoner in order to discuss his defence, that the depositions were neither long nor intricate, that they had been painstakingly read out in court and that Müller's defence had, in sum, had enough time to prepare. He considered the defence's request for postponement to be unreasonable. *All the judge has to do,* he argued, *is act like an ordinary magistrate.* He was not asking for a determination of guilt, simply for a committal to trial. *I dislike,* he continued, *to do anything which looks like bearing harshly upon this unfortunate man, but the case seems so plain and the man, if sent back, will be placed where will be found all the witnesses who can testify as to the facts and who will state any circumstances of exculpation, if any such exist.* The London detectives and witnesses were in New York at great expense, he argued. A postponement would cause great inconvenience.

And so the argument rocked backwards and forwards between the two lawyers while the witnesses and prisoner sat mute. Was the British Crown really so penny-pinching, wondered Blankman, and what of the interests of justice? Were the rights of the prisoner not to be protected? Were German and American citizens to be left wondering at the partiality of the law?

Commissioner Newton denied the request for postponement. The evidence was short, he said, and he could not believe that the interests of the prisoner would suffer by his refusal.

There were no witnesses for the defence and the defendant Franz Müller had no right in law to speak, except through his counsel. So, Chauncey Shaffer, known for his blistering oratory, went into battle. *There is something of sublimity in the energy with which the British Government has disregarded seas and oceans in their pursuit of this man*, he began. *I am not here to raise any ill feeling against that grand old nation but to judge that Treaty by the acts of the English nation itself.*

Shaffer intended to move for a discharge of the entire hearing on insuperable legal grounds. First, he argued that the extradition treaty of 1842 between Britain and America was an infringement of the American constitution and its amendments, *that no person shall be held to answer for a capital or infamous crime, save on the indictment ... of a Grand Jury.* How was it possible, he asked, that the Commissioner was being asked to surrender a man to be tried for his life when he had not been indicted? Further, in his view, the prisoner had already been convicted in the mind of the British public. There was no chance that he would receive a fair trial in London and to allow his extradition would be to *place him where his life and liberty will be imperilled.*

*I have, however, another proposition*, continued Shaffer, warming to his theme. *It is an elementary principle, recognised by the laws of nations, that a state of war suspends the operations of all treaties. You will say there is not war between the United States and England. Not in their sovereign capacity; but*

*there is war, what Grotius terms a 'mixed unsolemn state of war'*
*between the subjects of the nation on the one side ... and the*
*subjects of the nation on the other side, without any formal dec-*
*laration of war.* Harnessing legal theory and the antagonism
between the Northern States and Britain to his cause, Müller's
attorney declared that the extradition treaty of 1842 was nulli-
fied. Calling on such elevated authorities as Grotius, the
seventeenth-century father of international law, his arguments left
the majority of the courtroom impressed by his authority if baffled by his erudition.

Reminding the court of the events of the past three years,
Shaffer cited the routine sinking or pillaging of American vessels
and the suspension of trade and commerce between Britain and
America. He declared that the southern rebels were furnished
with arms and ammunition by the *neutral ports of Great Britain*
and that American subjects *whose hands are stained with blood*
were not returned. Shaffer believed that England claimed neutrality but acted like an aggressor. *No state of national neutrality*
*in effect actually exists, and the state of war suspends operation*
*of all treaties. They that would have justice,* he declaimed, his
voice soaring and his arms widening, *must do justice. England*
*must come here with clean hands.* In his opinion, the 1842 agreement was *a dead letter.*

The packed court burst into enthusiastic applause at Shaffer's
denouncement of the British government. Shaffer turned to the
question of the provisions of the treaty. *Though undoubtedly death*
*by violence has been proved, there is not sufficient evidence that it*
*amounts to murder,* he claimed. Further, *the Commissioner must*
*be satisfied beyond all reasonable doubt that not only was the*
*crime that of murder but that Franz Müller was the murderer.*

Reading out Thomas Lee's deposition, the lawyer endeavoured
to show that Müller – short, thin and barefaced – was clearly neither of the two men said by Lee to have shared a compartment
with Thomas Briggs on 9 July. Lee's evidence, Shaffer argued,

was crucial, yet he was not present to be cross-examined. In addition, there was no evidence submitted to prove that Müller was not at home on the evening of 9 July. (Here Marbury objected, citing witness statements that Müller had indeed been absent and that he was not seen until Sunday morning. His objection was sustained.)

Finally, Shaffer alleged that the sum of evidence so far brought forward against his client was circumstantial and allowed for other interpretations. *How are we to say he did not buy those goods not knowing them to belong to a murdered man?* he asked. Drawing his argument to a close, he asserted that it would be better that his nation should perish than that the constitution be violated by the treaty-making power of any other country. Müller must be released.

Shaffer then recalled Detective Inspector Richard Tanner.

Sitting within a yard of the inspector, Müller cast his eyes about the court. Was he still watching for the appearance of his resolutely absent sister?

Shaffer asked Tanner to describe the man before him. *I should judge him to be about five feet six and a half inches in height. He has no beard, nor any signs of ever having one. I should not call him a tall thin man, nor a thickset man.*

Did Müller bear any resemblance whatsoever to either of the men described by Thomas Lee?

*I don't think he will ever have any whiskers.*

*Can you see him clearly?* asked Shaffer.

*He is standing quite near to me, and there is no obstruction between us to my view of him.*

Shaffer had finished his galvanising defence. As he resumed his seat, spectators in the court shifted their attention to Francis Marbury. For a moment he was silent. Then he characterised his opponent as a blusterer, wasting their time with a bafflingly long and exaggerated speech, an address full of irrelevances and diversions. He suggested that Shaffer's loquacious ramblings stemmed from the fact that there was nothing in the facts of the case *out of which he could legitimately offer to the audience the entertainment which is always expected of him whenever he makes his appearance*. He had, said Marbury, resorted to verbal pyrotechnics only because he had no persuasively competing evidence to offer.

Point by point Marbury reprised the physical evidence against Müller and turned the defence's arguments. The question of the treaty's legitimacy was for the executive government. Despite the fact that the Hackney inquest had not yet drawn to its conclusion, Marbury considered that the *corpus delicti*, or body of evidence, had been fully established against Müller. The prisoner's absence from Park Terrace on the evening of 9 July was proved beyond doubt and he had suggested no other alibi that might prove his presence elsewhere at the time of the fatal attack. Useful though Mr Lee's evidence was, Francis Marbury reminded Commissioner Newton that Lee was unable to say whether one or both of Briggs' fellow passengers had left the carriage before the train pulled off.

*As I look upon Müller it appears almost inconceivable that he could have perpetrated the dreadful crime*, Marbury continued. *If I could escape from the evidences of his guilt which seem to gather from so many quarters, all converging and pointing to him, I should experience a sensation of relief.* He reminded the court that Thomas Briggs was a worthy, venerable man and that this crime was one of the most revolting in British criminal experience. Despite the clouds lowering about the head of the prisoner, who would not rejoice if he could prove himself to be innocent of the crime? Müller could not explain his whereabouts on the night of 9 July, he could give no convincing explanation for his ownership of the watch or the supernumerary hat. Had the crime taken place in New York then the magistrate would be compelled to commit him for trial. It was beyond doubt, he countered, that the certificate for the prisoner's extradition should be granted.

The courtroom was hushed. Commissioner Newton cleared his throat and prepared to speak. *Gentlemen*, he began, *I think my duty is plain. I do not desire to sit in judgement upon this man ... but I am bound to say that the combined circumstances, to my mind, appear so clear, and so distinct, that I can have no doubt. I shall be constrained to grant the certificate.*

Rising from his chair, Newton withdrew from the court. The journalists watched as, just perceptibly, Müller's jaw tightened. Tanner and his colleagues relaxed backwards, then leant forwards to shake hands with Francis Marbury and slap each other's shoulders. Shaffer and Blankman, who had waived their fees, shuffled papers, snapped their notebooks closed, wished their client luck and departed. *Müller did not seem affected in the least by the decision*, scribbled the reporter for the *New York Times*, *acting more like an indifferent spectator than a criminal on trial.*

*

Behind those small grey eyes, that detached exterior, it seemed that Müller must either be a simpleton or an innocent. New Yorkers argued over whether his composure evinced bafflement, arrogance or guilt and wondered at an absence in him of the kind of coiled fury that might mark him out as a murderer. Might it be that his stupor was evidence of bewilderment at his own act? If he was innocent, how could he remain so apathetic? Blank-faced and tight-lipped, he was pulled from the court into a police cab and driven to the Halls of Justice – the city prison known popularly as the Tombs.

Five blocks north of Chambers Street, built in the late 1830s on mouldering, boggy land and surrounded by distempered side-streets, the prison was a daunting granite structure in the style of an ancient Egyptian mausoleum. Great steps rose to a main entrance flanked by vast columns. Inside, its dank cells were reserved for prisoners awaiting trial on the gravest charges or those already convicted and waiting to be executed within the confines of a narrow inner court, witnessed by a group limited to twenty-five. There was no public executioner here to shuffle about on a raised scaffold, every move watched by unruly droves of hundreds or thousands.

Within the cavernous Tombs, the warders' steps rang on the walkways of the four iron galleries set one above the other, linked by zig-zagging staircases. On each side were rows of heavy black doors and behind each of these a small bare cell lit only by a high chink in the wall. Each one contained a bedstead, a table and a crude washing bowl. Wall hooks once provided for clothing had been removed to prevent suicide. Apart from the clatter of the warders' keys against the iron lattice of the walkways, the place was uncommonly quiet, run on the 'silent' system: all conversation between inmates was proscribed. Fearing that Müller would fall into a depression here, Tanner managed to side-step the rules by arranging for another prisoner to share his cell at night.

United States Commissioner Chas Newton retired to his office in Wall Street on the afternoon of his judgement to write to President Abraham Lincoln at the White House in Washington. His clerks were busy drafting a Certificate of Criminality and making handwritten copies of the Bow Street depositions along with a duplicate record of all the evidence and arguments presented during the two-day hearing. Once these were completed, Tanner would deliver them to Washington himself. When the warrant for extradition was in his hands, he would return to New York to claim his prisoner.

At the Everett House Hotel, congratulations over, Richard Tanner prepared another report for Sir Richard Mayne. He enclosed the newspaper articles from the weekend, telling the Commissioner of the strong language used by Shaffer in Müller's defence and the enthusiastic response it had received from the public. He planned to return from Washington in time to leave New York on the *Etna*, bound for Liverpool in a week's time.

Tanner was worn out from waiting through three weeks of sleepless nights and two things were troubling him. *Extraordinary as it may seem,* he wrote to Sir Richard, *strong sympathy is felt now for the prisoner and it is rumoured that an attempt to rescue him from my custody will be made.* He assured Mayne that all steps possible were being taken to prevent this but what also concerned him was entirely out of his control. Müller's defence had made much of Thomas Lee's statement, he wrote, and his instinct was that it could prove favourable to the prisoner during a London trial. Despite their success in America, the detective was worried by the possibility that an English jury might yet acquit Müller of the murder of Thomas Briggs.

# CHAPTER 20

## *Turning Back*

By Monday 29 August, Commissioner Newton's Certificate of Criminality against Müller was ready but it would be another twenty-four hours before the certified copy of the hearing transcript was finished for Tanner to collect and take to Washington.

The inspector left no record of the route he took to the capital – the slow journey by steamer or the faster, overland route – but he did make the return trip quickly, suggesting that he chose hazard and speed over relative safety. Train travellers faced dangers from both the northern and southern armies, and troops passed through New Jersey in their thousands. Goods trains transported materials, food and the many dead, while passenger trains were crammed with both soldiers and families en route to the battlefields in their hundreds to look for missing kin. The junctions were crowded and frantic; the lines, bridges and trains were all potential military targets. Only a month earlier, Washington had been encircled by the Confederate army.

On the last day of August, as Tanner was making his way to Washington, a journalist from the New York *Morning Star* sought permission from Marshal Murray to interview Müller in the

Mare Street Hackney, 1853. The church tower of St Augustine's is in the background. The line of the North London Railway runs overhead.

Hackney station and viaduct, 1851. Watercress fields stretched south from the line.

The only known image of Senior Banking Clerk Thomas Briggs, taken from an illustrated newspaper circa 1914.

Clapton Square N. E.

The west side of Clapton Square, Hackney: one of the best addresses in the neighbourhood.

Lombard Street, City of
London, 1849: a narrow,
curving thoroughfare whose
tall stone buildings dwarfed
the scuttling commuters.

Fenchurch Street Station: London's smallest terminus, tucked into the south-
eastern corner of the City.

Anxieties about the safety of the railways grew. *Left:* George Cruikshank depicts the steam engine literally eating up house and home in the late 1840s. *Below:* 'Going by train, sir?' – an undertaker presenting his card to a railway passenger, 1852.

Old Scotland Yard, the headquarters of the Metropolitan Police until 1890.

Richard Mayne, Metropolitan
Police Commissioner, circa 1869.

The only known images, taken from an illustrated
newspaper circa 1914, of Detective Inspector
Richard Tanner (*left*) and Detective Inspector
Adolphus 'Dolly' Williamson (*right*).

## THE MURDER IN A RAILWAY CARRIAGE.

The detective officers who have charge of this case have been pursuing their inquiries with the most eager activity, the proceedings before the coroner on Monday having apparently given a new impulse to their exertions. The fact of a person having been refused a loan by Mr. Briggs, and afterwards threatening to do him an injury, is not much relied upon, as the individual alluded to is a man in a respectable position, and his threat is believed to be simply one of those idle menaces in which disappointed people sometimes indulge without any intention to carry them into execution. The police are, however, far from giving up the clue which this piece of evidence may be supposed to afford.

A more important point with them at present is the clue which may be opened up to them by the evidence of the boy who, on the night of Saturday, the 9th instant, saw a man walk hastily, and apparently direct upon some object, up and down the Stepney platform, on the arrival of the 9·45 train from Fenchurch-street, and then enter a carriage in which an old gentleman (supposed to be Mr. Briggs) was sitting alone. The fact that the boy can easily recognise the man who so entered the carriage may, in connection with other circumstances, afford an important link in the chain of evidence.

Some very lamentable hoaxes continue to be played off on the police. A letter has been addressed to a near relative of the deceased, warning him that he was suspected of the murder, and recommending him to make himself "scarce," as the police were on his track, and would soon apprehend him. This letter bore the name of a late respected member of the police force, who was mainly instrumental in the capture of the Mannings. The poor man to whom it was addressed, and who had received another letter of a similar character, apparently from a different quarter, was thrown into great agony of mind by these communications, but did what every one should do under such circumstances, hurried off to Scotland-yard with them, where he was informed by the police of their real character and utter worthlessness.

The police express themselves sanguine of success, and are confidently of opinion that before the time appointed for the renewal of the inquest they will have the murderer at the bar of justice.

*Liverpool Mercury*, 20 July 1864.

## THE MURDER ON THE NORTH LONDON RAILWAY.

No additional facts of any importance about this horrible affair have transpired since yesterday. Late last night Sir George Grey announced the intention of the Government to offer a reward of 200l. for the apprehension of the murderer, and bills to that effect will be circulated throughout the country in the course of to-day. It is believed that the railway company will offer an additional reward of 100l. in furtherance of the same object.

Inspector Kerressey and Sergeant Lambert, of the K division, have at last succeeded in obtaining a correct description of the watch stolen from the murdered man. It is a gold lever, of old-fashioned manufacture, and bears the name of the maker, "S. W. Archer, Hackney, No. 1,487," the case being numbered 2,974. The gold spectacles, which were at first thought to have been stolen, were found in the pocket of the deceased. If, as has been stated, the outrage was committed between Bow Station and the place where the body was found, the time occupied by the whole affair was under two minutes, the time taken by the train to pass from one spot to the other being little more than a minute and a half. At present, however, there seems no reason for asserting that the assault happened after the train had left Bow. The hat found in the carriage bears the maker's name, "T. H. Walker, Crawford-street, Marylebone," but, beyond being spotted with blood, it has no marks upon it which could give any clue to its owner.

It is somewhat singular that about six years ago an attempted robbery and assault was made in a train passing the same spot. The thief jumped out and would have escaped had he not injured his knee in falling. Great surprise has been expressed that so fearful a murder should have been committed merely for the sake of an old-fashioned watch and chain, more especially as the murdered man's pocket-book, purse, diamond ring, and gold spectacles were left behind, and many persons are of opinion that the object of the murderer was not merely robbery. It is somewhat singular, too, that the perpetrator of the outrage, who must have been covered with fresh blood, should have been able to pass unnoticed by the persons about the station, and the ticket collector.

*The Times*, 12 July 1864.

National and regional newspaper headlines

## LLOYD'S WEEKLY LONDON NEWSPAPER.

### THE HORROR OF THE WEEK.

The public mind is unhappily seldom left at rest free from the horror created by the record of some foul and brutal crime, committed in the very centre and heart of our civilisation. No sensation novelist has yet invented a scene half so thrilling by its brutality and its blood, as that which was enacted, last Saturday night, on the North London railway, and near Victoria-park.

A gentleman, chief clerk in a great banking firm, left Peckham by omnibus, and travelled to the city, probably on some small matter of business. Having transacted this business, he went on to the Fenchurch-street railway station, and left that station at a quarter to ten, in a first-class carriage. That unhappy gentleman could never have dreamt, had he been the wildest of dreamers and speculators,

*Lloyd's Weekly Newspaper*, 17 July 1864.

One of Superintendent William Tiddey's expense forms. On 23 July he paid for several omnibus and cab fares, for Müller's lodgings to be searched and for the dust hole at 16 Park Terrace to be emptied.

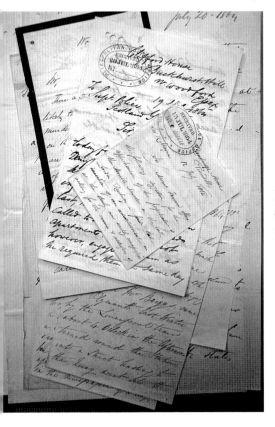

Letters addressed to the police, containing advice or airing suspicions, arrived from all over the country.

The London Docks, 1845. On the left, the North Quay and its warehouses, and on the right the River Thames snaking out towards the English Channel.

Steamship *The City of Manchester*, the boat Tanner took on his chase to New York.

Tombs. He wanted an answer to the question on every New Yorker's mind: what defence could the prisoner possibly offer against the weight of evidence against him? Shocked by Müller's wan appearance, the reporter asked him how he was and was told *I feel weak and bad. I am sick.* The prisoner wore the same threadbare but neatly brushed clothes in which he had appeared in court.

Müller talked first about his sister. He said she had come to New York fourteen years earlier, that the prison warden had been given her address, but that she had still not come to see him. Speaking of the night of 9 July, he swore that he had taken an omnibus to Camberwell New Road, to a public house where he drank beer until half-past nine. Returning to the Royal Exchange, he found that the last omnibus for Bow had gone and his only option was to walk, lame-footed, back to Park Terrace. He got there at past eleven o'clock, when the Blyths were already asleep.

Asked about the hat and watch, Müller answered swiftly that he had bought the hat in London a year ago and that the watch, along with a chain, came from a peddler at the London docks. They had cost all his money – four pounds, three crowns. With nothing left to get his ticket on the *Victoria*, he had pawned everything else he owned – both the chain he had got from Death's in exchange for the one he bought at the docks and his own old watch and chain. Eventually, he had accumulated the money he needed for his fare without having to pawn the heavy gold pocket watch sold to him by the peddler.

*Müller bore himself with great composure*, wrote the *Morning Star* reporter, *and was never at a loss to answer any questions that I put to him.* He was favourably impressed. But as he turned to leave, the warden took him aside. *He is a hard case, you may depend on it*, said the prison official. *His mouth shows that.* Prominently printed, the exclusive interview was lapped up by a city alive with the news of the extradition hearing. *There is interesting news enough, political and military*, the journalist wrote, but this story *will certainly be more interesting than comments upon 'the situation'*. In New York the supposed murderer was given equal prominence to the bloody events of the Civil War.

*

Richard Tanner returned at the end of the week with the President's signature on the warrant for Müller's extradition. Preparing to leave New York, he wrote a letter of thanks to NYPD Superintendent Kennedy, enclosing a ten-pound reward for Tieman, and visited Francis Marbury to request a reference for himself. *My opinion*, wrote the solicitor, *is that you have all performed the delicate and responsible task imposed upon you in a manner which is entirely free from exception and does credit to the force to which you belong.*

On Saturday 3 September at nine o'clock in the morning, Franz Müller was delivered into Tanner's custody at the Tombs and escorted to a closed carriage which drove fast towards the docks and the waiting steamship the *Etna*. Hoping to avoid an impenetrable mob, Tanner had let slip that they planned to embark on the *China* the following Wednesday. By this ruse he managed to have Müller, Death, Matthews and his colleagues below decks on the *Etna* before the truth leaked out and a great, disappointed crowd rushed on board the ship. Among those who embarked was a representative of the German Legal Protection Society in London who delivered a letter to Müller. It read:

> *Mr Francis Müller – I have been instructed by the . . . Society*
> *for the Legal Protection of Germans in London to*
> *communicate to you that* [they] *. . . have taken your case*
> *into their hands and have appointed Mr Thomas Beard, a*
> *solicitor . . . to act in your behalf . . . In the meantime it will*
> *be advisable for you not to make any communication*
> *whatever to the authorities, or to private individuals,*
> *without the previous advice of a solicitor . . . The German*

*Society still consider you to be innocent of the crime you are*
*accused of and have resolved ... to save no trouble or*
*expense to prove your being not guilty, if this is the case.*

At one o'clock in the afternoon the ship bearing the police, their prisoner and the two witnesses steamed out of New York Harbor. On board, Müller continued to protest his innocence but Tanner made certain to caution him to keep his own counsel. The law of England was clear: since 1848 it protected prisoners under arrest from involuntary self-incrimination by proscribing the police from any questioning following arrest.

Police and prisoners were all confined to the hospital quarters amidships, a secure room with six berths in which Müller could be left unchained but guarded. The German seemed not to dwell on his misfortune but to enjoy the comparative comfort of this journey to his earlier voyage on the *Victoria*, commenting on the delicious soups and fresh fruit prepared for him. Tanner lent him a copy of Charles Dickens' *Pickwick Papers* to help pass the time and Müller lay on his back, laughing heartily at the antics of Sam Weller and the complexities of his legal wranglings. After *Pickwick*, he was given *David Copperfield*, and settled back to let his mind slide away from his own immediate difficulties. Occasionally, reality seemed to intrude. Then he appeared to draw comfort from the fact that other, respectable people were on his side, taking out the letter from the GLPS, reading it, re-folding it and returning it to his coat pocket before diving back into Charles Dickens' world.

In the pause between New York and Liverpool, Müller was free from the quiver of intense scrutiny that had followed him from the moment of his arrest, from the obsessive recording of his face and his behaviour in reports that transformed the man into a cipher. Tanner, too, could finally unwind from the wearing anxiety of his chase.

\*

Britain's ravenous curiosity was buoyed by newspaper reports of the ongoing coroner's inquest in Hackney. Godfrey Repsch claimed that Müller told him that the chain and ring were bought at the docks and he related a curious story of Müller trying but failing to attach a black mourning band to his new silk hat during the week before he left, though he had refused to enlighten them about who had died. Until John Death and Jonathan Matthews returned from America, there was nothing more for the coroner to do and, since no one knew when they would be back, sessions were repeatedly rescheduled and postponed.

For seven weeks the papers had speculated about if, or when, Müller would be returned to England. At the end of August there was still uncertainty about whether the *Victoria* had even arrived in New York. Rumours began to circulate that she had been captured and sunk. Others speculated that, even if Müller had been arrested, the London detectives might have to make another round trip in order to collect more evidence to strengthen their case in the American court. At last, just short of nine weeks after the discovery of Thomas Briggs' body, Tanner's telegraph, sent via the *Baltimore*, arrived with news of the arrest. On Wednesday 7 September, with Tanner and his prisoner already three days out at sea, the country awoke to news that Briggs' hat and watch had been found on the suspect, that Müller had denied the charge and that he had declared that he could provide an alibi.

The New York papers brought by the steamship *Baltimore* to Liverpool on 7 September were devoured by a febrile national and regional press. The following day the minutiae of Müller's arrest and of the first day of his extradition hearing were being widely reprised. Columns headed *Scenes on the Deck of the Victoria* and *The Capture of Müller* dominated all other news. Particular attention fell once again on reports of his unprepossessing appearance. The *Globe* reminded its readers that *Müller may be innocent* and that he *will have a fair trial*, but its words sounded hollow. The paper appeared to forget that the prosecution must prove his guilt, suggesting instead that England waited for the German to prove his innocence. *The Times*, sure that *Müller's capture will excite an emotion which it is hard to analyse*, was optimistic that the news would halt potential murderers in their tracks, *serving to counteract the contagion of his example*. Britain could relax. The legal process that promised *vengeance upon a wrongdoer* promised to still unquiet minds and confirm *confidence in the supremacy of law over the destructive forces of human nature*.

If there was any doubt of Müller's guilt in the majority of minds it sprang only from disbelief that he had risked so much for such small gain. *It is a strange story, from beginning to end*, wrote *The Times, but the strangest part of it is the disproportion between the audacious enormity of the crime and the feebleness of the attempt to escape its consequences.*

The same paper noted that Müller's capture was facilitated by technological advance: by steam, the telegraph and photography. The telegraph – dubbed *God's lightning* by *Punch* – had been helping to catch criminals since the mid 1840s. Now, in the triumphant knowledge of Müller's arrest, the paper suggested that the progression of science was continuing to make the world a safer place, that modern invention could be harnessed to the cause of civilisation. It chose to ignore that the science that limited the chances of the murderer's escape had provided both the stage for his violent act and the means of his ensuing flight.

The day after receiving Tanner's telegraphic message, the Commissioner wrote to the Secretary of State asking permission both to submit their official reports of evidence against Müller and to prepare for his appearance at Bow Street Magistrates' Court when he arrived home. In anticipation of a trial, Stephen Franklin at the North London Railway's Bow works was instructed to make a perfect scale model of railway carriage 69.

Inspector Williamson and Superintendent Howie collated copies
of police reports, wrote lists of the witnesses for the prosecution
and prepared a statement of the crucial facts of the case:

   i.   *Briggs found on railway insensible about 25 past 10
      on 9th*

   ii.   *Müller exchanged chain about 10 a.m. on the 11th*

   iii.   *Müller pawned that chain about 12 p.m. on the Tuesday
      12th at Mr Annis*

   iv.   *Monday 11 July around 3 [p.m.] Müller gave paper box
      to Matthews daughter. Müller sold the pawn ticket for
      the chain at Mr Annis to Hoffa on Weds*

   v.   *Müller pawned own watch at Mr Barker Houndsditch on
      the 12th July and redeemed it on 13th July and the chain
      on the 13th and pawned them again same day at Mr
      Cox's Princes St Leicester Sq*

   vi.   *14th Müller embarked*

   vii.   *15th sailed*

The statement included a note emphasising that Thomas Lee had
waited to make his statement until 17 July. The police were worried about the effect of his evidence and, perhaps in the hope that
Lee's dubious moral position would undermine his testimony,
they highlighted the fact that *being a married man he had been
to see a girl and he did not wish it known that he was at Bow
Railway Station.*

Because the *Baltimore* had left New York before the conclusion of the extradition hearing, its outcome was still unknown.
Was Tanner already returning with the German? Or had the petition somehow failed? The docking of every transatlantic steamer
became an event. When the *Asia* arrived at Queenstown on the
southern Irish coast on Sunday 11 September, the great crowds
gathered at the docks roared their disappointment that the man
they had come to see was not on board. But the *Asia* did carry

the latest New York papers, which confirmed that an extradition warrant had been issued. Now there was certainty that the fugitive would be repatriated within a matter of days.

Müller's return was the subject of bar-room conjecture and breakfast-table postulation and a flood of correspondence from all parts of the country addressed to both the police and the Home Office was once again unleashed. At the Worship Street Police Court north of the City, another shabby drunk had been brought before the magistrates to answer claims that he was Müller's accomplice. Standing five feet nine or ten inches tall with straight red whiskers and a wiry frame, the man was said to have bragged *we were hard up; we wanted money; we went to Fenchurch Street, waited there ... and took two first class tickets to Hackney Wick ... I struck him twice; Müller struck him three times*. It did not take long for the Bow police to discover that the man, named George Augustus King, could not have been involved. He had been seen drinking in the Mitford Castle tavern from eight o'clock on the evening of the murder.

During the afternoon of Thursday 15 September, twelve days after setting out from Manhattan and more than eight weeks after he had left Liverpool in pursuit of Franz Müller, Detective Inspector Richard Tanner stood on the deck of the *Etna* as it approached Cape Clear, forty miles off the southern coast of Ireland.

# CHAPTER 21

## *The Appearance of Guilt*

As the *Etna* hove into sight at half-past two on the afternoon of Thursday 15 September, the telegraph station at Cape Clear alerted the authorities to her impending arrival. At eight-thirty the crowds gathered on every available lookout around Queenstown harbour cheered as a bright light shot up in the far distance and broke into a shower of embers. The *Etna*, as all ships were compelled to do, had signalled her approach.

An hour later the sea-swell was silvered by an almost-full moon. Steaming slowly towards Roche's Point, the ship passed the convict fortifications of Spike Island and the government storehouses before reaching its anchoring point outside the harbour. A steam tender took on the mail and thirty-five of her 205 passengers. Only one reporter (from the *Telegraph*) was allowed to jump on board. Within twenty minutes, the ship had resumed her course for England.

Having secured the opportunity for an exclusive interview with Detective Inspector Tanner, the *Telegraph*'s reporter made his way directly amidships and spent the next few hours closeted with him, listening as he related the details of their weeks in New

York, the facts of the arrest and the charged atmosphere of the Chambers Street court hearing. The next morning British newspapers alerted their millions of readers that Müller was expected to arrive in Liverpool that afternoon. Fearing unruly crowds, Tanner planned to keep Müller on board until Saturday morning when they would make their way quietly to Lime Street Station and the nine o'clock express to London.

As the *Etna* entered the Mersey estuary Müller changed into clean linen and his better clothes. To his threadbare light trousers, dark coat and waistcoat he added a black silk tie with white spots, a plain white collar and a gold stud. Combing his hair and donning a light, broad-brimmed straw hat procured by Inspector Walter Kerressey, he carefully packed up his few belongings and prepared to present himself as favourably as possible.

The Liverpool steam tug *Fury* got alongside the *Etna* off the Formby lightship at about half-past nine on Friday night, ferrying a small force of four detectives and two chief police officers. Passengers and crew crowded the side of the ship as Müller was led, without handcuffs, onto the deck and across a wide plank thrown between the two boats. This might have been his moment to attempt an escape and the *Telegraph* reporter, watching their every move, noticed that *the detectives stuck to him like leeches*, but Müller made no show of resistance. He shivered in his thin clothing, his hands in his pockets. Otherwise he appeared unconcerned as he stood on the deck of the tender, hemmed in on all sides by the Liverpool police.

In the dim light, thousands were crowding around the great landing stage, but the small boat steamed in the moonlight towards the north end of Prince's Pier instead. A dozen or so spectators had already gathered there and several hundred more had rushed down from the landing stage, making a dash for the waiting police vehicles and shouting for *Müller the murderer*. To distract them, several officers entered a police cab and drove off. At the same time, Tanner told Müller to take his arm – confusing

the issue of which of them might be the prisoner – and they struggled forward, falling into another police carriage as it was rocked
by the surging rabble. It swayed and threatened to overturn.
Müller was shaking. Then it lurched forward, racing away from
the yells and shouts and leaving the rest of the Liverpool police,
Clarke, Kerressey, Matthews and Death to follow in their wake.

At the main landing stage hundreds held their ground, refusing to believe that they had missed the arrival of the notorious
criminal. Others began to make their way into Liverpool,
towards the Central Police Station in Dale Street where Müller,
hustled through a private entrance to the side of the building, was
now settled in an inner room, with a plate of bread and butter
and a tankard of bitter ale. Outside, all were turned away.
Surrounded by officers, sergeants and constables, Müller was rattled. From time to time he raised his hands to mask his face until
Tanner cleared the room of everyone but the prisoner's guards.
A ramshackle bed was made from five chairs pushed together,
with a pile of books as a pillow; Müller carefully removed his
boots, collar, coat and neckerchief and folded them neatly to one
side before resting.

The sensation of the Müller story ensured that, throughout the
night and into the morning, all the roads around Lime Street
Station were gridlocked. In order to evade them, Tanner and his
group rose early and slipped unseen from the police station at
half-past seven in the morning, heading for Edge Hill Station further down the line. There they waited in a private room for the
arrival of the nine o'clock express. Müller had regained his
sangfroid and was even reading accounts of his capture in *Once
a Week*; pointedly polite to everyone around him, he shook their
hands and thanked them for the kind attentions he had received.
At the sound of braking wheels and simmering steam, conversation was interrupted. Crossing the platform with a hurried step,
the London police and Müller stepped into a reserved second-
class carriage while, behind them, the door was slammed shut

and locked. In London, Inspector Williamson and his men at Scotland Yard were preparing for the train's arrival at the Euston Square terminus, drafting constables to control the expected throng of spectators and determining the route of the police van from there to the Bow Street cells.

The morning papers wondered at the man's exemplary behaviour, and speculated about the trial. There were eight sessions a year at the Central Criminal Court and the next was due to begin on the following Monday – too soon for Müller's case to be heard. He still had to be formally identified by witnesses before the coroner in Hackney and the inquest jury had yet to reach its verdict on the cause of Thomas Briggs' death. If, as expected, the death was judged unlawful and if the jury considered that there was enough evidence to point to Müller as the murderer, then he would be sent to the magistrate at Bow Street in order to be committed for trial.

If Müller was remanded, time would still be needed for the prosecution and defence to marshal their arguments. The GLPS let it be known that they would employ the most learned and eminent serjeant, or Queen's Counsel, that could be found. Some said that their solicitor, Thomas Beard, had obtained a great deal of evidence favourable to the prisoner, including an alibi for the night of 9 July. Much depended on what Müller had to say for himself, and it was unlikely that a trial would be scheduled before the October sessions. Meanwhile, echoing the position taken by the *Telegraph* a month earlier, several papers were beginning to argue for British fair play. Accepting that an accumulation of facts appeared to support the assumption of Müller's guilt they also considered that *if he had been an innocent man he could not have acted more openly. The probability is that the police have got hold of the right man*, it wrote, *but still it is quite within the limits of possibility that a mistake has been committed.*

*Reynolds's* agreed that *several other papers have unceremoniously usurped the functions of a jury and seem to think that*

*Müller's trial thereby is a more useless and superfluous ceremony.*
Even those convinced of Müller's guilt were alive to the vagaries
of circumstantial evidence, remembering the hundreds of cases in
which the appearance of guilt had condemned a man to hang
only for evidence to emerge – too late – of his innocence.
Uppermost in many minds was the recent case of a traveller
found shot dead by the side of the road with his pockets plun-
dered. A wretched tramp with bloodstains on his clothing had
admitted to the theft but insisted that he robbed the body when
it was already dead. Nobody had believed him and he was summarily convicted and hanged. Later, a man convicted of another
murder confessed to the killing.

Everyone had their favourite tale of misguided capital justice,
but some feared that the errant nature of this particular kind of
evidence might be used by Müller's defence team to baffle justice.
People still fretted that Müller could not have acted alone in
those vital three minutes between Bow and Hackney Wick stations and that a violent accomplice was still on the loose. Others
wondered whether a single new fact, hitherto unknown or
undreamt of, might cause the chain that currently bound him to
fall away, leaving him free.

# CHAPTER 22

## A Very Public Ordeal

Throughout both Thursday and Friday nights, hackneys, drays, barouches and wagons crammed the approaches to Euston Square Station, clanking hooves and grinding wheels mixing with the shouts rising from the thick crowd of pedestrians. If the behaviour of the public in New York and in Liverpool was anything to go by, vast crowds of spectators, whipped into a frenzy of anticipation by the sensationalist reporting of the mass-circulation weekend newspapers, could be expected wherever a possibility of catching sight of Müller existed. This fact was likely to make both politicians, police and the middle classes extremely uneasy, for mobs were fickle: sometimes loud but peaceable in their craving for public 'entertainment' but occasionally rampaging, aggressive and criminal. Windows might be smashed, carriages overturned or children trampled; within the heaving crowds lurked drunks, fraudsters, pickpockets, thieves and worse.

Earlier in Victoria's reign, as the economic progress of the nation polarised the inequalities between the rich and the poor, riots had become a signal of inflammable class tensions and the working classes' demands for political reform. During the late 1830s and 'hungry 40s', as food prices rose and revolutions broke out in much of Europe, real fear had grown among those in power that a popular revolt was imminent. When the Lords refused to pass a new Reform Act extending the vote to more of the male middle classes in 1831, turmoil broke out. When the Act was finally passed a year later, it did not entirely halt demands both to reform corrupt electoral districts and to allow votes for all men over twenty-one. Anger grew with the passing of a harsh new Poor Law in 1843; demonstrations for better working conditions among the poor and starving became increasingly violent.

The constituency of these crowds was no longer confined, as in the first two decades of the century, to the local or to the working classes: the revolutionary language of the Chartists during the 1840s had, rather, united the discontent of both the lower-middle and the working classes, countrywide. When Friedrich Engels worked at a branch of his father's Manchester cotton mill between 1842 and 1844 he noted such appalling conditions among the workers and such *demoralised ... debased ... selfishness* in the bourgeoisie that he concluded that an uprising was imminent: *it is too late for a peaceful solution. The classes are divided more and more sharply, the spirit of resistance penetrates the workers, the bitterness intensifies ...* As the 1840s drew to a close, fearing the 'poison' of the French Revolution, the government struggled with a threat of radicalism that had the potential to burst out of control.

In the event, the repeal of the Corn Laws (which had held the price of corn artificially high) in 1846 did much to draw the sting of proletarian fervour. Rising employment and wages, improvements to scandalous factory working conditions and falling food prices during the early 1860s all somewhat appeased the mobs, though occasional, violent agitation for reform would continue until the Second Reform Act of 1867, which doubled the number of English and Welsh adult males allowed to vote. Even then, 60 per cent of males would remain unfranchised, harbouring a grievance that would rumble well into the twentieth century. Meanwhile, the taint of revolutionary aggression remained attached to the congregation of mobs, and the criminal element endemic in any large crowd made them deeply unsettling in their unpredictability. The publicity surrounding Thomas Briggs' murder and the capture and repatriation of Müller was likely to ensure the congregation of thousands wherever the prisoner appeared.

*

Camden Station was the last stop before Euston Square and railway officials, their friends and families and a gaggle of reporters swarmed the length of the platform. A telegraph sent from Liverpool had informed all stationmasters that Müller was sitting in the last compartment of the last second-class carriage, right at the rear of the train. As the express rounded the curve by the Chalk Farm bridge just after half-past two on Saturday afternoon and began to slow on its approach to Camden, a great surge was made towards the end of the platform. Faces pushed against the train windows but Müller, sitting between Inspectors Tanner and Kerressey, stared resolutely forward, refusing to turn his head. As several passengers departed from carriages further up the train, reporters struggled to get on board and claim empty seats. Tanner's colleague Inspector 'Dolly' Williamson pushed through the mêlée to enter the prisoner's carriage.

As the train pulled out of Camden a Black Maria – a windowless, horse-drawn police van with the royal crest emblazoned on its sides – drew up in Seymour Street alongside Euston Square Station, and backed into a narrow passage that opened onto the arrival platform. Railway directors and a knot of their officials waited on the platform, while a strong body of police struggled to contain the tremendous crowds pressing in from all directions.

Outside the station, vehicles were covered with human forms and inside the main shed men and children teemed over the roofs of standing train carriages. The whole station, reported *The Times*, was a veritable *scene of tumult*.

At 2.45 p.m the train appeared. A ripple passed through the crowd and *excitement overruled all propriety*, as *Lloyd's* later reported. Elderly men were knocked aside and women were shoved as the spectators clawed at each other to get a better look. The noise that went up was deafening.

The long express train shuddered to a stop just short of the buffers so that Tanner's carriage came to a halt at the furthest end of the platform immediately opposite the Seymour Street exit. The rear doors of the police van were open. As Tanner and Clarke emerged from their compartment, each holding one of Müller's arms, there was a single shout and then a chorus of groans and hisses. The German's efforts to spruce himself up had met with little success: his long black lounge coat looked seedy and his beribboned straw hat dirty. *The people seemed surprised at the slight, mean and shabby appearance of the man who had been so long the theme of universal discussion*, reported the *Manchester Guardian. Far below the middle height, excessively plain looking and ill-featured ... he really was not 'equal to the occasion' in the estimation of the crowd who freely commented on the disappointment which they experienced.*

Excitement quickly gave way to dismay. Was this really the man who had sparked such widespread alarm? Could a monster wear the appearance of such innocence? Dressed in tatty clothes, he looked far too slight to have thrown a large man from a train without assistance. Aware of violent pushing from every quarter, and of the edge of threat implicit in the crowds, the detectives almost ran across the exposed width of the platform, elbowing through departing passengers, lifting Müller up the steps into the van and stumbling in after him as it set off at speed.

At the magistrates' court in Bow Street the ordinary business of the day was taking place in packed courtrooms while the crowds outside thinned and regrouped. Heads and shoulders packed the windows of neighbouring houses. By three o'clock the air seemed almost frantic with expectation as a police van, guarded by constables on foot and followed by a breathless mob, drew up at the police station opposite, rocking violently under the press of people swarming around it. Several minutes elapsed while the police struggled to clear a route to the station door. There was a stir as the van door opened and then Müller emerged followed closely by Tanner, Williamson and Kerressey, with Sergeant Clarke in the rear. Among the black-caped officers and in the sea of black toppers, brown felt hats, caps or ladies' bonnets worn by the multitude, Müller's weather-beaten white straw hat emphasised his difference. Brimming with nervous energy, his step was jaunty and his manner seemed almost flippant as he was pushed towards the entrance to the police station, a boy among the burly officers who surrounded him.

Inside the police station, Thomas Beard, his clerk and Dr Ernest Juch, editor of the London-published German newspaper the *Hermann*, watched as Müller was charged *with having wilfully murdered Thomas Briggs on the night of the 9th July last.* A note was made that a hat and watch were found in his possession when arrested. Dropping his head, Müller gave as his address the Blyths' home at 16 Park Terrace, Old Ford, Bow, then he was led out of the busy room and conducted across the yard outside towards a cell where Dr Juch and Thomas Beard were allowed to join him. A German-speaking police officer stood guard outside. Since his committal to the New York Tombs twenty-one days earlier, this was the first time Müller found himself in the company of people who might help him. Asked how he was, he burst into tears before replying quietly, *very bad.* To Juch's reassurances that he would be protected, Müller simply repeated, *I am quite innocent of the crime and I shall be able to prove it.*

Far from the boiling, dust-filled city of New York in which he had never been free, back in the centre of London with its chilly mists and its skies heavy with clouds, he would sleep alone that night for the first time in weeks. As evening fell, he was given a blanket and a bolster and seemed cast down again by this small act of kindness. *You are very kind*, he said. *The police are very kind, particularly Mr Tanner all the way home from America. Of course, you must do your duty.* It seemed that this apparently sociable and naïve young man expected to be treated harshly.

Hoping that the famous prisoner would be taken across the road to the courthouse for committal that afternoon, people were still kicking their heels in the streets around Bow Street, braving the intermittent rain. They called for Matthews, but he had made his own way home from Euston to Paddington. When Tanner left the police station at about five o'clock, accompanied by Inspector Williamson, he was cheered lustily. At Scotland Yard more people had gathered to applaud the now-famous, clever plain-clothed policeman who had tracked the villain and brought him home. As the crowds along the routes from Euston Square to Bow Street and Westminster began slowly to dissipate, he and Williamson went over the investigation together, preparing for the reopening of the coroner's inquest and the magisterial hearing that would set the law in motion. It would be several hours before Tanner would at last be free to head home to his wife and two small children.

\*

In his cell at Bow Street police station, Müller spent Sunday quietly. He wondered aloud why he was not being held at the Stepney station in the neighbourhood of his old lodgings with the Blyths, adding quietly to his guard *it's of no consequence. I shall get justice wherever it is.*

At Scotland Yard the police were busy. It fell once more to

Superintendent Tiddey to ensure that all the case witnesses were available on Monday morning, while Daniel Howie was put in charge of double-checking all the facts for the Treasury solicitors. The measurements of the railway line were repeated, reports on tests for blood were filed, lists of all twenty-one witnesses with their addresses and summaries of their statements were collated. The model of carriage 69 was collected from the railway workshops at Bow and the watch found in Müller's trunk on the *Victoria* was taken to Samuel Tidmarsh – who had regularly cleaned and repaired Briggs' watch – for identification. Then the watch, the three chains, the jewellers' pasteboard box, the hats and the pawn tickets – all crucial evidence – were packed up and secured, ready for the opening of proceedings.

The *sensation* – as it was repeatedly called – was unfolding before the eyes of the nation and the excitement of the public was said to be *unprecedented*. The speed of the attack, the viciousness of the injuries, the status of the victim, the mystery surrounding the hat left in the train, the disappearance of the attacker and the coincidental involvement of two clerks in Mr Briggs' bank had all provoked amazement. Matthews' startling revelations, the hurried pursuit of the fugitive and the long-awaited arrival of Müller in New York had each pumped new blood into the story. *The complete novelty of the outrage in this country*, wrote the *Daily News*, was *a fact which in itself suggested the probability ... that a foreigner had been concerned in the murder.*

For two months the name of an obscure, impoverished German tailor had been uppermost in the nation's thoughts. This *waif and stray of a foreign land, floating in the scum of the London Maelstrom*, as the *Telegraph* put it, might have entered the New World with as little attention as he had left it, one drop more in the tide of immigrants seeking elusive fortune. Instead, millions of people across the world had waited intensely for the outcome of his pursuit across the Atlantic and questions of international importance were raised on his behalf. His name had

BOOK THREE

# JUDGEMENTS

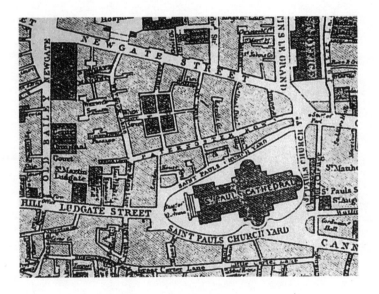

# CHAPTER 23

## *I've Come to Tell the Truth*

Müller was to appear before the magistrate at the Bow Street court at eleven o'clock on Monday morning. By seven there were already five hundred onlookers, and Superintendent Durkin feared that the numbers could become unmanageable. Deciding not to wait any longer, he ordered lines of his constables to stand shoulder to shoulder, forming a passage across the width of the street. Müller ignored the jeers as he walked the short distance.

By ten o'clock, smart carriages lining the routes to the court indicated that the upper classes were in attendance, anticipating something more dramatic than anything provided by the theatres of nearby Drury Lane. The spectator benches were packed with English and foreign press, artists from the illustrated papers and dignitaries with empty diaries, including young Prince Humbert, heir to the Italian crown, with his aide-de-camp and the Italian minister.

An hour later a sudden and impressive silence fell over the commotion as Müller, looking white and sad, was accompanied to the dock by his gaoler. The point of this hearing was to decide whether to proceed to trial after hearing outline evidence from both sides. Representing Müller's interests, Thomas Beard would pit himself against Mr Hardinge Giffard for the Crown. Giffard was not a senior lawyer but his competence was beyond doubt. The forty-one-year-old son of the editor of the *Standard* newspaper, he was destined for a glittering career as Solicitor General in Disraeli's government of 1874 and, later, to be Lord Chancellor.

Beard first ensured that all the witnesses, apart from Inspector Tanner, were removed from the room pending their own depositions: a proper precaution already rendered useless by the repetitive and detailed news reporting of the evidence in the case. Over the next three hours the crammed court would hear the testimonies of Briggs' nephew-in-law David Buchan, his son Thomas James, John Death the jeweller, Ellen Blyth, Elizabeth Repsch, Sergeant George Clarke and William Timms, the railwayman who had discovered the body. Step by careful step the old ground was slowly re-walked. The watch, chains, black bag and walking stick were each identified by the various witnesses, attracting considerable interest from the crowds as they were each handed up to the witness box for careful scrutiny.

Apart from Müller, the man everyone most wanted to see was Jonathan Matthews. His evidence had been given only once before in London, at the first depositions taken in the same court at Bow Street two months earlier on 19 July. Hundreds of words had been written about his testimony and the curiosity surrounding him was intense. Stepping out from the witness room, he took his place in the box.

Shrewd Thomas Beard centred his questions on Matthews' claims that he had bought a hat for Müller at Walker's in Crawford Street. How was it possible to purchase a hat for another man? he asked. How could he be so certain of the marks on it? Could he identify the hats of any other friends with such precision? How many hats had he bought for himself since owning the one he claimed Müller admired? The cabman faltered: he was unable to say exactly what had become of the hat he had bought for himself from Walker's in Crawford Street, or what colour its lining was. He could not be sure, either, how many hats he had bought since, nor from whom or at what cost. He thought he had left the old hat at Down's shop in Long Acre, but he could not swear to it.

Beard's interrogation needled him.

*I can't say more*, he lashed out, under pressure, *I've come here to tell the truth and not to be badgered and bothered in this way.*

Beard deferred further cross-examination. Matthews had showed himself to be a man with a sharp enough memory relative to the hat he identified as Müller's, but vague when it came to his own.

Beard also laboured the questions he put to Thomas James Briggs regarding his father's silk hats. Were they not generally taller in the crown than the one found in Müller's box?

*Yes, somewhere between an inch and two inches higher.*

Thomas James did not know if his father had been in the habit of inscribing his name inside his hats. Pressing his point, Beard wondered whether he could, then, identify this hat as belonging to the victim? *No, I could not positively identify this hat as the one my father wore on 9th July.*

This was progress. Beard chose not to cross-examine either John Death or Elizabeth Repsch, the tailor's wife. But he succeeded in encouraging Müller's friend John Hoffa to confirm that Müller had been limping on 9 July and that he was wearing a slipper on his injured foot when he left the Repschs' house that evening. It further counterbalanced the weight of evidence accumulated against his client. If doubt already existed over Müller's ability to overpower Thomas Briggs in the short time between leaving Bow Station and passing over the Duckett's Canal bridge, an injured foot would have both hampered the attack and made his escape more tricky to conceal.

Anticipating that his client would be remanded for trial, Beard had already decided to reserve the part of his defence concerning proof of an alibi. For now it was simply crucial to do everything in his power to destabilise the evidence of the prosecution witnesses and nurture seeds of doubt. Throughout the hearing, Müller had scarcely looked at the witnesses nor did he react as their names were called. Only once did he appear agitated. After an hour of standing in the dock, the magistrate's offer of a chair caused him to flush rapidly; his shoulders contracted with apparent embarrassment. Was this another indication that the German, schooled in hardship and unaccustomed to consideration from his superiors, was moved by simple, thoughtful acts?

It helped Thomas Beard's case that Müller's conduct appeared so at variance with his guilt. A growing minority were finding it difficult to reconcile his stature and demeanour with the amount of strength and resolve needed to commit the appalling deed. As the hearing drew to a close at two o'clock Müller was remanded for a week pending his attendance before the coroner in Hackney. Beard was satisfied that he had begun to make inroads against the Treasury's prosecution.

Müller remained in the dock until a path was cleared to a waiting police van that hastened along Bow Street and through the afternoon traffic as dull drops of rain began to drum on its roof. On the northern edge of the city another locked room awaited in the three-storey House of Detention in Clerkenwell designed for the incarceration of remand prisoners. Crossing the courtyard towards its pillared portal, Müller was conducted along a wide, high corridor floored in asphalt with whitewashed walls, then into a broad hall where he was assigned a prisoner number. Then he was led to a reception cell on the floor above.

His property was removed and his name and age recorded. After washing, a bustling warder in blue uniform read out the rules, then Müller was examined by a surgeon and allocated a small cell with a window, a warm-air grating in the corner, a seat fixed to the wall and a hammock. A blanket, a towel, soap and a comb were supplied and his clothing was taken for fumigation before being returned to him to wear at his trial. He was told that visits and letters were prohibited, that tobacco, swearing, whistling and shouting were forbidden and that regular attendance at divine service was required. His meals would consist of eight ounces of potatoes, one and a half pints of soup and a pint of gruel daily, with an additional six ounces of meat on Tuesdays, Thursdays and at the weekends; on Sundays he would be given a sweet cup of cocoa and an additional ration of bread.

To ensure against the possibility that he would try to defy justice by committing suicide, two officers were placed on constant watch outside his cell.

*

The next morning, the inquest jury were empanelled once more in Hackney. In the body of the room, every seat was filled. Waiting for the legal representatives and witnesses to arrive, *the question of the guilt or innocence of the accused man ... was discussed with a singular degree of anxiety.*

Jonathan Matthews was the first to be called. The cabman's experience at Bow Street the previous day had prepared him for fierce interrogation and he seemed more in control of his testimony. The audience was rapt as he repeated the circumstances surrounding the purchase of a hat for Müller and the reasons he was able so easily to identify it several months later. When passed the hat, he pointed out that the slight extra curl to one side of the brim was still evident.

*What was the colour of the lining of your own hat?* asked Beard.

*I told you before,* said Matthews insolently, *that I could not tell you.*

*Never mind what you said yesterday, have you no recollection of the colour of the lining of your own hat?*

*None whatsoever.*

His Walker hat, said Matthews, was worn out within four or

five months of its purchase and he bought the next at Down's in Covent Garden's Long Acre some time during June, paying five shillings and sixpence and leaving the old hat behind at the shop. Holding up the hat said to be Müller's once more, Beard asked the question no one had yet put to the driver.

*Is not that the hat?*

*No*, said Matthews, *I am sure it is not.*

*Just try it on*, said Beard after a lengthy pause.

Beard was taking a risk, knowing that it could either work strongly to his client's advantage or substantiate the claims of the man whose story did so much to condemn. Taking it up with both hands, Matthews pulled the hat onto his head with a flourish, letting it fall a little forward over his eyebrows. It was evidently too large. Playing up to the jury, he shrugged back his shoulders in triumph.

*There*, he exclaimed. *Is that a hat to suit me?* He laughed, and the court laughed with him.

Beard made himself a note that the lining of the hat had come away – and he wondered whether, once it was refixed, the hat might fit Matthews more snugly. Then he set out to nail Matthews with the same questions that had begun to make the witness squirm the day before. Having had time to think about it, Matthews now remembered buying yet another hat, soon after the one from Down's, at a shop in Oxford Street. He still could not say what had become of either of them.

*Do you persevere in the statement that the hat you purchased at Walker's was the hat you left at Down's?* asked Beard sarcastically.

*I do.*

He would return to this theme, but now Beard quickly changed direction. Was Müller not intimate with Matthews' sister-in-law, and had there not been an argument between them that led to a falling out? Matthews rejoindered that he believed there had been some agreement between Müller and this woman, but again he could not swear to it. *They were never at my house together. I heard from him that there had been some misunderstanding between* [them] *but I have never had any misunderstanding with him on my sister-in-law's account.*

Now Beard came from another angle, demanding that Matthews account for his own whereabouts on 9 July. *I was driving my cab*, he replied. It was hired by the day, but since the owner had gone out of business and disappeared, he was unable to substantiate his claim. Nor was he able to say whether he worked during the week following the murder. Pushed harder by Thomas Beard, the witness admitted that he was not completely certain after all that he was out driving that day. *I might have laid up all day in bed*, he said, explaining that if he was not in bed he was driving; if he was not out with the cab, he was in bed.

Beard had only one more question: *Was any one present at this pretended examination of the hat at your house before the murder?* No, admitted Matthews, *I cannot say that there was.*

Sticking to the decision he had made at Bow Street not to question John Death, Thomas Beard declined to cross-examine the jeweller on his statement concerning the exchange of chains. Nor did he further question the dead man's son over his identification of the articles that had belonged to his father – the watch and hat found in Müller's box in New York or the chain given up to the jeweller in Cheapside. Thomas James' uncertainty that this was his father's hat was continuing to work to their advantage. Earlier that morning Briggs' son had re-examined the silk hat and had told the coroner that it was *considerably shorter, and the lining inside has been cut short and sewn together again under the brim. The underside of the brim is parramatta, and my father usually wore silk.*

When the last witness stepped down, Coroner Humphreys told the jury that their job was nearly done. They would reconvene in six days' time, at eight o'clock on the following Monday morning. Franz Müller would be called to appear before them in order for his identity to be fully established; then the inquest jury would retire to consider their verdict.

# CHAPTER 24

# *First Judgement*

No one outside Müller's legal team knew how he intended to defend himself but *it is not expected*, reported *Reynolds's Weekly Newspaper*, that he *will disclose the nature of the defence ... until the trial.* It was said that the prisoner was eating well but that his spirits were low as he continued to claim his innocence to the officers guarding his cell.

Snippets of new information that suggested developments in the prosecution's case began to appear in the press. Inspector Tanner had questioned a shopman employed by Digance hatters in the Royal Exchange (Thomas Briggs' hatters) and the man was said distinctly to remember selling the hat found in Müller's luggage to Mr Briggs, recognising it by a peculiar alteration made in the lining to make it fit more comfortably. It was also reported that Mr Digance was in the habit of marking the inside brim of all the hats he sold with the date of their sale. *Should that be so,* wrote *The Times, and the date be found, it will materially affect the issue.*

It also appeared that several people were rushing to gain from the poor tailor's infamy. The sale of souvenirs relating to *causes célèbres* was a highly profitable business and copyright piracy was rife. Press reports now confirmed that Thomas Beard was acting on behalf of Mr A. L. Henderson, a 'photographiartist' (as he called himself) in the City. Henderson accused another man of copyright infringement in the printing and sale of photographs of Franz Müller and the forgery and sale of a carte-de-visite made earlier that year for the German. Henderson contended that Müller had paid him to take his likeness in December 1863 but had left one print behind, along with its negative. A week or so after the detectives left for New York, realising the value of this image, Henderson had registered copyright and began to publish it. *The sale of the photograph*, claimed Beard, *had been such a great success that it had caused parties to pirate.*

Over the intervening weekend most of the illustrated papers carried drawings of Müller copied from Henderson's photograph, alongside representations of the surging crowds on his arrival at Bow Street police station the previous Saturday. *Not even in the annals of crime can be found a case that has created more general interest than this of the murder of Mr Briggs*, wrote the *Penny Illustrated Paper* under their portrait of the prisoner. *It has every element of the sensational kind that a sensation-loving public can possibly desire ... Doubt hangs over the affair ... Müller's own behaviour remains as wonderful as ever. He has continued to act to the last exactly as an innocent man might be supposed to act.*

Quiet and respectful, Müller's character was particularly at odds with the bravado of Matthews and it was said that Müller had complained to his German-speaking police guard about the cab driver's evidence at Bow Street that week. He was apparently bitter about his old friend's falseness, claiming that Matthews knew very well that the hat he bought for Müller was worn out and that one side of its brim had been broken the last time the two men met. It was even reported that Müller had once threatened to have one of Matthews' brothers-in-law arrested and that

Matthews' evidence was thus born of spite. Most exercising was a rumour that *the solicitor for the defence is in possession of certain facts which are expected to materially shake the testimony given by Matthews.*

*

A dense fog hung low over London on Monday morning as Müller was removed from his cell in Clerkenwell to a police van, accompanied by Detective Inspector Tanner and Inspector Kerressey. Extra police had been mustered to keep the approach roads to the Hackney town hall clear. Six separate mounted patrols diverted and managed the suburban traffic. Thirty constables guarded the entrance to the main building; twenty more were inside and fifty police patrolled the area around Hackney Station, within 150 yards of the hall. By half-past seven, all two hundred places in the inquest room were occupied and the corridors and staircases were crammed, while outside the police struggled to maintain an access route. At eight o'clock Müller arrived under police guard; the witnesses were ordered into an adjoining room, and the questions began. George Blyth was called first, and then his wife Ellen. Eliza Matthews spoke plainly about Müller's visit to her on Monday 11 July and the circumstances surrounding their possession of the cardboard box from Death's shop. John Hoffa, John Death and the Repschs identified the prisoner. Then a juryman asked Müller to put on the crushed hat found in carriage 69. Tanner stood to hand it to him and he pulled it onto his head.

There was a flurry in the court as it fitted.

After Humphreys reimposed silence on the room, Thomas Lee's deposition was read to the jury and Müller's solicitor Thomas Beard laboured over the evidence regarding the two men seen in Briggs' compartment at Bow Station on the night of the murder. *Is the prisoner one of them? ... Is he like the man or not? ... Will you not swear the prisoner is the man?* he asked

Map of New York, 1847. A warren of southern streets gave way to the twelve parallel avenues that stretched north to 44th Street.

Broadway, 1862, bewilderingly alive with snapping reins and shying horses, fine shops, bright clothes, vagrant children and burly cops.

*Above:* 300 Mulberry Street, Manhattan, 1863. The New York Police Department's headquarters.

*Right:* 'Müller was arrested and his luggage searched', from an illustrated newspaper circa 1914.

*Below:* 'The Tombs', New York's prison: a daunting structure in the style of an ancient Egyptian mausoleum.

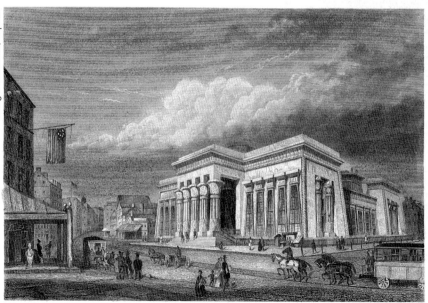

A 'Black Maria' or police van, circa 1862.

The verdict of the Hackney inquest. The victim's name was almost recorded as Thomas Müller, before the surname was scratched out and amended to Briggs.

The House of Detention, Clerkenwell, 1862. *Above:* a bird's-eye view. *Left:* interior.

Newgate gaol from the corner of Newgate Street and Old Bailey, 1862. The dome of St Paul's Cathedral is just visible in the top left corner.

Serjeant William Ballantine, part of the prosecution team.

Lord Chief Baron Pollock.

Serjeant John Humffreys Parry

Members of the legal teams, taken from an illustrated newspaper circa 1914. *Left to right:* Mr Giffard, the Solicitor-General, Lord Chief Baron Pollock, Baron Martin, Serjeant Parry and Mr Beard.

The Old Court at the Old Bailey, 1862.

Baron Martin donning a black cap to sentence Müller to death, 1864.

Sketches of some of the witnesses from an illustrated newspaper circa 1914. *Left to right:* John Death the silversmith, cabman Jonathan Matthews and his wife.

The cell for condemned prisoners, Newgate, 1850.

Crowds throng the Old Bailey to witness an execution at Newgate, 1863.

Sir George Grey, Home Secretary.

Franz Müller, 24, German tailor.

'Dead Man's Walk', the underground passage between Newgate and the Old Bailey through which Müller walked on each day of his trial, and where his body was buried.

*Above:* The Memorial on Müller's behalf, delivered to Sir George Grey by solicitor Thomas Beard.

*Left:* Some of the many pamphlets printed after Müller's trial.

repeatedly. Over and over again Thomas Lee simply answered, *I cannot so swear*.

Lee's refusal to put Müller in the train with Briggs that night went some way to redressing the advantage lost as Müller stood before the court with the broken Walker hat sitting comfortably on his head. Rising swiftly, Hardinge Giffard wrested back the advantage: under fire from his interrogation, Lee let slip that he was not, after all, entirely sure that either of the men he saw had whiskers. A rippling *Oh!* swept through the court.

Reprising the post-mortem results and directing the jury that they must consider only the material facts presented before them, Humphreys advised them that Thomas Briggs had certainly been robbed and that his death was the result of malice. He reminded them that a hat presumed to be Müller's had been left in the compartment while Mr Briggs' hat had disappeared, later to be found on the prisoner. The jury's duty was to consider, on the basis of the evidence, whether a crime had been committed. Further, if they concluded it likely that Müller had played any part in the murder of Mr Briggs then they must return the inquest's verdict of wilful murder against him. The jury retired.

Twenty minutes passed before they returned, preceded by the coroner. They found that *the deceased died from the effects of foul violence administered in the railway carriage on the 9th July and we find that Franz Müller is the man by whom the violence was committed.* Before proceedings were brought to a close, however, the foreman of the jury asked to make a statement on behalf of them all. They wished to call the attention of the government to their dissatisfaction at the present state of security on the railways. No delay should be allowed – they said – in enforcing the railway companies to adopt more efficient methods of protection of life, character and property.

The room emptied. Police and witnesses were all running late for their next appointment at the Bow Street Magistrates' Court. Dispersing, they left the thirteen men of the inquest jury waiting to discharge their final duty by adding their signatures to an indictment, stating on their oaths that *Franz Müller, late of Bow, did feloniously wilfully and of his malice aforethought kill and murder against the peace of Our Lady the Queen her Crown and dignity the said Thomas Briggs.*

In the rush, did any of the jurymen notice that a mistake had been rapidly corrected in the official documentation? So closely did the names Franz Müller and Thomas Briggs elide in the public mind that in the space reserved for the name of the victim 'Thomas Müller' was recorded, before the clerk dashed it out and corrected it to Briggs.

*

Those fortunate enough to secure a seat on the public benches at the Bow Street court earlier that morning had endured a long and uncomfortable wait. At ten past eleven, more than an hour late, the witnesses arrived, grumbling that they had been given no pause to rest or take refreshment and that, summoned hither and thither across the capital, their lives no longer seemed their own.

*When did you first hear of the huge reward?* solicitor Beard asked of both Godfrey and Elizabeth Repsch once each had given their evidence to the magistrate. Neither was able to say. How were they able to remember with such precision the trousers Müller had worn on any day prior to Saturday the 9th, or even after it? Could they describe in detail the lining or shape of any of their own hats, or the hats of their friends, or even of the new 'guinea' hat Müller was wearing when he visited them the week after the murder? Again, neither the husband nor the wife was able to do so.

Reporters came and went, taking copious notes for the several editions of the day's newspapers. Beard pushed Toulmin – the Briggs' family doctor – about finding grit in the wounds on the victim's head, suggesting that death had been caused by the fall from the train. Toulmin countered that the great quantity of blood found on the carriage seats and the nature of the forceful, blunt wounds demonstrated that a violent attack had occurred before the fall. Called next to testify, young Dr Brereton concurred that these were the blows that had fractured the skull and that they were more likely to have caused death than the fall from the train.

Müller appeared at last to have snapped into life. Gone was the unmoved and unmoving defendant: following the verdict of the inquest, he seemed finally to have woken up to the gravity of his situation. He listened to Dr Brereton's descriptions of Thomas Briggs' injuries with equanimity but when any other portion of the evidence told against him he became animated, scribbling notes for his solicitor and engaging him from time to time in earnest discussion. When Matthews took the stand, Müller's face lit with anger and his eyes never left the witness throughout his testimony as Thomas Beard once again harried the cab driver to account for his whereabouts on 9 July. Again he could not.

*You ought to know exactly. You have reason to remember it*, reproved Beard. It made no odds. Matthews remained obstinate and unyielding.

*Yes, I know I have*, he barked.

Late into the afternoon a new witness was called by Hardinge Giffard. Daniel Digance was asked to take the stand. Rumours that the police had procured new evidence from Thomas Briggs' hatters were confirmed as he swore that he had made hats for Briggs for the last thirty-five years, that Briggs preferred the best-quality, twenty-one-shilling hats and that his most recent purchase was in September 1863, almost exactly a year earlier. Referring to the hat found in Müller's box, Giffard asked, *Does the measurement as to the fit of the hat correspond with the order given by Mr Briggs?*

*Yes, precisely*, replied Digance.

Further, Digance remembered that Thomas Briggs complained after a few days that his new hat was a little loose and asked that a folded band of tissue paper be lodged under its brim to alter its fit. Taking up the hat in question, the hatter showed that *the paper has been removed, but there are some fragments of the tissue left, showing where the paper has been.* This unexpected development elicited another loud exclamation from the public seats.

The fact remained that this hat was much lower in the crown than the style favoured by Briggs, allowing uncertainty to remain as to its original owner. Digance's hatmaker, Frederick William Thorne, was called next and his evidence was damning. He recognised the hat as one of his by his handwritten mark but he believed it had been cut down. *The work has not been done as a hatter would do it. A hatter would have stuck it together with a hot iron and gum. That would necessitate the use of a block. This has been sewn round.* He said that the lining, too, had been altered in a manner not used by professional hatters. He thought that the stitching used to alter the hat was uncommonly neat. *It was evidently done,* he said pointedly, *by some one accustomed to sewing.*

After five gruelling hours, at a little after four o'clock, the lawyers were done. As the magistrate Mr Flowers asked the prisoner whether he had anything to say, Müller looked up sharply. *I have nothing to say now,* he demurred in a loud but respectful voice, laying particular emphasis on the final word.

There had been no surprises. Having read over and signed the depositions, the magistrate ruled that the prisoner should be committed to take his trial on the charge of wilful murder.

\*

An hour later, Müller was being led under strong guard out of the court towards a waiting police van. With loud groans and yells, the crowd broke through the ranks of the police stationed at some distance above and below the court to keep them back. Pushing and shoving, sweeping through the barrier, they made a rush at the van, reaching it just as the doors were closed. As it drove away with Müller inside, half the multitude pursued it, rushing down the street and banging on its side before the horses pulled ahead and began to draw clear.

It was unclear whether the mob had intended to lynch the prisoner. What was obvious was that it was wound to a fury so intense that it would take time to abate. In the meantime, those who had not given chase remained outside the court, howling, stamping their excitement, and stubbornly refusing to be moved on.

# CHAPTER 25

# A Pint of Meat and Vegetable Soup

Making its way east through the ashen light of the late afternoon the police van clattered to a halt outside Newgate, the most fearsome prison in Victorian imagination. For more than a thousand years a gaol had stood on the site of the City's westernmost gate, a mere ten minutes' walk from the Bank of England and St Paul's Cathedral. It was a monstrous building designed to call forth horror, its scowling bulk, pitted granite flanks and chilling, ironspiked walls emphasising the inevitability of punishment for crime.

The schoolboy Charles Dickens had gazed at this exterior with *mingled feelings of awe and respect*, noting *how dreadful its rough, heavy walls and low massive doors appeared ... looking as if they were made for the express purpose of letting people in and never letting them out again.* This building had been one of the landmarks in the narrow radius of Müller's former London life but the familiar was made strange by his arrest. He could hear the resounding boom of St Paul's bells. His friends still toiled in nearby Threadneedle Street amid the human din and harsh rattle of hooves and wheels. They moved, anonymous in the feverish crowd of clerks, lawyers, vagrants, day-workers and prostitutes, passing from grand buildings to mean dwellings in squalid courts, while he followed only the orders of his captors.

Rain had turned the cold streets pewter. Omnibuses passed on their journeys between the Bank and the West End. Bewigged lawyers with bundles of papers tied in red tape, clerks in their black gowns, and employees of the neighbouring Central Criminal Court hurried past in the shadows of the austere building, as Müller entered the gaol through the iron-bound, nail-studded oak wicket gate. Directed by warders, he passed through two more barred doors and along sombre stone passages lit with dull lamps, arriving at the whitewashed Bread Room. He stood as his details were entered solemnly in the vast, vellum-bound register, a florid copperplate hand noting his name, height, age, birthplace and occupation. It was recorded that he was committed by Mr Flowers from Bow Street and by Mr Humphreys the coroner, pending trial on the charge of wilful murder against Thomas Briggs. Spaces for the trial date, the judge's name, the verdict and the sentence remained blank.

Newgate housed several hundred prisoners in recently 'improved' single cells, each of them awaiting their trials at the opening of the next court sessions. If they were found guilty, they would be removed to other prisons; if convicted of murder they stayed to await their execution. Conducted along flagged corridors, Müller traversed narrow stone stairways and winding passages, through a succession of locked iron doors, each opened by an identically uniformed turnkey. Small windows gave onto open courts but admitted little light or air to diffuse a broth of smells that thickened throughout the place. He passed a room with glass panelling used by solicitors to meet with their clients, crossed a court and entered a glass-roofed gallery ranging up over four floors with cells branching off on either side.

Müller's cell was about seven feet wide, thirteen feet long and ten feet high. It contained a table that folded up against the wall, a small three-legged stool, a copper washbasin under a tap in the wall and a water closet or lavatory. Three triangular shelves in the corner held a Bible, prayer book, plate, mug and bedding. The floor was asphalt with a grating to admit heated air. A gaslight with tin shade was fixed to the wall. At one end was a high window with fixed panes and crossed iron bars.

The prisoner was given a pint of meat and vegetable soup and eight ounces of bread. His breakfast would be a pint of gruel alternately seasoned with salt and molasses, and on four evenings each week his dinner would consist of a pound of potatoes and three ounces of meat. While he waited for his trial in the adjoining Central Criminal Court, he would exercise daily in an open yard under forty-foot walls surmounted by iron pickets, walking three yards apart from his fellow prisoners. He would also attend services and sermons in the small chapel, sitting every morning (and twice on Sundays) on a low form behind railings. He would only be allowed visits from the prison authorities or members of his defence team. Because his case was considered 'remarkable' an officer was put on guard outside his cell around the clock. Sometimes, Müller would talk to him.

*

The second act of the strange drama that had absorbed so much public interest had drawn to a close. Only the third and last act remained to be played out and attention turned to the anticipated trial. The next day, Tuesday 27 September, the *Daily Telegraph* judged Thomas Beard wise to have reserved the substance of his defence, though it also believed the case against Müller might have been strengthened during Monday's two hearings. The absence of any real motive for the crime (the intricacies of the various pawnbroker deals revealed that Müller had enough money for his fare without resorting to the sale of the watch, *ergo* he need not have stolen it) and the difficulty of reconciling his behaviour with that of a guilty man both told in the prisoner's favour. Nevertheless, while the negative evidence in Müller's favour was strong, most thought that the positive evidence outweighed it.

There were some who considered that Beard's reluctance to offer evidence in defence was a sign of weakness, an indication that nothing had been discovered to substantiate an alibi. Müller had not contested Matthews' story about the purchase of the Walker hat. The new evidence of the two hatters appeared to prove that the hat found on Müller really had once belonged to Thomas Briggs, its alteration effected by someone clever with needle and scissors. These people believed that, if the defence was not more cunning, Müller would undoubtedly hang.

*Taken from life expressly for this exhibition*, a model of Müller had been added to Madame Tussaud's waxwork museum in the Baker Street Bazaar in Portman Square, open daily from ten o'clock until five, and again in the evening from seven to eleven, admission one shilling (children half-price). Established in 1843 and known first as the Separate Room and then as the Chamber of Comparative Physiognomy, the re-named Chamber of Horrors offered an alternative to the wax models of statesmen, royalty, warriors and thinkers. Here, three-dimensional likenesses of renowned ruffians and criminals catered to the Victorian appetite for the odd, the deformed and the monstrous. Indeed, all over London – in side-street exhibitions, peepshows, penny-gaffs and dank upstairs rooms – 'living skeletons', Siamese twins and humans with 'enormities and deformities' were paraded for cash, feeding a rampant appetite for morbid entertainment.

The Chamber of Horrors was, advised *Cruchley's London: A Handbook for Strangers*, viewed at its alarming best in the gloomy hours of night. The public could stare at the figures of notorious Victorian murderers such as Courvoisier, Frederick and Maria Manning and James Mullins – all translated into wax within days of their arrests, trials or executions – and at blood-curdling casts of guillotined heads from the first French

Revolution. Never mind the fact that the *Spectator* (much like the critics of 'sensation novels') dubbed it all *a disgrace to our nation*, there was a strange thrill in being able to look the freakish duplicate of a killer in the eye.

Tussaud's effigy of Müller was widely reported to be an excellent likeness and it may have been the reason why the Briggs family decided to write a letter for publication in the daily papers. Concerned that the public seemed to have accepted the impression that Briggs was a large, strong man who could have been overwhelmed only with great difficulty, they wanted to put the record straight. *An argument has been founded favourable to Müller*, they wrote, *that so slight a man as he would hardly have ventured to attack one so powerfully made.* [We] *write to say that Mr Briggs' height was not more than 5 feet 8½ inches; his weight about, but certainly not over, 11 stone, and his muscular development not above average for men of his size. He had further been weakened by a very serious illness, from which he had not long recovered, and was in his 70th year.*

Hitherto, the family had refused to react publicly to the tragedy overtaking their lives. The Unitarian codes of conduct regarding hard work, sober living, compassion, tolerance and restraint, added to class codes of polite behaviour, all ensured that they maintained their silence. It was the supposed criminal, Müller, rather than the respectable, self-improving victim, Thomas Briggs, whose name edged its way into every conversation. All that Briggs had stood for seemed to have been defeated by the dominance of conjecture about the prisoner and his motives; Briggs' industrious decency paled into insignificance before the crime and its implications for society as a whole.

Despite a few vague suspicions aired against the family at the start of the police investigation, they had been proved beyond reproach, yet considerably more sympathy had begun to attach itself to Müller than to the Briggs' personal grief. As tension mounted over the date of Müller's trial, the family could no longer read newspaper reports and speculations without being piqued into reaction. While they were at pains to stress that they had no desire to prejudice Müller's case, they thought that *the public should be made aware that what has been relied upon by many as an argument in favour of the accused is founded upon a misapprehension.*

\*

Inspector Tanner and his team were still fixed on plugging gaps in the investigation, finally asking the chemistry professor Dr Henry Letheby to provide a second opinion on whether the stick belonging to one of Müller's co-lodgers at 16 Park Terrace bore any signs of human blood. Members of the public continued, sporadically, to come forward with their own tales. One, Mr Flemming, told the Westminster police on 7 October that he had also seen Thomas Briggs on the night of his murder sharing a compartment with two other men. Flemming said that he saw them at Fenchurch Street Station but, since Briggs was occupying Flemming's favourite corner seat, he had gone into the next carriage along. It took over a week for the report to be written up and sent to the Commissioner. Mayne forwarded it to Inspector Tanner. It was then, apparently, filed without further action.

At the end of the third week of October the Home Office confirmed that Müller's trial would take place during the October sessions commencing the following week, on Monday the 24th. The judges on the rota were the Lord Chief Baron Pollock, Mr Baron Martin and Mr Justice Willes and the prevailing impression among the journalists was that the first two of these would sit together.

Lord Chief Baron Frederick Pollock was one of England's leading and most learned judges. With a long face and a deep vertical furrow between sharp eyes, he was approaching the end of a glittering career – as Attorney General in Sir Robert Peel's first

Tory administration, as successful defender of the Chartist insur-
rectionists, and as the presiding judge in the murder trials of the
Mannings in 1849 and of James Mullins in 1860. Scholarly, pol-
ished and impressively strong-minded, Pollock had a reputation
for demanding hasty verdicts from his juries and for focusing on
substantive justice over bravura legal showmanship. Beside him
in co-judgement would sit Ulsterman Samuel Martin. Pollock's
former pupil and now his son-in-law, Martin was also impatient
of pedantic legal stickling but was less predictable in his judgements and could veer between the imposition of the harshest
penalties and a striking liberal-mindedness. The practice of trying
capital cases at the Central Criminal Court with two judges was
an ancient one, already in decline, but it offered the advantage of
allowing them to confer over complicated points of law without
undue delay. The two courts of the Old Bailey had a substantial
calendar to get through in the forthcoming sessions: one charge
of murder, two of manslaughter, one of attempted murder, one of
rape, four of feloniously wounding, one of arson, four of bigamy,
eight of burglary and the rest of counterfeiting, forgery, stealing,
threatening and other misdemeanours. There were 114 prisoners
and no time for delays.

The previous year, eminent nineteenth-century judge and legal
historian Sir James Fitzjames Stephen wrote that the five
common rules of evidence in the English criminal court were that
the burden of proof was cast upon the prosecutor; that evidence
must be confined to the points at issue; that the best evidence
must always be given; that hearsay was inadmissible; and that
confessions under police questioning should not be considered as
evidence. Most importantly, he stressed that the presumption of
innocence was enshrined in all criminal trials: *crime must be
proved beyond all reasonable doubt ... The word 'reasonable' is
indefinite. It is an emphatic caution against haste in coming to a
conclusion adverse to a prisoner.* Juries, in other words, should
convict only when they believed that no reasonable hypothesis

existed to explain the facts of the case other than the prisoner's guilt.

Better, it was repeatedly avowed, ten guilty men should escape than one innocent man should suffer. Yet the reality was that Victorian trials often moved at extraordinary speed. Charles Cottu, sent by the French government to England several decades earlier to inquire into the British judicial system, was shocked by precipitate trials. He believed that the English were practically *indifferent whether among the really guilty such be convicted . . . so much the worse for him against whom the proofs are too evident, so much the better for the other in whose favour there may exist some faint doubts*. English criminal trials, reported Cottu, were less about justice than about setting examples to the criminal classes in order to inspire in them *a wholesome terror of the vengeance of the law*.

In Müller's trial, as in all those scheduled for the October sessions, both the prosecution and the defence would be required to present their cases swiftly. Witnesses might be called to attest to the prisoner's good character but the law was clear: evidence of character meant evidence of reputation as opposed to disposition and – confusingly – previous 'good deeds' were considered irrelevant. The body of circumstantial evidence against him was considerable and damning. It was the kind of indirect evidence that inferred rather than proved his guilt, yet the majority of English judges were intolerant of the widespread public opinion that indirect evidence was too fallible to justify a capital conviction. They argued robustly according to their experience: that murder was rarely witnessed, that men did not commit crimes openly and that circumstance and presumptions were the raw materials out of which substantial proof was often made. Like Judge Stephen, even liberal-minded judges were impatient of defence barristers using the phrase 'circumstantial evidence', to *puzzle juries*, believing that it provided *them with a loophole for avoiding a painful but most important duty*.

Müller's trial would doubtless centre on the concept of 'reasonable doubt'. All twelve men of the jury must unanimously be convinced of his guilt in order to convict. Should a single man harbour uncertainty, should just one of them shrink from the burden of sending a man to the gallows, then the duty of the jury as a whole was clear: they would be required to return a verdict of not guilty.

# CHAPTER 26

## *The Great Müller Case*

Straw was laid on the narrow roadway of the Old Bailey on the morning of Monday 24 October to deaden the noise of carts and cabs and it was soon filled with people, signalling the start of the sessions. Within the building, attention centred on the grand jury. Twenty-four men, aged between twenty-one and sixty, each a tradesman or professional, had been summoned by the sheriff; those who failed to appear were heavily fined, while all those who turned up – subject to a quorum of twelve – were required to decide by majority vote whether enough evidence existed in each case to justify a trial. Weak or baseless cases would be dismissed while, for all the rest, they would pass a 'true bill' of indictment. Only then could the prisoner be arraigned and asked to state his plea.

The recorder of the court outlined all the important cases that morning, telling the grand jury that there was *only one trial for wilful murder and the circumstances of that case have become familiar, unfortunately, to most of the public. But for the purposes of the present inquiry it was probably sufficient to say that they would be aware Mr Briggs was murdered in a railway carriage on the night of the 9th July.* He reminded them of the main thrusts of the evidence and explained that they would hear a general overview of the facts including summary testimony from the key witnesses. They must then judge whether a prima facie case was made out for the prosecution and, if so, return a true bill allowing the trial to begin.

Freezing rain fell steadily outside the narrow window of Müller's Newgate cell, chasing the falling leaves into the court-yards of the gaol. The outlines of the capital were muted as cloud, sleet and fog met smoke and mud. On Tuesday 25 October several of the prosecution witnesses gave their evidence privately to the grand jury. The following day it returned a bill of indictment, or true bill. The day after that, Müller's lawyers would fight for his life.

*

More than three months since the death of Thomas Briggs, a horde described by *The Times* as *numerous and urgent, almost beyond precedent* began to gather outside the Sessions House from three o'clock on the morning of Thursday 27 October. Ten policemen guarded the outer door and only those involved in *the great Müller case*, as the *Telegraph* dubbed it, were allowed to pass inside. Once admitted, they waited in the narrow passage with rising impatience for the similarly guarded inner door to be opened. By nine o'clock the fifty public seats within the court had been filled. MPs and aris-tocrats pressed together on the reserved bench, beside Police Commissioner Sir Richard Mayne and a handful of men believed to be Thomas Briggs' relatives. Chairs had been squeezed into every available corner. Seats were improvised on every ledge. Outside, knots of disappointed spectators rushed towards every arriving cab in the hope of glimpsing one of the witnesses. Pubs and taverns in the area enjoyed a roaring trade.

Important trials were always conducted in the Old Court, a space endlessly criticised as small and dingy. The Lord Mayor with all the pomp of his office, the sheriffs, the aldermen of the City of London in purple silk and fur and the recorder were arranged either side of the two judges' raised, crimson-cushioned bench. Before them in the open space of the body of the court, solicitors and wigged, black-gowned barristers huddled round an unsightly deal table covered in green baize and littered with briefcases and papers. Behind them were cramped benches for reporters, friends of the judges, and hangers-on.

Two narrow benches for the twelve jurymen were ranged to the right of the judges. Before them was the commodious dock. With a wooden bar to its front and a rear staircase leading to the cells beneath, it contained three seats: one for the governor of Newgate, another for the warder and a third for the prisoner who had only recently been released from the obligation to stand. The public were accommodated in a limited number of wooden pews rising in tiers above and behind the dock.

The courtroom had three large and three smaller windows and was lit by gas lamps, notwithstanding which the dark, wood-panelled room was gloomy and badly ventilated. Seven separate doors led from it, each reserved for the particular use of the judges, jury, witnesses, counsel, solicitors, prisoner or public. The witness room on one side was so small that it was often left simply to the women, male witnesses sent to wait in the draughty passageways or at Allwood's coffee and dining rooms across the road. Called into court, each witness would have to pass directly in front of the prisoner in the dock, taking a seat to his right-hand side.

On the open floor of the Old Court, the battle between prosecution and defence would be waged between members of a serious-minded, close-knit clique well used to pitting their wits against each other. The Solicitor General Sir Robert Collier – an eloquent, brilliant advocate noted not only for his versatility but also for his accomplishment at billiards – would lead the prosecution with William Ballantine, the counsel once mooted as the

GLPS's favourite to defend Müller, undertaking most of the work. Ballantine – credited with being the original of Trollope's scruffy Chaffenbrass in *Orley Farm*, published two years earlier – had failed in his defence of the murderess Maria Manning but he was a stellar counsel, dominating juries with his curiously hesitant drawl and his charm. With a name as a *verdict getter*, Ballantine had a violent temper and excelled at bullying, bitterly sarcastic cross-examination. He never gave an inch.

With the addition of prosecution juniors known for their accurate, precise and painstaking work, these men constituted a formidable legal team but the GLPS had not let Müller down. Leading his defence, Serjeant John Humffreys Parry was a brilliant counsel. Chief prosecutor in the trial of James Mullins, side-whiskered, heavy-lidded and with bushy black brows and a thrusting chin, Parry was known as one of the most dramatic and successful advocates of his generation. Renowned for his 'admirable' voice, the clarity and simplicity of his statements and his affecting tact, he frequently got the better of Ballantine in court. Despite the fact that he had won many convictions for murder when acting as prosecutor, he was also one of a very small group of lawyers opposed to the death penalty on the grounds that real villains were often acquitted by juries squeamish about sending a man to the gallows. It was an understanding of human nature that he had previously used to his advantage.

Just as the police had been proscribed from questioning Müller after his arrest, English law held that, in capital cases, prisoners and their spouses were *incompetent witnesses*. Aside from making their pleas of guilty or not guilty right at the start of a trial, defendants were never allowed to speak. The imposition of silence was designed to protect them from self-incrimination under cross-examination but it also effectively barred them from articulating their own version of events. Forty-one witnesses for the prosecution and eight for the defence would successively be questioned and cross-examined, but Müller would not speak, forced by the law to rely on what his barrister, John Parry, would say on his behalf.

Gathered in one place for the first time, the array of trial witnesses represented a cross-section of the working life of London rarely seen outside a Dickens novel or Henry Mayhew's journalism. Ticket-takers and railway guards, pawnbrokers' assistants, clerks, cabbies, watchmakers, hatmakers, jewellers and tailors would all take the stand and, to satisfy public demand, the papers planned to run several extra editions each day with reports published in instalments. All would be sent across the country and to the continent by the operators of the electric telegraph.

Everyone knew the bare facts of the case: the blood-spattered state of carriage 69, the discovery of the Walker hat, bag and cane, the theft of Thomas Briggs' watch and chain, and the silk hat and gold watch found in Müller's possession on his arrest in New York. The case against the prisoner included the Blyths' testimony that he did not return home until after eleven o'clock on the night of the attack, John Death's evidence that Müller had exchanged Briggs' stolen chain at his shop in Cheapside and Matthews' assertion that he had purchased the Walker hat on behalf of the tailor. There was the fact that Müller's foot was injured, and the often-repeated pawnshop deals that suggested that he was in need of cash in the week before he left.

The potential fallibility of these kinds of 'proof' had been widely debated. It remained to be seen whether the prosecution had uncovered something less equivocal that would absolutely fix Müller at the scene of the crime. Would they be able to identify a murder weapon and conclusively link it to him? Would the various testimonies of their witnesses ultimately combine to prove the impossibility of this man's innocence?

Would John Parry have enough solid information regarding an alibi to counter the prosecution's claims? Or would he, instead, rely on disabling their case by the introduction of doubt? No blood had been found on any of Müller's clothing and a number of witnesses confirmed that the injury to his ankle had occurred several days before 9 July. Would Parry be able to show that the tailor had bought the watch and chain at the docks as had already been suggested? Most crucially, what would the jury make of Thomas Lee's statement about the two unidentified men? Was it possible that Lee's testimony alone would introduce enough uncertainty to force the jury's hand? None of the court reporters underestimated Parry's ability to stand his ground before the collective force of Sir Robert Collier and William Ballantine.

Earlier that morning Müller, neatly dressed in a plain brown 'cutaway' coat buttoned tightly to the chin, had been led through the subterranean stone tunnel running between Newgate and the Old Bailey. Weak light filtered through the metal grilles overhead. Heavy, barred gates were unlocked and resecured as he passed. Arriving in a paved room beneath the courtroom, he waited behind sturdy iron gates at the foot of some steps. When the call came at ten o'clock, this grave and boyish man mounted the stairs accompanied by the governor of Newgate and a warder, and emerged into the court. All eyes turned.

Stepping forward, taking in the judges in their long wigs and crimson robes and the crush of lawyers with their mass of papers, Müller rested his hands on the bar of the dock, resolutely refusing to look to his left or right.

# CHAPTER 27

# *The Trial: First Day*

*Franz Müller, you are indicted that you did, on the 9th July, in the present year, maliciously, wilfully, and of malice aforethought, kill and murder Thomas Briggs. Are you guilty or not guilty?*

*Not guilty.*

*You are entitled to be tried by a jury partly composed of foreigners.*

Serjeant Parry (for the prisoner): *He wishes to be tried by twelve Englishmen.*

This took the court by surprise. Aliens were entitled to be tried by a jury *de medietate linguae* – one half consisting of foreigners of any nationality. Müller's wish not to take up the prerogative was so unexpected that a murmur ran through the room. It was a smart tactic. Parry was creating the impression that Müller would behave with all the unflinching honour expected of an Englishman, reinforcing the powerful effect of his calm, passive exterior. He might be a foreigner, but he did not behave like a scoundrel.

The next hour was dull. Parry had the right to object to any members of the jury but he was bullish and instead demanded that the names of all potential jurors be drawn by ballot in order to ensure that the final group included men taken from the panels of diverse neighbourhoods and counties. A compromise was reached. After several objections twelve men were sworn, all from the lower-middle classes: small-businessmen including a lodging-house keeper, a tobacconist, a grocer, a blacksmith, a tallow chandler, a victualler and a handful of accountancy clerks. They ranged in age from eighteen to forty-five.

The Solicitor General rose to open the case for the Crown. Cool, rational and restrained, he went straight to the nub. *Gentlemen, this is a case which has excited unusual and painful interest,* he began, *one which ... has been canvassed and discussed in almost every newspaper, I might say almost every house in the kingdom; and it is one on which some persons might be inclined already to form an opinion.* He entreated the jury to discard everything they might have heard or read and to try the prisoner on the evidence alone.

This was traditional etiquette in the opening of a capital trial: the promise of reason over emotion, the elimination of the possibility that the prisoner would be made a scapegoat. Drawing attention to the *utmost* skill and eloquence of Müller's defence, Collier aimed also to remove residual pity for the apparent powerlessness of the prisoner at the bar. Then, by recognising the painful duty of the jurors, he emphasised the grave responsibility of their task. Over the next hour he dwelt on the seriousness of the crime and on the esteem in which Thomas Briggs had been held. Outlining the basic facts against Müller, he promised to exhibit Briggs' stick and his hat, watch and chain. He lingered over descriptions of the victim's injuries and, indicating the model of carriage 69, he pointed out each place where blood was found – human blood, without a doubt, on the evidence of Dr Letheby who would shortly be called to testify. They would see the stick found in the carriage: a stick that may have received its bloody stains merely by being present in the carriage but which

may also have been *powerfully wielded by the murderer ...
swinging it around with great violence to inflict the injuries Mr
Briggs sustained.*

Collier spoke of *the plain and simple facts*, in rhetoric designed
to transfix the assembly. He enumerated the witnesses, outlining
how each one of their depositions would substantiate a sequence
of accusations. He would show how close Müller lived to the
route of the North London Railway and to the place where the
body was discovered. The evidence of Mr and Mrs Repsch,
Jonathan and Eliza Matthews, the silversmith John Death and
others would each forge and prove a link in the chain of facts
that told against him.

Taking care to avoid any reference to the statement made by
Thomas Lee, Collier set about deflating doubt about whether *the
violence was committed by one person only or by more than one
person*. It was his opinion that just one man was responsible for
the deed, for he believed that a number of thieves would have
rifled Briggs' pockets and stolen his other valuables. In the
absence of any motive other than theft he posited that *the murder
was the result of some sudden determination*, an impulsive rather
than a premeditated act. What it came down to, he stated with
some force, was that the stolen items were found on Müller and –
more – Müller's own hat had mistakenly been left behind at the
scene of the crime. He would set out to prove this beyond doubt.
He would show that Müller had no alibi and he would recount
Müller's movements during the week following the murder
including visits on which he showed off a new watch, chain and
hat, offering several different accounts about their origin. He
would show that a series of pawnbroker deals involving the
stolen goods could be traced back to the German tailor, proving
that he was in great financial need prior to the fateful weekend.

Collier's speech was punctuated with the words, *Gentlemen,
the case does not rest here.* He stacked the weight of circumstantial evidence until Müller appeared irrevocably pinioned by

it. *Undoubtedly*, Collier continued, *the evidence in this case is what is called circumstantial evidence chiefly, but I may remind you that it is by circumstantial evidence that great crimes are most frequently detected. Murders are not committed in the presence of witnesses and to reject circumstantial evidence would be to proclaim immunity to crime … Gentlemen, I venture to think that if these circumstances are proved to you by witnesses, a stronger case of circumstantial evidence has rarely, if ever, been submitted to a jury.*

Faced with any reasonable doubts, he intoned, then the jury must acquit, but again he emphasised that the proof against the defendant was formidable. His opinion was irrelevant, he thundered disingenuously, but theirs counted: if they were convinced that the prisoner had indeed maliciously and violently murdered Thomas Briggs then they must not hesitate or shy from their duty. Silently looking each of them in the eye, Sir Robert Collier then turned and resumed his seat.

Müller was listening attentively, scribbling notes for Parry or leaning over the dock to speak with him. The spectators shifted their gaze momentarily towards the dock and then, as the prosecution's first witness was summoned, turned their eyes back towards the stand.

One after the other, David Buchan, Caroline Buchan, the Fenchurch Street ticket collector Thomas Fishbourne, the clerks Harry Vernez and Sydney Jones, guard Benjamin Ames, engine driver Alfred Ekin, his train guard William Timms and the Bow police constable Edward Dougan were prompted by Serjeant Ballantine to repeat the stories they had told so many times before. None deviated from the substance of their past scripts and there was little for Serjeant Parry to establish in cross-examination. He focused only on David and Caroline Buchan, attempting to confirm the existence of threats made to their uncle. Both replied that they believed them to have existed but admitted that their knowledge was based on the reports of others. Asking Caroline, *was it a person to whom he objected to send money?* Collier objected and was overruled, but Parry decided against repeating the question. Was this because he believed that he had planted the first seed of reasonable doubt? Or, given earlier newspaper reports that the man supposed to have threatened Briggs was a respected member of his community, did Parry know that this line of questioning was unlikely to yield results?

Of the doctors who had seen Briggs' wounds at the Mitford Castle tavern and then performed the post-mortem, Parry cross-questioned only Francis Toulmin. The Briggs' family doctor described the wounds to the top of Thomas Briggs' head as being *inflicted by a blunt instrument, used with considerable force – the wound on the left ear I believe to have been also inflicted by a blunt instrument, but of that I will not speak so certainly; that was my impression.*

Parry wondered why, if these blows were so violent, they were no deeper than half an inch? Was it not also possible that some of the injuries were caused by the fall from the train and was it not also true that the victim was considerably taller (at five feet eight inches) and heavier (at almost twelve stone) than the accused? Parry avoided mentioning the fact that Briggs was probably sitting when he was attacked and skirted the issue of the amount of blood in the carriage. He aimed only to suggest that Toulmin's conclusions were by no means certain.

For the prosecution, Ballantine next asked Inspector Kerressey to describe the state of the carriage, the patent hook left in Briggs' waistcoat buttonhole and the jump link discovered in the floor matting, aiming to establish that the victim's watch and chain were violently wrenched from his person. Then Parry sprang from his seat, moving Kerressey's evidence onto uncomfortable ground:

*Do you know of a man called Thomas Lee?*
*I know Thomas Lee.*

*Was he examined by the coroner in your presence?*

*No, he was not.*

*Did you not hear ... in the course of your enquiries in this case, that Mr Briggs was seen alive on the night of the murder at Bow Station, and that there were two people in the carriage with him?*

The Solicitor General objected on the grounds that the question tended to introduce hearsay into the evidence. Parry countered tersely: *I apprehend that if he heard, in prosecuting his enquiries, a fact of so important a character as this, and that fact was kept from the jury in the opening speech for the Crown, I have a right to ask the witness whose special duty it was to investigate the case, whether it did not come to his notice.*

Refusing to allow the defence an advantage, Judge Pollock ruled that the question could not be pressed. Was his judgement already formed? Parry was forced to retreat, scuppered from raising the spectre of those two men in Briggs' compartment. Until Lee could take the stand for the defence, the issue of whether Briggs had company in the train on the night of his murder was inadmissible. The police knew that there were at least four people whose own experience strongly corroborated Lee's statement but they were under no legal obligation to reveal this to the defence. Parry was unaware that Lee's story had been substantiated by others. Had he known, he might have been able to force Inspector Kerressey to admit under oath that an alternative scenario for the murder existed. Instead – potentially damning for Müller – what the alert jury was most likely to remember from Kerressey's deposition were his closing words: *I am sure the [inside] handle of the door was bloody. There was no blood on Mr Briggs' hands.*

Ballantine called the chemist Dr Letheby to describe the blood spatters on the glass and upholstery of the carriage, to confirm that their pattern was consistent with blows to the head and to testify that, from the existence of coagulum within it, the blood *had been living when it came on the glass.* Then it was the turn of John Death to recount the events of Monday 11 July. He said that the chain Müller had exchanged with him on that day (labelled Number 1) was missing the jump link designed to connect its two halves. Instead there was a common pin bent to form a loop and a piece of string.

Parry might have sought to question Death's identification of Müller by asking whether the jeweller had not repeatedly seen Müller's photograph during the voyage with Tanner to New York. Instead, Parry said that Müller admitted to visiting the shop but that it had been on an earlier occasion. Asking Death to look closely at the chain labelled Number 3 (Müller's original, pawned chain), Parry wondered whether it was not the case that Müller had brought this chain to be mended during November 1863 and that he had paid one shilling and sixpence for the work? Death was sure that was not the case. Had Müller not returned during June 1864 to offer that chain for exchange? Again, Death was certain that he had never seen the prisoner before 11 July.

*Take that chain*, ordered Parry, *and look at it carefully again and tell me whether a link has been broken.* Death examined the piece of jewellery labelled Number 3. Yes, he admitted, it showed signs of being mended. Was it not taken in for repair at his own shop? No, he was sure that he had never seen that chain before. Parry tried one last time. Was it not possible that he had served Müller as a customer weeks prior to the murder? Death said that he had no such recollection.

As the day inched forward Müller's landlady Ellen Blyth told the court that he had worn the same clothes on Sunday 10 July as he had worn on the previous evening and that he had been lame in his right foot since 7 July, wearing a slipper instead of his usual boot on his bad foot. Questioned about the prisoner's laundry, she admitted that she had washed six shirts for him before he left on the *Victoria* that week but said that all of them were new and none showed any traces of blood. George Blyth then swore that the dark coat taken out of pawn by Hoffa and delivered to Scotland Yard was *very like* the one Müller wore on both days that weekend. Yes, they had walked with Müller on Sunday evening in Victoria Park, for close to three hours between six and nine o'clock. Under cross-examination, Parry strangely declined to ask either of the Blyths whether Müller had found the walk uncomfortable with this wounded ankle. Nor did he ask whether they recognised the battered hat with the striped lining.

Mrs Repsch was next. She also confirmed that Müller had injured his foot on Thursday 7 July and had taken to wearing a slipper on it. Also that when he worked at her house on the following Saturday Müller *wore a slipper during the day, on the right foot, in fact, he wore two slippers, because he was in the habit of taking off his boots when he came to my house, and putting on his slippers ... I did not see him leave that night, I was out when he left.*

Given the left slipper to examine, Mrs Repsch identified it and said, *I found* [it] *after he was gone – the right slipper was gone. He had his boots with him during the day, two boots – whether he came in them or not on the Saturday morning I can't say – he might have had one in his pocket – the two boots were by the side when he changed them, to put on his slippers – when he left neither of those boots remained, they were both gone – he took away both boots, and one slipper.*

Mrs Repsch testified that she thought Müller over-fond of finery and said that he had lied to her about being sent to America by Mr Hodgkinson. She was certain about all the details of Müller's hats and particularly the lining of the one bought for him by Matthews: *It was a striped lining, a broad brown stripe, and a broad blue stripe edged with black and white – my attention was drawn to the lining from its being a peculiar lining – I never saw a hat lined with such a lining before ... I have frequently seen him take off his hat, and I have frequently had it in my hands.* Shown the crushed hat recovered from under the seat in the bloody carriage, she was firm: *To the best of my belief this is the hat – the lining is the same, and the merino also.*

Asked about the dark trousers Müller had supposedly worn on Saturday 9 July, she hissed accusingly that she had never seen them again. She also spoke of the new guinea hat he wore after the murder and the chain (Number 2, procured from John Death in exchange for Thomas Briggs') that Müller had shown her on the morning of Monday 11 July.

Coming from her dark alley on the margins of a slum, Mrs Repsch was the least likeable of the array of witnesses compelled to stand and answer questions in the packed, hot court. Parry kept her longest to face his questions, hammering away at the fact of Müller's bad foot, expressing disbelief that she could identify the crushed hat so clearly but could not describe the lining of her own husband's. Could she then describe John Hoffa's hat since he, too, was a constant visitor to 12½ Jewry Street?

*No, I don't know what sort of lining it has, not yet what sort of lining there is in any other man's hat what comes to see my husband. It was the peculiarity of the lining in Müller's hat that took my attention.*

*Did you ever ask the prisoner to lend you five shillings?*

*No, sir.*

Then she hesitated, coloured, swallowed and corrected herself.

*Yes, I did.*

*Did Müller not refuse you most particularly because he wanted to buy a new hat? Did you not say to him, 'Pooh! You may as well get one next week'?*

*I don't think I did – I cannot swear it, because I do not remember it – I cannot swear it did not pass – I don't remember his saying it.*

In fact, on further consideration, Mrs Repsch thought that Müller *had* lent her the money but that she had paid it back to him. She thought he had never spoken of a new hat before she saw him on the 11th with the silk topper.

Was not her deposition motivated entirely, flashed Parry, by hope of the reward? Had not her husband known Matthews for six years? Did they not see the Matthews quite often? Despite her denials, as Parry swung away from Elizabeth Repsch the unarticulated suggestion that the Matthews and the Repschs were in league against Müller for their own profit hung in the air.

It was nearing quarter past four when Müller's friend Hoffa was called. Beyond admitting to seeing Müller with a new chain and hat in the week of 11 July he was of no use to the prosecution. In particular, he had no idea what Müller was wearing when he left Jewry Street on Saturday evening. Responding to Parry's questions, though, Hoffa said that his friend had announced his intention to sail for America at least a fortnight before he left, that he had seen Müller with enough money for his passage prior to the 9th, that he had been lame for several days and that he believed he had gone to see his sweetheart on the evening of 9 July. He understood that she lived in Camberwell. Parry was interested in the question of funds: what had happened to Müller's money? Why had he had such difficulty in finding enough to pay for his fare? Hoffa only knew that the prisoner had been to the docks several times early that week and he thought he must have bought the new chain, watch, ring and hat there.

Finally, harking back to his cross-examination of John Death, Parry asked one more question: had Hoffa asked Müller to try to exchange a chain for him earlier that summer? *Yes*, said Hoffa, *but nothing came of it and he brought it back to me.*

Parry's questions had succeeded in suggesting the thread of a theory in support of Müller's innocence. He had backed away from pressing the Buchans on the threats made to their uncle, had declined to argue with the medical men over the cause of Briggs' death and had not succeeded in getting Kerressey to acknowledge Thomas Lee's statement. But he had attached considerable importance to the fact of Müller's lameness and he had attempted to show that John Death misidentified Müller having done business with him in the months prior to the murder.

If Hoffa had been the last witness of the day, the jury may have left the court allowing that some small doubt attached itself to the prisoner's guilt. Following the testimony of John Death, though, Judge Martin had summoned the jeweller's brother. Robert Death had just arrived and there was sufficient time for him to take the stand. Ignorant of Parry's line of questioning earlier in the afternoon he was also shown chain Number 3 (Müller's chain) and denied ever having seen it before: *it is such a peculiar one that I should remember it if I had.*

It was a quarter to five o'clock. Robert Death's corroboration of his brother's statement that Müller had never been in their shop before 11 July weakened Parry's contention.

The court was adjourned, the judges rose and the room began to empty of its chattering crowd. The jury, forbidden from separating and cautioned against speaking to anyone outside their group for the duration of the trial, were sent to lodge in the London Coffee House in nearby Ludgate Hill, where they would be watched by officers of the sheriff.

Franz Müller was led quietly back through the underground passage to his Newgate cell.

# CHAPTER 28

# The Trial: Second Day

When dawn broke at a little after quarter to seven on Friday 28 October Müller was already dressed and ready, his habitual reserve replaced by an anxious watchfulness. Jonathan Matthews, his most damaging detractor, would be called today. The prosecution would then rest its case – the worst of the trial over.

Proceedings resumed at ten o'clock. First to be called was Müller's old co-worker John Henry Glass, followed by three pawnbrokers' assistants from separate businesses in Houndsditch and Minories. Central to the prosecution's case was the need to establish that Müller had been short of cash – that he could not have paid for his ticket to America in any other way than through robbery, and that it was not possible that he could have afforded to buy an expensive watch, chain or ring from a vagrant at the docks. Glass testified that Müller had earned about thirty shillings a week – just enough to cover his rent, food and clothing. The prisoner's habitual need to pawn his belongings further evinced that he had not earned enough to put aside any savings.

The testimonies of Glass and the pawnbrokers' men proved that in early June Müller had pawned his old watch and chain at

Barker's in Houndsditch, raising three pounds. Following Müller's supposed exchange of Mr Briggs' chain with John Death on Monday the 11th for another worth three pounds, ten shillings, he had taken this 'new' chain on Tuesday to Mr Annis' pawnbrokers in Minories and received thirty shillings for it, using the money to reclaim his own watch. On Wednesday 13 July, Glass lent Müller one pound in order to redeem his old chain. Now the two men took Müller's old watch and chain and pawned them both in Leicester Square for four pounds – about three weeks' salary. Glass bought the ticket from Müller for five shillings. Undoubtedly, therefore, Müller owned four pounds and five shillings on Wednesday 13 July, besides some few shillings he had raised with the help of Elizabeth Repsch who had pawned one of his coats. On that day, he purchased his ticket for the *Victoria*.

The various transactions showed that, had Müller come by Thomas Briggs' possessions by robbery, he had profited only a paltry thirty shillings from his dealings. When added to the money raised from pawning his old watch and chain, this just covered the price of a ticket to sail while allowing him to keep Briggs' valuable gold pocket watch. Set against this, Hoffa had previously testified that he had seen Müller in possession of two or three pounds in the days before 9 July – enough, with a bit of scrambling, to pay for the passage without resorting to crime.

Broadly, the convoluted deals were easy enough for the court to understand, though the maths was tricky to remember. Two things counted. First, all three very different chains were held aloft in court, each representative of stolid respectability against impoverished graft; all three were glittering reminders of a motive for murder. Secondly, Parry would need to establish that Müller had funds prior to the 9th, in order to have bought Briggs' stolen watch and chain in good faith. Since the prosecution did not recall John Hoffa, he was unavailable for cross-examination and his testimony would have to wait for the defence. Meanwhile, the impression that Müller had been in desperate need prior to 9 July was allowed to settle in the minds of the jury.

Despite the array of circumstantial evidence against Müller, the prosecution were unable to place him at the scene of the murder. Additionally, on the first day of the trial, the Blyths and the Repschs had given conflicting accounts of the clothing worn by him on and after 9 July. According to Elizabeth Repsch, a pair of dark trousers was missing but the remainder of his coats, shirts and trousers appeared to be accounted for, and none showed any evidence of blood. It had also been proven that the injury to Müller's foot took place on Thursday the 7th and that he was still using a slipper on Saturday the 9th. Despite the fact that he went walking with the Blyths on Sunday evening, this suggested that he had been unable to move fast.

The broken Walker hat and the 'cut-down' silk Digance hat remained in full view on the lawyers' central table, symbols both of a violated man and of his attacker. The identification and ownership of each lay at the heart of the case.

The prosecution now turned its attention to the first of these hats. Several spectators stood to get a better look as the insolent cabman, whose appearance had been awaited with excitement, was summoned. Matthews entered the court to a buzz of interest, looking altogether more nervous than on any previous occasion. In the dock, Müller visibly brightened. Leaning forward with strained attention, taking up his pen, he passed notes to Parry throughout the hour of Matthews' examination.

Matthews mumbled as he outlined the circumstances surrounding his purchase of a hat for Müller from Walker's of Crawford Street, the distinguishing curl to the brim, and the thumbmark on the underside. His evidence was peppered with interjections from Parry urging him to *Speak up, sir, do!*, and when Ballantine's questions were done Parry rose to cross-examine. Müller had admitted that Matthews once bought a hat for him. Parry's intention now was to disprove that the hat in court was the one.

*Allow me that hat, please*, he snapped, turning it over in his hands calmly as he took possession of it.

*I believe your own hat is like it?*

*As nearly as possible.*

Musing on this answer, Parry repeated it aloud. But if Matthews was expecting a repetition of the bludgeoning he had taken from Müller's solicitor Beard in the earlier hearings, he was now surprised. Instead, Parry asked for copies of the depositions given by the cabman both to the coroner and the Bow Street magistrate. Instead of fixing ownership of the hat on Matthews, he aimed to show that Matthews' evidence varied each time he was under oath.

*Can you tell me how many hats you bought within six or twelve months of the 9th of July?*

*I cannot tell you.*

*What has become of your last hat at the time of this one?*

*I cannot say. I think I left it at a hatter's shop where I bought another.*

*Where did you buy the hat you now wear?*

*In Oxford Street, at Mr Mummery's.*

*Have you not stated that you left it at Mr Down's in Long Acre three weeks before 9th July?*

*I said that I left one there. I did not say the time I did so … I did not state the time.*

*Did you not say this: 'I purchased the hat at Down's Long Acre. I left the old one there.'*

*I did say so.*

*That is not true?*

*No, it was not it exactly. It was longer ago. I cannot remember exactly.*

Parry's team had discovered that Down's hatters had gone out of business. Matthews could not have bought his new hat there at the time he said, and could not have left his old one behind. What, then, had become of Matthews' Walker hat? And how could he account for what appeared to be lies under oath?

Under Parry's badgering, Matthews sputtered that, until he came to consider it on his return from New York, he had not realised how many hats he owned. He admitted that his evidence to the coroner had contained mistakes. He could not remember what he did with his Walker hat and was unable to describe the lining in any of his own hats, despite being so particular about the lining in Müller's. Initially he swore that he was *not a public house visitor, perhaps I may go there sometimes*, but he soon confessed that he usually visited an inn daily. Moving on swiftly, Parry then expressed sarcastic astonishment that a cab driver in London could claim to have heard nothing about the murder until over a week after it occurred. His questions came like bullets.

*Do you take in a newspaper? Did you not see notice of the murder in large, conspicuous letters on the placards? Do you attend the station at Paddington? Do you pass the police station every day?*

*Now, can you tell me what you were doing on Saturday the 9th of July?*

*I was out in my cab, I find.*

*Did you not say before the coroner 'it is impossible for me to say where I was'?*

*I did say so. I have made enquiries since.*

*So, since you were before the coroner, you have been making enquiries with a view of giving evidence here?*

*I had lost my pocket book, but I have found it since.*

Matthews produced a letter, dated 29 September, from his employer. Parry took it, but declined to read it.

*I believe your master failed, or was 'sold up' to use your own expression?*

*He sold off.*

*This is another mistake, then?*
*Yes.*
*Is it a mistake in the depositions?*
*Yes.*

Parry had been hammering away for close to an hour. Had the cab driver ever been insolvent? Had he ever failed in business? How many creditors did he have? Had he not said that were he to get the reward it would hardly cover his debts? That if he had waited a little longer the reward would have mounted from three hundred to five hundred pounds? However much he denied the insinuations, Parry's contemptuous repetition of the same questions often led Matthews to back down, changing his answer and – Parry must have hoped – shaking his credibility with the jury.

*Were you ever in prison?*

Matthews admitted that he had been, in Norwich in 1850 for absconding from his employment as a coach driver. He admitted he had gone on *a spree*, was convicted and served twenty-one days in gaol. Parry knew that this was only half the truth.

*Were you not convicted for having feloniously stolen a posting book, value eight shillings; a spur, value two shillings; and a padlock, value sixpence? Was not that the conviction?*

*That was what they brought in because they found them in the box, unbeknown to me ... I did not know they were there.*

It was not a very serious charge but it did mark out Matthews as having been convicted in the past for theft. Parry now returned to the business of the hats, asking Matthews – twice – whether the lining of his Walker hat was the same as the lining of the hat exhibited in court. Twice Matthews responded that it was merely *similar*.

*Did you not say that the lining of both hats was the same, as nearly as possible?*

Matthews faltered unconvincingly. *I cannot say exactly.*

Another *Oh!* went up from the court.

Under re-examination, the Solicitor General attempted to

restore Matthews' credibility. Was it correct that Matthews was now thirty-eight years old, that he had been only nineteen or twenty at the time of his *spree*, and that he had never been in any kind of trouble since? Had he since had the chance to write to his previous employer to confirm whether he was working on the night of the murder?

*Yes*, replied Matthews, *and I was on the cab-stand from seven o'clock until eleven o'clock at the Great Western Railway ... Then I went homewards. I bought a joint of meat and took it home. I went to the stable yard, and left the cab in Lisson Grove, I then went home.*

Matthews was dismissed. Parry had ensured that he left the court with the impression both that his evidence was variable and that he had been assisted prior to the commencement of the trial in order to make his story more credible. At the same time, the country's anticipation that lurid details of the man's criminal past would emerge had not been met: a minor offence committed by a young wastrel, his previous conviction did not define him as a person of abandoned character. Parry had not managed to prove him a delinquent, but Matthews' shuffling and prevarication, the improbability of his statement that he had not heard of the murder until after Müller had sailed and his imputed desire for the reward had injured his standing as the prosecution's central witness. As the *Daily Telegraph* reported, *his character is, to say the least, not altogether of a description to give additional weight to his testimony.*

There was nothing new in the evidence given by Matthews' wife. The sun went down, the light dimmed and the courtroom's stuffiness increased as the gas lamps were lit. The owner and the foreman of Walker's hatters were called and a peculiar fact emerged which appeared to take both the prosecution and defence by surprise. It turned out that the broad-striped lining of the hat found in the carriage was rare, a piece of French fabric included in a batch of samples that had only been large enough to use on two – or perhaps four – hats. This was extraordinary.

It meant that potential ownership of the broken hat found at the crime scene was limited to fewer than five people in the entire country. Caught off guard, neither the prosecution nor the defence appeared to recognise its significance and neither thought to make use of the fact for their own advantage.

George Clarke was called, then Inspector Richard Tanner. When Müller's travelling trunk was brought in and its meagre contents displayed, a juryman asked to be shown the tailor's shears and they were passed around the jury box and examined carefully. This was odd, since the prosecution had never suggested they could have been used to kill Thomas Briggs: on the contrary, Briggs' wounds had been imputed to a heavy, blunt instrument.

Lastly, Daniel Digance and then his hatmaker Frederick Thorne took the stand. Both testified that the silk topper found in New York had been sold from Digance's shop. Both believed it had been made for Thomas Briggs due to its size and the fragments of tissue paper still adhering to the lining, but since the part that would have borne his name had been cut away neither was able to swear conclusively that the hat had ever belonged to the old man.

A small piece of theatre remained.

*Do your hats make it into the second-hand trade?* Parry asked Daniel Digance.

He took offence, replying frostily, *My trade is of a first-class not second-hand. I know nothing of the second-hand trade in hats.*

Solemnly, Parry then began to hand a series of old hats one by one to the witness, telling him as he did so that each one had been bought in the second-hand markets. Peering at their linings, Digance was forced to confess that all of them bore the mark of his own shop in the Royal Exchange.

\*

The prosecution's case ended so abruptly that several of the spectators seemed unaware that the defence had begun until they noticed a change in the tone of Serjeant Parry's delivery. The hectoring of his cross-examination had modulated to a low and almost inaudible voice that had the effect of stilling the fidgeting public as they strained to catch his words. Apparently overwhelmed now that the array of evidence marshalled against him had finally been exhausted, Müller ceased to scribble feverish notes, dropped his head into his hands and stooped down behind the front of the dock until he had almost disappeared from sight. Half an hour later, when he recovered his nerve and lifted his head, Parry was still only halfway through his opening address.

The prosecution had failed to put Müller at the scene of the attack, or to identify a murder weapon, and Parry had performed well in his cross-examination of the hatter Daniel Digance, making him look both a snob and a fool. His routine with the hats had been carefully choreographed, proving beyond doubt that the one found in Müller's possession might easily have been bought in the second-hand trade. Lodged in the jury's minds was the testimony of several witnesses that the prisoner had hurt his foot some days before the attack on Thomas Briggs, eliminating conjecture that it was injured during the jump from the moving train.

On the other hand, Parry had been unable to undermine materially either Jonathan Matthews or Elizabeth Repsch's statements about Müller's ownership of the battered hat and he had missed an opportunity to emphasise that the hat might, just as convincingly, have belonged to Matthews. It all now rested on what new evidence he might submit for the defence. Would he be able to present an alternative scenario for the discovery of Briggs' watch in Müller's travelling trunk? Would he offer a convincing alibi? Might Thomas Lee's statement about the two men allow Parry to insinuate into the case enough uncertainty to set his client free?

Parry began with a measured attack on the unscrupulousness of newspaper reports, reminding the jury that *what has been*

*written has been read probably by every one of you gentlemen –
certainly by almost every person capable of reading a newspaper
in the country.*

*Gentlemen*, he continued, *the crime of which this young man
is charged is almost unparalleled in this country. It is a crime
which strikes at the lives of millions. It is a crime which affects
the life of every man who travels upon the great iron ways of this
country. A thrill of horror ran through the whole land when the
fact of this crime was first published. Gentlemen, this is a crime
of a character to arouse in the human breast an almost instinc-
tive spirit of vengeance. It is a crime which demands a victim.*
Parry considered that the press had prejudiced the case *on a massive scale*. The jury, he warned, must exert every effort to make
a passionless analysis of the evidence. The law must bypass
vengeance and aim only for unqualified truth.

Parry knew that the prosecution's case was founded on circumstantial evidence and suspicion and he was at pains to
admonish the jury against conjecture. They must, he declaimed,
be as satisfied of Müller's guilt as surely as if their eyes had seen
him do the deed. The evidence must be complete. It must be certain. Any doubt whatsoever rendered *the chain of evidence
incomplete and the jury ought not, and cannot act upon it.*

He reminded them that he had tested the prosecution's case,
questioning the competence of witnesses, demanding facts over
hypotheses and suggesting competing theories to demonstrate
how much doubt lay at the heart of the case. Neither of the two
hats, he asserted, could be positively identified as having
belonged either to Müller or to Mr Briggs. That Müller had once
owned a hat like the one found in the train was not proof that
the broken hat belonged to him. The silk hat might easily have
been purchased in the second-hand trade where it was custom-
ary to cut them down or alter their shape and where many were
stuffed with tissue paper to make them fit. Further, it was not
unlikely that Müller had bought Briggs' chain and watch at the

docks. Knowing that they may have been attained illegally, it was natural for him to have denied the fact at the time of his arrest.

Parry professed disingenuous indignation at the suggestion that Jonathan Matthews was on trial or that he had been involved in the murder. But he alerted the jury to the fact that Matthews' evidence was so unreliable that *no body of sensible men would for a moment pay any attention to it ... He is evidently actuated by a desire to obtain the reward and that has animated his whole conduct. I should be very sorry to charge him with being a party to the murder, but I should be very wicked if I were not to say that suspicion is pointing to him.* He reminded them that Matthews was unable to corroborate his account of where he was on the night of the murder. Additionally, Matthews appeared to have tried to mislead them all with his story about leaving his hat at Down's while admitting that he also had a hat *exactly like* the one now in court. Matthews' hat had a similarly striped lining: what had become of it? Matthews, concluded Müller's counsel, *tells an untruth both before the coroner and the magistrates and never corrects that untruth until now when he knows we have a witness to show that Mr Down went out of business ... Is Mr Matthews trustworthy?*

Parry accepted that a suspicion existed that the smashed hat belonged to Müller, but he warned the jury that suspicion was insufficient. Müller's vain boastfulness around his friends and his varied stories were not proof of his guilt. Additionally, Hoffa saw him with money before the murderous Saturday. If he had not bought the watch and chain with it, then what did become of those pounds? Since none of the witnesses could agree about what Müller wore on Saturday or during the following week, Parry contended that the prosecution had not established that a pair of dark trousers was missing. Indeed, he reminded them, several witnesses had testified that Müller wore both the pairs of trousers he possessed after the 9th and that neither showed signs of blood or of having been cleaned. These facts and others, cautioned Parry, were open to interpretation and, since a verdict of not proven was not allowed under English law, the jury's only course was to find the prisoner not guilty.

The barrister went on to characterise Müller as a *mere stripling* of a lad whose many friends had testified to his *kind and trusting nature*. Was it possible that powerful, sober Mr Briggs had been overpowered and dragged across the compartment by this pale youth? Parry claimed that the prisoner maintained a calm containment that none of the police involved in the investigation, nor his gaolers, had ever seen slip. Openly expressing his intention of going to America some weeks before 9 July, Müller had taken passage in his own name and sent a letter confirming the name of his ship to the Blyths. Were these the actions of a criminal?

Thus far, it appeared to the spectators hanging on Parry's words that the barrister would rely solely upon the weakness of the prosecution and the undisguised conduct of his client. Then, to the court's evident satisfaction he announced that he would call the *unimpeachable gentleman* Thomas Lee to prove that when the train left Bow Station two men had shared Briggs' compartment. Further, he would prove an alibi through the testimony of a lodging-house keeper and an omnibus conductor who would swear that Müller was elsewhere at the time of the murder – in Camberwell, exactly as he had told Hoffa he would be when he left the Repschs.

Had Parry been defending a less serious charge than murder he would have been allowed to summarise the defence's case again at the end of the trial. But in murder trials, this was proscribed – unfairly in the view of many prominent legal minds, who felt the proceedings were thereby weighted in the Crown's favour. Knowing, then, that this was his only opportunity to address the jury, Parry's impressive, hour-long oratory drew towards its conclusion with a moving entreaty to find the evidence against his innocent client unsatisfactory. Relying on his experience of juries acquitting rather than sending a man to his death, he advanced on the twelve men in the jury box and appealed to their religious sensibilities. *Gentlemen, if ever there was a case in which care and caution ought to be exercised by Christian men ... it is a case like this, where the life or death of a fellow creature hangs upon the balance ... You possess a transcendent power to bid that young man to live or to die.*

It was five o'clock by the time Parry returned to his seat. The next day he would call a handful of new witnesses. Eager to conclude the trial and concerned that the jury would be left with insufficient time to agree their verdict before Sunday interrupted them, Judge Pollock ordered the court to reconvene an hour earlier than usual the following morning.

At seven minutes past five o'clock Müller was removed from the dock, apparently exhausted and depressed by Parry's emotive entreaty. By dusk on Saturday it would all be over.

## CHAPTER 29

# *The Trial: Third Day*

Thomas Lee's evidence was known to be crucial to Müller's defence. When the trial reopened on Saturday 29 October, he was Parry's first witness.

Lee's story was unwavering. As the 9.45 p.m. train from Fenchurch Street arrived at Bow Station on the night of 9 July, he had spoken briefly to Thomas Briggs.

*How long had you known Mr Briggs?*

*For about three or four years, I should think.*

*When did you last see him alive?*

*On 9th July, Saturday evening, at the Bow Station, in a first-class carriage, about ten o'clock, I think – it was a carriage of a train coming from Fenchurch Street – it stopped at the Bow Station. It was about three or four carriages from the engine, I think.*

*Did you speak to him?*

*I said, 'Good-night, Mr Briggs.' He answered, 'Good-night, Tom' – he was sufficiently intimate with me to call me in that way.*

*Was anyone else with him?*

*The train stopped rather longer than usual that night ... there were two persons in the same compartment of the carriage with Mr Briggs. There was a light in the carriage. I believe Mr Briggs had his hat on, or else I should have noticed it; I should have noticed it certainly. One of the persons was sitting on the side of the carriage, next to the platform, opposite Mr Briggs, the other was sitting on the left-hand side of Mr Briggs, next to him, on the same side of the carriage.*

*Did you see them clearly, then?*

*I saw sufficiently of those two persons to be able to give a description of them afterwards, one in particular – the man who sat opposite Mr Briggs – was a stoutish, thick-set man with light whiskers, and he had his hand in the squab or loop of the carriage, and it was rather a large hand. I had only a casual glance of the other man: he appeared a tall, thin man, dark.*

*And to the best of your judgement, is the prisoner either of these two men?*

*I would not swear that. I should rather think he was not.*

When the defence finished its questions, the jury had one of its own to add. When Mr Briggs travelled late on the railway, Lee had stated that he often slumbered between stations. Was he in the habit of having his hat on, or off, they asked. *He used to have it on*, said Lee. The jury might have wondered, therefore, why Briggs' silk hat was not also crushed by the blows from his assailant.

Collier stepped forward to cross-examine. Lee was a powerful witness and Collier went straight for the one weakness in his testimony – that he had not come forward voluntarily and that it had taken more than a week for him to tell the police what he had seen. He urged Lee repeatedly to tell the court where he had been that evening and why. Lee refused to be mauled, remaining stalwartly unemotional as he replied, *I went to Bow for amusement.*

*Why did you not give information to the police as soon as you heard of the murder?*

*I did not wish to be bothered.*

*You did not wish to be bothered?*

*I did not consider my evidence material. I did not see that there was any need.*

Despite Collier's expressions of disbelief, Lee adhered to his contention that, once asked to testify, he had done so willingly and honestly and that he was as sure now about what he had seen as he had been three months before.

Parry's next witnesses were two second-hand hat dealers who testified about the fashion among young men for 'cut-down' hats. One said that stitching them down was common and the other concurred. Both added that a stitched hat would sometimes be varnished with gum or shellac but that it added to the expense. Their evidence confirmed what Parry had already established in his cross-examination of Digance: that hats like the one found in Müller's box were a fixture of the second-hand market.

To establish Müller's alibi, Parry needed to call only four more witnesses. The first was Alfred Woodward, a clerk for the Electric and International Telegraph Company. Woodward's records showed that a telegraphic message was delivered to Müller's friend Miss Eldred at Stanley Cottage, James Street, Vassall Road in Camberwell during the afternoon of 9 July.

Next Parry examined Mrs Elizabeth Jones, a small-time brothel keeper, and Mary Anne Eldred, a young woman who lodged with Jones and who, she said, had received regular visits from Franz Müller for nine months prior to the date of the murder. Mrs Jones testified that on the day the telegram was received Miss Eldred had gone out at her habitual hour – nine o'clock in the evening – narrowly missing the arrival of Müller who had hung about for ten minutes or so before leaving to walk the three-quarters of a mile back to the nearest omnibus stand at Camberwell Gate. She told the court that this journey would normally take between fifteen and twenty minutes and she repeated that she remembered very clearly that Müller had called on the day the telegraph arrived for Mary Anne; he had been lame and wore a slipper. Responding to a question put directly by a juror, she confirmed that Müller had been wearing a hat.

Jones' testimony appeared to establish that Müller had been in Camberwell at ten past nine on 9 July, but her profession presented a difficulty. Under cross-examination the prosecution bullied her remorselessly, chipping away at the reliability of her memory and that of her kitchen clock. Was this the kind of woman, they imputed, the court should believe?

Then came Müller's 'girlfriend', Mary Anne Eldred, who took the stand shaking visibly and who was so profoundly deaf that it was only by speaking very slowly and loudly that Parry could make his questions understood. She stated that Müller visited her often and that he had asked her to go to New York with him several weeks before 9 July. She said that she always left the house at nine o'clock in the evening. Asked about the telegram, she told Parry that she had only remembered about it ten days earlier: gentlemen from the GLPS had been to see her in an attempt to fix Müller's alibi and had prompted her memory. It had taken her a while to find it, but when she did, the paper was sent directly to Thomas Beard since it proved the date of Müller's last visit. Cross-examining, Collier was brutal. What time did you dine that day? When did you breakfast? What time did you get up? When did you go to bed? To each question she stammered, *I don't remember, I can only guess, I can't exactly tell.* Under the Solicitor General's furious onslaught, Eldred's initial appearance of certainty began to crumble.

Yet Collier could not materially shake the evidence either of Eldred or of Jones. *Stupid and confused as these two witnesses were*, wrote the *Telegraph*, they gave the impression that they were speaking what they believed to be the truth. The weakness of the alibi remained. Even if it was true, it was not entirely incompatible with the prisoner's guilt. When it came to timekeeping, Collier had successfully imputed that Eldred was fatally unreliable and that her powers of perception and memory were flawed. Müller might have been in Camberwell on the night of the 9th, but Collier had effectively demolished any confidence that an exact time could be fixed to his presence there, and exact times were crucial if Parry was to establish that Müller could not have been on Thomas Briggs' train.

It did not help that before she was dismissed, a juror asked Eldred whether she was *in the habit of noticing Müller's hat*. She said that she was not. Dropping her eyes and turning to leave, Eldred looked up at Müller. The German in the dock and the young deaf prostitute smiled sadly at one another.

Parry's final witness was Charles Foreman. The omnibus conductor told the court that his last 'bus left Camberwell Gate at about ten minutes to ten, arriving in King William Street about twenty past the hour. Prior to that, an omnibus left the Camberwell stand at seven o'clock. It meant that if Müller had been at Stanley Cottage after seven – and he had not left the Repschs' in time to get there earlier – he could not have made it back to the City from Camberwell Gate in time to reach Fenchurch Street before Briggs' train departed. *I remember*, said the conductor, *that I had a gentleman ride in my omnibus on my last journey ... from Camberwell Gate to the City, who appeared to be lame and wore a slipper. It was in the summer*. The problem was that he could neither remember the month nor the day of the week. Further, although his customer had been young and fair the conductor remembered him as rather stout. That description did not correspond to the slim young German now on trial for his life.

Serjeant Parry had no more witnesses to call. By comparison with the twelve hours taken by the prosecution so far, arguments for the defence had lasted a mere four.

\*

Parry might have done enough to establish the element of uncertainty that would liberate his client, but the Crown still had the advantage. Müller and his legal team were now constrained to listen as Collier summed up the arguments for the prosecution. He applauded the zeal and proficiency of his learned brother Parry and expressed himself satisfied that the defendant had been fortunate in the provision of such an eminent team. Müller had been given the best possible chance, suggested the Solicitor General, but the fact remained that murder had been proven against him.

The hats, he submitted to the jury, told the story. He contended that the hat found in the carriage belonged to Müller and that this was a fact rather than a probability, proving that Müller had been present at the time of the attack. He reminded them that only one or two such hats were ever made with that same lining (dismissing the evidence given that it might have been four). What of Mr Briggs' hat? It had been missed and it was most conclusive that the murderer had gone away with it and cut it down. Both Mrs Repsch and Mrs Matthews saw Müller wearing that hat from Monday 11 July. *My learned friend, feeling the gigantic difficulties – which I candidly admit – of the case he had to grapple with, did not feel himself able to propound to you any theory of Müller's innocence consistent with the fact of his hat having been found in the railway carriage.* The facts regarding the hats were strengthened by Müller's possession at that time of a new chain – a chain which John Death had given him in exchange for one wrenched from the unconscious body of Mr Briggs.

Matthews might, Collier conceded, be motivated by the reward – but that was, after all, the point of rewards. The jury had seen the walking stick and they had examined the tailor's shears but he felt himself under no obligation to prove the murder weapon. Müller was young and strong while Thomas Briggs had been recovering from illness and was elderly. As for Lee's evidence, Collier suggested that the man was not trustworthy enough to take the stand. Ultimately, he now believed that the evidence, circumstantial though it was, turned out to be even stronger than he had suggested in his opening speech. The words *fact* and *proved* punctuated his argument, overwriting the possibilities of suspicion and probability. The hats were – he said – at the centre of it all and the hats proclaimed Müller guilty.

Most damaging, Collier then turned the evidence intended to prove Müller's alibi to the prosecution's advantage. Since Eldred was such an unreliable timekeeper, he posited, was it not possible that she had gone out on Saturday the 9th at half-past eight, or even a quarter to nine? If Müller had arrived soon after, and left within minutes, it would have allowed him time to take an earlier omnibus (he declined to remind the jury that only one 'bus ran between seven and ten o'clock at night) and his arrival at King William Street or Fenchurch Street Station would then have coincided almost exactly with the arrival of Thomas Briggs on his journey home.

After breaking for an hour, the judge Lord Chief Baron Pollock began his summation to the jury at two o'clock. Müller rose from his seat, leaning against the front of the dock, motionless. Several reporters now noticed that, while Parry had described him as puny, the prisoner in fact had *an expanded chest*. They would later leave the court to describe to their readers *his large, massive, sinewy hands folded on the dock and the peculiar determination of ... his closely compressed lips.*

Judge Pollock's summation began by focusing on the hat found in the carriage and the watch and chain. *These,* he intoned, *are the three links in the chain of evidence for the prosecution, each distinctly apart from each other. It would be for the jury to say whether* [Müller] *had given a satisfactory account for them.*

Although Parry had been at pains to establish with the jury that the law cast the burden of proof on the prosecution and that the case against Müller was, at worst, inconclusive, Pollock's own advice differed. In effect, he now diluted the standard of proof as he had famously done at the Mannings trial in the late forties by directing the jury that they need not be as certain as if they had seen events with their own eyes. They must simply exercise, he advised, as much caution as they would in their ordinary, everyday business dealings. In effect, the judge ruled that the jury's decision could be based on probability rather than on certainty.

Pollock reminded the twelve men of the jury that Müller was said to have been lame but that his lameness had not affected his ability to take a walk on Sunday with the Blyths for three hours from six o'clock. Then he demolished Müller's alibi, believing that the assembly must feel *great compassion for the situation in life which* [Eldred] *has filled. Her evidence consisted, certainly, very much more in saying what she could not than to saying what she did recollect.* Pollock's vitriol was reserved instead for Mrs Jones: a madam about whom it was *impossible to speak ... with the same degree of forbearance.*

Listening to the venerable judge, Müller must have suspected that Pollock was shivering the theories of his defence to atoms. After an hour's solemn summation, at almost three o'clock, the jury retired to consider. Müller sat quietly as whispers rose to hearty conversations. An arm's length from the dock the lawyers round the green baize table talked to one another at the tops of their voices – *the scene in court*, reported the *Telegraph*, *was very like that presented by a betting ring before a great race is going to be run.*

Conspicuously alone, Müller seemed to be making a desperate effort to appear composed. From time to time, Thomas Beard leaned over to speak to him, attempting to support his client during the awful interval of suspense.

Jury deliberations were often quick – in 1864 juries were still denied fire, food or refreshment in an effort to discourage delays – but after scarcely a quarter of an hour the twelve men of the jury filed back in, taking the court by surprise. Following them into court, Judge Pollock entered without Baron Martin. Müller was asked to stand. The call went up for silence.

*Gentlemen, are you agreed upon your verdict?*

*We are.*

*How do you find the prisoner at the bar – guilty or not guilty of the murder with which he is charged?*

There is no record of whether any of the jurymen looked at Müller standing immobile in the dock, waiting for the verdict that would decide his fate.

*Guilty.*

*That is the verdict of you all?*

*Yes.*

*

The jury believed that the hat left in the carriage was Müller's hat and that he therefore must have been there. They presumed that his possession of Briggs' hat and gold watch at the time of his arrest was the direct result of his crime. They did not believe that Müller's visit to Camberwell precluded his ability to have been on the North London Railway at the time of the murder. They disregarded the evidence of Thomas Lee perhaps because he could not satisfactorily account for his delay in coming forward: a whiff of shiftiness, cast over him by the prosecution, had stuck. Parry had failed to cast suspicion on Jonathan Matthews, or to make enough of the existing injury to Müller's foot. He had not convinced the jury that Briggs' death had resulted from injuries sustained as he fell from the train, nor that there was enough doubt surrounding the murder weapon or the true ownership of the hats to force an alternative verdict. He seemed also to have forgotten to make it clear to the jury that the evidence of the omnibus conductor independently substantiated the claim Müller made in his New York press interview that he had been in Camberwell on the night of the murder.

The jury was unanimous, and they made no recommendation to mercy. The second judge, Martin, arrived back in court in his billowing robes as the Clerk of the Arraigns spoke towards the dock: *Prisoner at the bar, you have been convicted of the crime of wilful murder. Have you anything to say why judgement of death should not be given?* Involuntarily, Müller's firmly compressed upper lip began to twitch. He shook his head.

Placing a piece of black cloth over his wig, Martin addressed the prisoner. *Prisoner at the bar, you have been found guilty by the jury of the wilful murder of Mr Briggs ... It is usual with judges to state, in passing sentence, if they entirely concur in that verdict, and they do so for two reasons ... I am authorised to state that we are perfectly satisfied with that verdict and I state so in order to remove entirely from your mind the possibility that you will live in this world much longer ... I beseech you to avail yourself of the means of making your peace with your Maker. I wish to remove from your mind any hope of alteration of the sentence. I feel no more doubt that you committed this murder than I do with reference to the occurrence of any other event of which I am certain but which I did not see with my own eyes ...*

*The sentence is that you be taken from here to the prison from whence you came, that from thence you be taken to a place of execution, that there you be hanged by the neck till your body be dead; that your body when dead be taken down and that it be buried within the precincts of the prison where you were last confined. And may God have mercy on your soul.*

Dry-eyed, Müller watched as the usually intransigent Judge Pollock unaccountably pressed a large handkerchief to his eyes to obscure his tears. Two warders standing behind Müller advanced to take him by the arms but, shrugging them off, he stepped forward with extraordinary self-possession. Then, the one man who had been barred from speaking throughout his own trial, with one hand almost covering his mouth said in a very low, trembling voice and in broken English: *I should like to say something. I am satisfied with the sentence which your Lordship has passed. I know very well it is what the law of the country prescribes. But I have been convicted on false evidence not a true statement of facts, whatever my faults may be.*

Only those sitting nearest to the dock heard his words, hardly audible among the clamour of the room. The judges had already turned to go.

Steadily, the spectators streamed out, turning their backs on the dock and their attention towards dinner. A thunder of cheers went up outside as news of the verdict rippled out onto the crowded streets around the Old Bailey, the roars thrumming into the unseasonably cold dusk. In the dim light of the court, Müller heard it. His stern self-command faltered and then snapped. All hope gone, he began to weep.

# CHAPTER 30

## *The Shadow of Doubt*

Müller had the presence of mind to turn and bow to his counsel before the grip of a warder's strong hand directed him back down the steps and along the tunnel to Newgate. He waited as each gate was unlocked before and resecured behind him, making his way not to his old cell but to another, assigned specifically to condemned prisoners.

The new cell was long and narrow – about nine feet high, nine deep and six broad, with a door four inches thick. There was a small window and a fireplace. To one side was a long wooden settle and on the table lay a Bible and religious tracts, a spoon and fork but no knife. He would change into dark grey prison dress. The warders watched as the cold realisation of his fate broke through the walls of his shock and Müller gave himself up to waves of fear and grief.

Two days after the conclusion of his trial, on Monday 31 October, Müller turned twenty-four. News of the verdict had spread like wildfire and *The Times* reported that public interest in the case had rarely been *equalled . . . the prisoner having excited the utmost curiosity wherever the incidents have become known.* To them it all seemed stranger than fiction. Who would have dreamt that when each man bought a new hat within weeks of each other their purchases would ultimately lead to the identification of the one as the murderer of the other? English law had been seen to be upheld and the nation could congratulate itself on the scrupulousness of its judicial system even while it debated the weakness of the defence, the slipperiness of circumstantial evidence, the *foolishness* of Mr Lee or the probability of premeditation. There was some confusion over the actual words spoken by Müller following Judge Martin's sentence, speculation about who would receive the reward and wonderment that a determined and desperate killer could appear so cool and unperturbed.

The real problem was that neither Müller's arrest, nor his trial nor the sentence under which he now laboured provided the absolute resolution that the nation sought. The big questions – the how and the why – remained unanswered so that while the editor of *The Times* expressed the view that *there ought not to rest on the mind of any human being* [any] *doubt that on the night of the 9th July last Müller did assault and rob this old man in the railway carriage and leave him dying between the rails,* there was still a general feeling of dissatisfaction. People felt that the trial had reached a truth, but not its entirety.

The indirect nature of the evidence on which he had been convicted left people nervous and things remained unexplained. How was it possible for an attack of such violence to be perpetrated in a matter of minutes and attract no attention? Why were Müller's clothes not covered in blood? What was the murder weapon? Who were the two men seen in carriage 69 that night? What should they really think of the proof that Müller's ankle was injured days prior to the attack, slowing him down and making him conspicuous? The judges were certain that the prosecution's case had been made beyond reasonable doubt but the *Telegraph* recognised that *the public will feel a lurking doubt whether we have at present got to the bottom of the mystery.*

There was only one sentence for murder – death – and only one escape: to appeal to the Queen's mercy through the office of the Home Secretary. Appeals usually took the form of a request for the death penalty to be commuted to lifelong imprisonment with hard labour. They were not unusual – solicitors regularly complained of perjured evidence, unexamined witnesses and over-hasty trials – and only two months earlier the Home Secretary, Sir George Grey, had agreed to reduce Mary Hartley's death sentence for the murder of her illegitimate child to one of a life of penal servitude. Despite this recent decision, though, most appeals were rejected. Grey was disinclined to neutralise verdicts by acting as a thirteenth juryman, both reticent about being seen to interfere with the process of the law and in favour of demonstrating to the 'mob' its swift retribution.

The consensus was that the date of Müller's execution would be delayed for the longest allowable period in order for the GLPS and Thomas Beard to request a reprieve. That would be in three Mondays' time, 21 November. In fact, first thing on the Monday after the trial, the sheriffs advised Müller that the date had been set a fortnight hence.

Müller would be hanged by London's public executioner, William Calcraft, a short, thickset, shambling man with straggling grey hair and beard who had served since 1829. Unlike his successor William Marwood, Calcraft was notorious for favouring the clumsy 'short drop' method, making no attempt to calculate from the prisoner's weight and height the length of the rope needed swiftly to dislocate their spine. Instead, by using a short rope, he frequently left convicts to struggle as they died slowly from strangulation.

Eight years earlier, William Bousfield had managed to draw up his legs and lodge his feet on the side of the drop to prevent himself being throttled. Pushed off by one of the prison turnkeys, Bousfield found purchase for a second time before Calcraft dashed down the steps to hang onto his legs. Still he managed to raise himself. On the fourth fall he submitted, but writhed violently for more than ten minutes before he died. Horrified, the prison officials withdrew from the scaffold and the crowd erupted into enraged yells. The *Morning Chronicle* would report that *the effect was rather that of a slaughtering than an execution* but it was neither the first nor the last time that Calcraft failed to dispatch his victims with speed.

Each bungled occasion prompted short-lived outbursts of editorial feeling but scorn was traditionally voiced less at the hangman's errors than at the behaviour of the crowds. In the previous century, Dr Johnson had asserted that if executions did not draw spectators then they did *not answer their purpose*. During the nineteenth century, that point of view began to lose its force and the question of whether the public spectacle of judicial killing exercised any deterrent effect began vigorously to be debated.

The earliest record of parliamentary dissent was recorded in 1819. Twenty-one years later the House was given its first vote on the abolition of capital punishment. It failed. As the 1840s progressed, arguments about the effectiveness of capital punishment were energised by the bestiality of the vast hordes that congregated for the executions of notorious murderers including the Swiss valet Courvoisier for the murder of Lord William Russell in 1840, and husband and wife Maria and Frederick Manning nine years later.

Witnessed by several writers, philosophers and politicians, they generated an outpouring of written and visual material, including a tirade from William Makepeace Thackeray after attending the murderer Peytel's execution in France in 1839. Describing the savage spectacle, Thackeray was unconvinced that any of the spectators had been *deterred, or frightened or moralised; he had gratified his appetite for blood, and this was all*. Unable to reconcile capital punishment with Christian morality, the novelist asked, *Who gave you the right to do so? You, who cry out against suicides as impious and contrary to Christian law? What use is there in killing him? You deter no one.*

A year later, Thackeray's horror was compounded by the *sickening, ghastly, wicked scene* of Courvoisier's execution in London. *Where is the reason for the practice,* he wrote in *Fraser's Magazine, knowing ... that revenge is not only evil, but useless? ... I came away ... that morning with a disgust for murder, but it was for the murder I saw done ... So salutary has the impression of the butchery been upon me ... that I feel myself ashamed and degraded at the brutal curiosity which took me to the ... sight.* Charles Dickens agreed, writing of the *odious levity,* the lechery, ribaldry, vice and drunkenness of crowds that had turned Courvoisier's death into a shameful theatrical spectacle. Yet by the Mannings' execution a decade later, Dickens had abandoned his abolitionist stance in favour of private executions, arguing that – far from demonstrating the resumption of order by the ruling classes and instead of providing an antidote to the anxiety of the age – public executions served no useful reformative purpose. Worse, they brutalised and corrupted.

1864 had so far provided few opportunities for London mobs to congregate at the ghoulish spectacle of public death. In February, a crowd of thirty thousand had jeered at the 'exhibition' of five foreign sailors being hanged simultaneously for murdering the captain of their British ship. Just a few thousand gathered for the executions of murderers John Devine in May and Frederick Charles Bricknell at the start of August.

Their crimes paled, though, beside the widespread horror occasioned by the murder of Thomas Briggs on his suburban train and, with the date now set for Müller's sentence to be carried out, the sheriffs exhorted him to spend his time in preparation for his death. Above all, what they wanted was a confession. To meet God with a lie on one's lips and a stain on one's heart was to invite an everlasting damnation dreaded by most Victorians. A confession would also serve a wider purpose:

illuminating the motive behind the murder and clarifying whether it really had been the act of a single man; it would erase any doubt about his innocence and minimise the potential for riots at his death. Fearful of allowing him false hope, the prison authorities considered it crucial that Müller should not be told of the efforts by the GLPS on his behalf.

\*

Sixty-five-year-old Sir George Grey, a trained lawyer and lifelong politician, had held the position of Home Secretary twice before. Grave, patrician and somewhat dismissive, he ran a department that was the repository of every petition concerning prisons, asylums, the police and the country's institutions. In preparation for the anticipated legal arguments for a reprieve – known as a 'Memorial' – he followed custom by asking both trial judges for their opinion. Both Pollock and Martin confirmed their faith in the conclusive evidence of Müller's guilt. As far as they were concerned, no legal reason existed to justify either a postponement of the execution or a reprieve.

The anxiety for Müller to confess contained a perplexing inconsistency. If the public mind was destabilised by doubt, should those very uncertainties not have played to his benefit in court? The newspapers were, on the whole, convinced that a Memorial would fail: even if his alibi could be strengthened, even if the dubious docks peddler were to be found, what could explain the possession of those two hats? The *Daily News* believed that the process would only strengthen the *circumstantial evidence on which the jury proceeded. It is seen that it is not a chain which breaks at its weakest point but a solid pyramid of facts rising to an apex of conviction.*

Yet letters in their hundreds began arriving at the Home Office, some from abolitionists petitioning for Müller's reprieve on religious grounds *lest the curse of innocent blood should be brought on the whole nation*, and others from correspondents who wondered why Thomas Lee had never properly been believed. All of them raised questions. If the convict had jumped from the train how was it possible that he had escaped injury? Given the saturation of pre-trial publicity, was it possible to find an unbiased jury? Should Müller not have been allowed to speak in his own defence? Was it right to believe Mrs Repsch's and Matthews' testimonies without asking either the Blyths or Hoffa – who knew him better – the same questions about the ownership of the Walker hat? Had Judge Pollock's summation been impartial and fair?

The facts of Müller's good character and of his diminutive stature were pressed in his defence while Matthews' reputation elicited furious censure. There were letters expressing anger that the police had failed to pursue statements made during the summer months. Others focused on Müller's denial upon his arrest that he would not know his way to either Bow or Hackney Wick stations, pointing out that his lodgings were not close to either while the omnibus from the City passed conveniently close to his door. All these correspondents believed that irretrievable sentences demanded infallible judges, and that a shadow of doubt had attached itself to Müller; all demanded a postponement of his sentence in order to reinvestigate the facts.

No details of Müller's immediate family had been included in the material sent from Germany. In New York he had mentioned, and watched for, a sister who had not appeared. Now, interleaved among the bulging papers shuffled by Home Office staff into paper files, were short notes from Sophia Pearson of 15 Shaftesbury Terrace, Pimlico. Pearson claimed to be another of Müller's sisters and wrote to Sir George Grey that, on the Monday following his conviction, she had presented herself at Newgate in the hope of visiting her brother but had been *thrust from the Door like a Dog and told I was Drunk. I then walk* [sic] *to and fro the street pleading to God to save and protect poor Müller.*

Grey's secretary wrote cursorily to advise Sophia Pearson to apply to the prison authorities, and then he washed his hands of her. Turning to every quarter – including the Queen – for help but, receiving no further replies, Pearson's letters grew desperate as the days passed. *Grant me an interview with poor Müller*, she wrote. *I have waited 12 hours in the deepest suspence* [sic] *no answer came. So this is what is called justice to the condemned man. I plead in the name of God.* As the days passed, Müller received other visitors while she was refused and ignored, questioning whether there were *two rules – one for the Rich and another for the Poor?* Her words fell on deaf ears. The letters petered out. Presumably she was forced to give up hope and, for a second time, no sister appeared to comfort Müller in his adversity.

Thomas Beard, meanwhile, laboured over the preparation of his petition. What he needed was new evidence to corroborate Müller's presence in Camberwell and to substantiate the claim that the condemned man bought Briggs' watch and chain at the London docks.

Despite Parry's attempts to show that Müller had bought the silk topper in a second-hand market, Beard knew that Müller had claimed that he had bought it at Digance hatters in the City and that he had described the shopman who served him. Since Digance had employed only one assistant for the last twelve years, Beard brought that man to the condemned cell in Newgate on the Thursday after the trial. The interview lasted only minutes and it was a failure. Neither man was able to recognise the other.

Beard was also pursuing rumours that on the day after the murder, a Mr Poole from Edmonton had been startled when his window was smashed by a parcel thrown from the windows of a cab passing rapidly by on the road from London. Giving chase, he overtook the vehicle and found it to contain four men including one whose head was bandaged. The men paid Poole for his trouble but when the parcel was subsequently examined it contained a pair of trousers stained with human blood. The GLPS were attempting to trace those men.

During the week following Müller's trial, Thomas Briggs' watch, chain, hat, stick and bag, as well as the contents of his pockets on the night his body was found, were finally returned to his widow at 5 Clapton Square. A cheque for five pounds, five shillings was sent back to Scotland Yard addressed to Detective Inspector Tanner *as a small token of our appreciation of the courteousness and delicacy with which he has conducted the case in all communications with the family*. The Treasury added a further five pounds for *his help in this case*.

At the same time, Jonathan Matthews wrote to the Commissioner, Sir Richard Mayne, to ask for financial help. He claimed that he had been given seventeen shillings and sixpence for loss of employment while attending the trial but that he owed a great deal of rent – twelve pounds and eighteen shillings – and he complained of mobs collecting in front of his house to sing ballads about him and Müller. Matthews' pleas were ignored. According to police records, local constables could find no evidence of intimidation by gangs and concluded that *he has no truth in him*. The cab driver's reputation was in tatters.

## CHAPTER 31

# Condemned for a Thumbmark

After the rush to judgement that had characterised most news-paper reports prior to Müller's trial, printed pamphlets now questioned his guilt. Several anonymous tracts appeared with titles like *Who Murdered Mr Briggs?*, *Müller's Guilt or Innocence?*, *The Great NLR Tragedy* and *Was Mr Briggs' Death a Murder?* A traditional element of the paraphernalia surrounding notorious crime, they sold in their hundreds of thousands, and they all fostered uncertainty about Müller's guilt.

The same unanswered questions flared. Should Lee's evidence have been discounted? Did Müller's alibi warrant further inves-tigation? Why was there no blood on his clothes? Had he had enough money for his fare before the murder? Was Matthews to be believed? Where was the murder weapon? Public blood-thirstiness had led to the prejudgement of Müller's guilt so that the trial had been a farce, its outcome directed by society's crav-ing for vengeance and its demand for the apparent reimposition of security. Would Müller, then, be *condemned for a thumbmark when many thousands of other hats also have thumbmarks?*

Would the country stick to *an omnipotent faith in Digance and HIS hat and Matthews and HIS hat*?

It was not only the profit-seeking press. Armchair detectives, abolitionists and the devout all took up their pens to write to the Home Office or the papers and even eminent lawyers were excited by the case. James Walter Smith, an Inner Temple barrister practised at expressing his discontent with the English system of criminal justice, published a document asking *Has Müller Been Tried?* Positing that Briggs' death could have been caused by the fall from the train, he criticised Digance for concealing that his clients' names were inscribed three inches up inside his hats while Müller's hat was cut down only by an inch and a half at most. He wondered why the police had not taken seriously reports of the man with the head wound seen in Victoria Park or the parcel thrown in Edmonton and he repeated a question of burgeoning significance to the public: why had no one asked the Blyths whether the carriage hat was Müller's? *All of these questions*, he wrote, *bear as much weight as the circumstantial evidence heard in court*. Smith considered that the poor tailor was paying the penalty for the German war against the Danes.

Privately, London solicitor James Aytoun sent carefully considered arguments to the Home Secretary outlining his belief that more time should be allowed to investigate Müller's alibi and that the prosecution's case, resting on the two hats, could easily be undermined. Hearing that the Blyths were denying that the broken hat had ever belonged to Müller, he posited that *in a civil case this kind of new evidence would demand a new trial ... In France if similar happened the verdict would be referred to the Court of Cessation and set aside*. He believed that to refuse a delay now would be equal to judicial murder. A Temple barrister called W. F. Finlason also wrote to Sir George Grey that a growing body of legal minds thought Pollock's failure to advise the jury about the importance of Matthews' evidence – *and therefore the importance of his credibility* – had impaired the impartiality of the trial.

Press prejudice, the perilous difficulty of circumstantial evidence, the inability of the accused to speak in his own defence, the lack of a proper Court of Appeals and a growing scepticism of the probity of capital punishment were all raised as arguments in the convict's defence. In the absence of any apparent motive for the murder and in the face of the incompatibility of the crime with Müller's character, questions were also asked about why the defence of insanity or temporary insanity had not been introduced at trial.

An insanity defence would have proved thorny, however. In 1843 a deluded Daniel M'Naghten had tried to murder Prime Minister Robert Peel, killing his secretary instead. When M'Naghten's lawyers argued successfully that he had not understood the nature of his act, a legal precedent was established, encouraging a surge of insanity pleas to be lodged by defence counsels on behalf of their clients. But there was a problem. No clear definition of insanity existed and the rule recognised no middle ground between the extremes of madness and its opposite. Lawyers disagreed with medics and early psychological scientists about how the nature of madness diminished criminal responsibility and most judges remained unconvinced by the argument that an impulse could not be resisted based only on the evidence that it had not been.

Recent cases proved the difficulties of diving into these controversial waters. In 1856 James Hill was tried for decapitating his nephew in a fury entirely out of character. His defence succeeded in having him committed to a lunatic asylum rather than condemned to death. Three years later James Pownall – a man with a history of infrequent violence but who seemed in every other way entirely rational – was also acquitted of murder in Gloucester when the jury found evidence for homicidal mania. More often, legal counsel failed to make the defence stick. In

1863 Robert Burton was executed for the murder of a boy in Maidstone despite the fact that many doctors viewed his crime as desperate, self-centred and motiveless, and attributed his violent impulse to insanity.

It would be almost twenty more years before courts began to accept new definitions of mental disease, accepting that juries should be allowed to *return any one of three verdicts: Guilty, Guilty but the power of his self-control was diminished by insanity or Not Guilty on the grounds of insanity*. In the meantime, despite Müller's good character and apparent lack of real motive, Parry must have known that a plea of insanity was very unlikely to succeed.

\*

The pamphlets and legal rumblings, most of them reprinted in various newspapers, might have been altering public opinion towards Müller, but to Thomas Beard they were immaterial and he set out, instead, to procure new statements. John Hoffa's was designed to negate the supposition that Müller could have taken a change of trousers with him when he left the Repschs. Hoffa swore that Müller had carried no parcel with him and that his pockets were not large enough to carry spare clothing. Another statement was taken from a boot maker at the London docks who described a peddler frequently hawking dubious goods in that area and who had disappeared around 13 July. Jacob Weist, a porter at the docks, then confirmed what no one at the trial had been able to do – that he saw Müller at the docks on the morning of Monday the 11th, early enough for him to have bought Briggs' stolen watch and chain before visiting Death's Cheapside shop.

Late on Tuesday 8 November, less than a week before the date set for Müller's execution, Beard went before the magistrate at the Worship Street Police Court in the City with the Blyths and a third new witness in order to make further declarations.

At last Ellen Blyth answered the question neither counsel had put to her at the trial: *Franz Müller never wore any hat which in any way approached a shabby hat. He was careful of them and always protected them from the rain with an umbrella.* Both Ellen and her husband George swore on their oaths that neither of them recognised the broken hat found under a seat in carriage 69.

Beard had also secured the assistance of a character styling himself André Massena, Baron de Camin. Camin stated that on 9 July he had got lost walking from Mile End to Hackney Wick Station. Arriving at the embankment between Hackney Wick and Bow stations he had seen a man, bloody from head to foot, staggering from the line where it met the canal. He complained that he gave his statement immediately to Sergeant Clarke who had failed to pursue it. Camin's testimony was heady stuff but it was also problematic. When Inspector Williamson asked Clarke about de Camin's affidavit, the policeman could neither remember it nor find a report in the files to confirm his story. Further, Beard seemed to be unaware that Camin was an inveterate publicity-seeker and reputed fraud – less a Baron of note than an English actor motivated by money and fame.

The lengthy Memorial finally prepared by Müller's solicitor asked for a reconsideration of Müller's guilt on the grounds that new evidence had emerged which, had it been set before the jury, would have strengthened his defence. It submitted that the parcel thrown through the window at Edmonton, and the state of the men in that carriage, threw suspicion elsewhere. Additionally, a new report from a chemist in Victoria Park stated that two rough men came to him late on the evening of the murder July asking him to administer to a severe head wound. Sending them away, the chemist had made a statement to the police on the following day but *as they could not make my description tally with that of Müller, whom they appeared to have made up their minds must have been the guilty party, they let the matter drop.* Both theories supported Thomas Lee's evidence that there had been more than one person involved in the crime and that neither was Müller.

Beard also submitted further proof of Müller's alibi. Dr Ernest Juch, editor of the *Hermann*, had visited Müller before his trial and was then told by the prisoner that when he was returning from Camberwell on 9 July he had stopped for a beer in a public house two hundred yards or so from the Camberwell Gate. Müller had told Juch that as he left the pub at about twenty to ten there had been a disturbance when a small child was bitten by a dog.

The statement alone proved nothing, but a second affidavit corroborated the story. A man called William Curtis said that on 9 July he was at the Red Lion pub on Walworth Road close to Camberwell Gate when, at about twenty minutes past nine, a foreigner came in and asked for a glass of ale. The man had been wearing a red carpet slipper on his right foot, had fair hair and was about middle stature with dark clothes and a lowish-crowned hat. Curtis knew the date by business that he had in town and he also remembered the incident with the dog and the child. If Müller was still in Camberwell at half past nine, then his intention to take the late omnibus was corroborated and he could not possibly have made it to Fenchurch Street Station by the time Briggs' train departed.

There was more. The conductor of the omnibus leaving Camberwell Gate at 9.40 p.m. had been traced and he also remembered the incident with the dog. On that journey, he recalled that there had been five passengers including a man with fair hair wearing a red slipper on one foot. Checking the 'way-bills' of the omnibus company, Beard discovered that on the night of 9 July the conductor of the last 'bus from Camberwell Gate to the City had recorded five passengers. Not only did this incident with the dog fix the date as that of the murder, not only was it clear that one of the passengers had injured his foot, but Müller had independently stated to Ernest Juch that there had been four other passengers in his 'bus that night and he had described them. On the basis of these new facts, Beard requested time for further investigation.

Details of the contents of the Memorial had already been sent to the press when it was presented to the Home Office at two o'clock on the afternoon of Thursday 10 November, less than four days before Müller was due to hang. Expecting the deputation, Sir George told his secretary that he would decline to meet them since *I feel little confidence in the accuracy of any report they might choose to make.* Instead, Grey retreated to his estate in Northumberland until Saturday. Waiting for his return, the GLPS and Thomas Beard faced two days of keen suspense. In case new evidence should come to light, they advertised in the papers that they would sit *en permanence* at Seyd's Hotel in the City until Grey's ruling was announced.

*

The second week of Müller's confinement in the condemned cell drew to a close and he still refused to make the confession the country craved. Both the Blyths and John Hoffa had been allowed to visit him and his warders were now almost certain that he had wind of the efforts being made on his behalf. Confusion reigned: *it is surely worthy of most serious consideration whether a regard to the character of English justice does not demand further inquiry ... before a human being is launched into eternity*, wrote the *Evening Star* on 10 November. *It would be criminal to refuse the indulgence of time to establish the truth.* A certain amount of sympathy was developing even in circles where the certainty of Müller's guilt had been most obstinately believed. Perhaps, after all, there was as much circumstantial evidence in his favour as against it. The London correspondent for the *New York Times* thought that *though there is a general and determined conviction of his guilt, there are too many doubts for the quiet of the public conscience ...* [and] *the dissentient minority is rapidly increasing.*

Desperate to set eyes on the condemned man, some of the middle classes obtained permission to visit Newgate and, with the judicious offer of a shilling, were allowed to peep through the observation hole in the door of his cell. In the minds of several religious ministers allowed to visit officially, conviction of Müller's innocence was also settling. The Reverend Mr Battiscombe, minister at the German Chapel in Blackheath and a clergyman for thirty years, assured the Home Secretary that *no one has more strongly felt than I did – at first – that Franz Müller was guilty.* He described two long meetings with Müller during which he pressed the prisoner to confess. Müller's refusal, he believed, sprang from the German's fervent belief that *God had permitted that to occur which had befallen him … in consequence of the … gay, prayerless and sinful life he had led.* Battiscombe believed in Müller's deepening religious belief and that he expected to enter Paradise with no stain on his conscience. The churchman's letter (also sent to and reprinted widely in the daily press) asserted that Battiscombe had *never … seen a person of whose sincerity I have felt more affirmed.*

On the afternoon of Friday 11 November workmen began to erect hoardings in front of the Old Bailey and barriers along the approach roads in expectation of huge crowds at the planned execution on Monday morning. Throughout the day the men divided the open space in front of the gaol into pens designed to prevent the crowd boiling over. They blocked up the doors leading to the courts and Sessions House and set planks along the roofs to prevent anyone climbing up for a better view. They boxed in the railings in front of the church of St Sepulchre and constructed timber barricades that stretched out from Newgate Street and the Old Bailey down Giltspur Street towards Smithfield and Ludgate Hill. *The Times* recorded that well-dressed sightseers milled about on the rain-greasy pavements, the sound of hammers echoing round them. Shops, it wrote,

were being boarded up and places at the windows of surrounding buildings were already being sold for up to four
pounds.

\*

The day following Müller's trial, on Sunday 30 October, a treaty
of peace between Prussia and Denmark was concluded in Vienna.
The Danish concession of lands along its frontier marked the first
success in Prussia's goal to unify the German states, an ambition
that would – within seven years – fundamentally change the balance of power in Europe. Despite the promise of peace marked
by the Viennese treaty, British suspicion about Germany's aggressive intentions and concern at her growing economic prosperity
was unlikely to abate. For the first time in her industrialised history, Britain faced a Continental rival.

There was widespread English antagonism towards Germany,
yet three enormous bundles containing hundreds of signatures
from the people of Frankfurt on behalf of Müller were delivered
to Sir George Grey at the Home Office during the weekend.
Opinion was growing in Germany that Müller had been made a
scapegoat and that his trial had been unfairly conducted by a
pro-Danish nation too eager to fasten its prejudices upon a
German. Feelings were running high. Brushing aside the pres-
sures of international politics, Grey sought instead the opinion of
the judges for a second time. Then he sat at his desk scribbling
for several hours as he responded to each one of Thomas Beard's
contentions, weighing in the balance the opposing dictates of retribution and deterrence against mercy and understanding.

Towards midday on Saturday 12 November, Sir George Grey's
secretary copied out his official response to the Memorial. In his
office in Basinghall Street, Thomas Beard anxiously anticipated
this final judgement.

# CHAPTER 32

## *City of Devils*

With two days to go before the execution the possibility that an ignominious public death would be inflicted on an innocent man stirred the public's disquiet and Franz Müller waited. On Friday 11 November he had spent an hour with his friend John Hoffa, repeating over and over again that he had been convicted on false statements. He wrote letters. The governor of the prison and the undersheriffs and aldermen all visited. Sheriff Dakin was disturbed: he, too, was beginning to believe in Müller's innocence and had gone to the unusual extreme of seeking a meeting with Mr Henry at Bow Street Magistrates' Court on the matter. This was so unprecedented that the magistrate wrote to Sir George Grey, urging upon the Home Secretary the expediency of giving time for the sifting of new evidence.

Müller prayed regularly and fervently with both the prison Ordinary Dr Davis, the Reverend Battiscombe and Dr Louis Cappel, the Lutheran minister of the East End German Georgenkirche in Alie Street, Goodman's Fields. Cappel's initial certainty of Müller's guilt was also wavering.

After the freezing temperatures of the previous fortnight it was

turning milder. The weather had broken and frost was replaced
by an intermittent rain pattering through the bare trees. Fogs rose
from the river, mingled with the soot from house and factory and
cloaked the city in a yellowing, soapy atmosphere. It was as if, as
Miller wrote in his *Picturesque Sketches of London*, *all the
smoke from hundreds of chimneys ascended, rotted and then
descended all at once – choking* [and] *foul tasting.* With visibil-
ity limited to a yard ahead, pedestrians groped their way gingerly
along the greasy pavements, feeling their way along walls in an
attempt to avoid being knocked down. Street vehicles and riverboats collided. A drawback of industrial progress, these
dangerous 'pea soupers' were disorienting and depressing.

At three o'clock on Saturday 12 November, just as Hoffa left
Müller's cell after making an emotional farewell, Thomas Beard
arrived at the gaol. He brought with him the communication
from the Home Secretary. Sir George Grey wrote that, *after carefully considering the statements and comparing them with the
report of the evidence given at the trial, and after full communication with the learned judges before whom the proceedings took
place,* [I] *see no ground which would justify* [me] *in advising Her
Majesty to interfere with the course of law in this case.*

Beard explained that this was the end, that Grey's refusal of
either postponement or reprieve meant that his legal efforts were
now exhausted and that nothing now could prevent the execution going ahead on Monday morning. Dejected but composed,
Müller told his solicitor that he had not expected it to be otherwise.

*I should be a very bad fellow if I had done it*, he said.

*Were you aware*, asked Beard, *that efforts were being made
for you?*

*Yes, I did think so.*

Shaking hands with the man who had failed to save his life,
Müller then assured Thomas Beard that he had made his peace
with God and then watched his solicitor depart for the last time.

Turning to sit at his table, he took up his pen and began to scratch line after line of writing on the sheets of paper made available to him. His warders presumed that he was constructing a formal confession.

In arriving at his judgement, Grey had taken his cue from the conviction of the judges presiding over Müller's trial. A private, draft statement filed among the Home Office papers shows that he was suspicious of the statements given by the Blyths, *so identical in their terms* that they appeared to have been *prepared by the solicitor and subscribed by them*. He did not believe that the evidence of ownership of the Walker hat had been shaken. He questioned the respectability of Thomas Lee and the memory of Mary Anne Eldred. Dismissing the statement of 'Baron de Camin', he questioned why neither Jacob Weist – the docks porter – nor any of the witnesses who claimed to be able to substantiate Müller's alibi had been subpoenaed to appear in court. Tellingly, these notes were made on the very day the Memorial was delivered to Whitehall, suggesting that he had reached his own conclusions far more swiftly than he had made out.

The Home Secretary's judgement was coloured, too, by his belief that were he to overturn the verdict on the basis of new evidence he would set a precedent for facts to be withheld from future trials in order to form the basis of appeals. If the investigations of Müller's defence were incomplete why, he wondered, had they failed to request a postponement of the trial? His draft statement concluded with his belief that his interference would not be in the interests of society as a whole – that *it would be dangerous and prejudicial to the due administration of the criminal law.*

\*

Sir George Grey was conscious that disquiet about the reality of capital punishment was growing among a section of the population who argued that it was a leftover from more brutal times,

unfit for a progressive society. Marshalling the writings of
Dickens and Thackeray from the 1840s, they were increasingly
vocal about their desire for abolition. Against this, the politician
had to balance the strident morality of the Victorian age and its
demands for retribution.

What was to be done? Successive governments had striven to
impose order on the capital's seedy alleys, its rookeries and stink-
ing slums. Clearances and evictions had made way for the new
roads and railways that sliced through the streets, for new hospitals, docks, warehouses, theatres, parks and houses. Murder,
however, evaded attempts at sanitisation. The pressing difficulty
was in reconciling the drunken crowds that bayed for death at
the foot of the scaffold with the notion of an advanced civilisation that held itself as an example to the rest of the world.

Four years earlier, in October 1860, ex-police sergeant James
Mullins had been convicted of the murder of seventy-year-old
Mary Emsley, a case on which the young Richard Tanner had cut
his teeth. The jury had ignored the judge's opinion that the case
against him had not fully been made and, protesting his innocence, Mullins had been executed in November before a Newgate
mob of twenty thousand. It was, wrote *The Times*, *the greatest
crowd assembled there at an execution for many years past* and,
as Mullins stood on the scaffold, it *surged about in wild excitement and raised an indescribable murmur*. The ensuing outcry
had forced attention back on the capital punishment issue.

The debate was finely balanced. Although the movement for
total abolition had gained force in the two decades since 1840,
several instances of 'misplaced leniency' on the part of the Home
Secretary had swung public opinion back towards a rigorous prosecution of the law. During the summer of 1863 Victor Townley
had been convicted of murder but was saved by his family's ability to have him privately committed to a lunatic asylum. The
argument ran that while the Townleys had the wherewithal to
effect Victor's escape, a working-class man without powerful

friends would have swung. Sir George Grey was strongly criticised for failing to take the right action and, smarting, he had grown less inclined than ever to approve applications for reprieve. In January 1864 a bricklayer, Samuel Wright, was arrested, tried, sentenced and hanged within three weeks of killing – possibly in self-defence – his notoriously violent girlfriend. Despite widespread protest and appeals for leniency, Grey had refused to interfere in the process of justice.

It was against this background that the Memorial on behalf of Franz Müller failed. But Grey's determination not to budge was countered by those who now wondered afresh to what extent hanging demonstrated the might of the law against the wickedness of crime. How far did it qualify as an effective deterrent? The appetite for public hanging was waning.

The authors of the sensation novels of the early 1860s understood this lurking distaste for public death. Their murderous villains rarely paid the ultimate public price for their crimes but were consigned instead to the 'natural' justice of fires, street stabbings or drawn-out decline in foreign mental institutions. In Ellen Wood's *East Lynne*, Sir Francis Levison's capital sentence was reduced to penal servitude on the basis that his act was not premeditated, but her readers were left in little doubt that with his fine white hands and his terror of hardship, Levison would not last long. Only the impoverished hunchback 'Softy' in Mrs Braddon's *Aurora Floyd* was made to climb the steps to the gallows – which was ironic, since he was a man so mentally impaired that a plea of irresponsibility should probably have held sway.

Following Dickens' belief that public executions created *a city of devils*, a House of Lords Select Committee of 1856 had recommended the introduction of private executions, believing that scandalous scenes at hangings threatened to undermine the principle of the law. It was ignored. In May 1864 the government had been pressured into establishing a Royal Commission to report further on the issue: its members were appointed by Queen Victoria on Friday 8 July, one day before the murder of Thomas Briggs.

In early August, as the police waited for the arrival of Müller in New York, the *Manchester Guardian* had written of a growing squeamishness towards public hangings, reporting that a *great change has come over the public opinion in regard to the matter. There is much less faith among us now than there was a few years ago in the power of moral means to repress the more brutal forms of crime.* The newspaper believed that by allowing the process of execution to remain a frightful mystery and by removing the supporting presence of friends in the crowd, terror would spawn in the murdering mind. It suggested that the prison bell should toll, a black flag should be raised and a limited number of spectators – jurors, judges, witnesses, press and the like – should be admitted in order to remove any public doubt that the execution had taken place. Private executions, it concluded – like those in America – would provide *a system more in harmony with the civilisation of the day.*

These contemporary arguments made Franz Müller's impending execution the subject of intense concern. On Monday 14 November the apparently imperturbable young man – believed by a growing number to be innocent of murder – was scheduled for his own very public death.

# CHAPTER 33

## *St Sepulchre's Bell*

In the prison chapel on the morning of Sunday 13 November, sitting in the condemned pew positioned under the scanty pulpit and in full view of the other prisoners, Franz Müller heard a part of the burial service and prayers for his soul. Throughout the day the visits of sheriffs and aldermen were interleaved with those of the religious ministers who had befriended him. The country steeled itself for the execution and hundreds of applications were made to the governor of Newgate for access to the gaol on the following morning. Only a small group of pressmen were to be admitted.

At Windsor Castle the Queen received a telegraphic message from Wilhelm I, King of Prussia, pressing for the execution to be delayed. His representation to Victoria was regal but also personal: the two royal families were related by the marriage of Victoria's eldest daughter Princess Victoria to Wilhelm's son Friedrich. Nevertheless, Queen Victoria asked for it to be forwarded to the Home Office with a note expressing her amazement at the appeals. *She is sure no such appeal is necessary to induce you and the judges who tried the man to do whatever is right.* A letter was also sent to Sir George Grey by Richard Stevens, a tailor in the City who had worked with Müller from November 1863 to 7 May 1864 and who never *during the whole time ... and my opportunities of seeing his hat saw it with a peculiar lining by which Mrs Repsch and Mrs Matthews declared that they identify it. But on the contrary I solemnly and sincerely declare that such a lining did not in any way correspond with the lining* of Müller's hat. Stevens, also, begged for a stay of execution.

The GLPS had only one place left to go: 5 Clapton Square. At half past ten on Sunday night, three representatives of the society arrived there and asked for an interview with Thomas Briggs' widow, Mary. They were refused entry but, labouring under the misconception that the Briggs family were dissatisfied with the verdict, the three men remained on the doorstep for the best part of an hour as they recapitulated arguments in Müller's defence. They had new evidence, they said, that the dimensions of the crumpled hat did not fit the marks made by the hat that had been stored in the box Müller left behind in his room at the Blyths'. They implored Briggs' sons to come with them to Sir George Grey to plead for respite. Indelicate and immoderate, their request caused outrage.

Müller's desperate countrymen withdrew defeated as the still-grieving, usually tight-lipped Briggs family gave vent to their restrained scorn in a letter sent for publication to the editor of *The Times*. *From motives which I believe will be understood by ... nearly all your readers,* they wrote, *the family of the late Mr Briggs have refrained from addressing to you any remarks on the recent proceedings of the committee of the German Legal Protection Society, and had a right to respect in return for their forbearance that their privacy would be respected. But one of the last acts of some members of the above society appear to me to have been so foolish, unwarrantable and cruel that I consider it my duty to make it known ... You cannot doubt, Sir that the widow and children of the murdered man would be the last to*

*wish that an innocent man should be punished for the crime*
[but] ... *I put it to you and the public whether they should not
have been spared so indelicate and ill-timed an appeal.* It was the
last public statement about events that the family would make.

*

Late on the afternoon of Sunday the 13th, heavy rain scattered
the growing crowd from the muddy streets around the prison. By
eight o'clock, though, the Old Bailey was impassable, the small
'pens' filling up while itinerant preachers on the margins ser-
monised about evil. By the time the public houses and tap rooms
closed at eleven o'clock, between four and five thousand people
had formed a dark ridge before the prison and a strong force of
police, drafted from six of the Metropolitan divisions, battled to
keep passage open for the scaffold. The white barriers showed up
in the wet darkness like a network of bones above the mud and,
unseen in the clouded sky, the full moon passed through the
shadow of the earth. In the early hours of Monday morning,
almost exactly thirteen weeks since Briggs had died, a blackened
deal frame was brought out from the yard in the Old Bailey,
drawn by two carthorses. Over the next few hours the dull thuds
and rasps of the workmen's tools echoed from the walls of the
gaol as the scaffold was erected outside the old, low Debtor's
Door.

At five o'clock on Monday morning Müller woke to the sound
of driving rain, hammers and the stamping feet and swelling mur-
murs of the crowd outside. He dressed with scrupulous care in
the clothes he had worn in court, took breakfast and was joined
by the Reverend Davis with whom he prayed. The countdown to
his execution had begun, a well-rehearsed progression of precisely timed events designed to ensure that nothing occurred to
disturb his equilibrium. In the hope that he would confess, every
visitor impressed upon him the finality of his position.

An hour later, the rain stopped. The German minister Dr

Cappel arrived to administer the Sacrament and the multitude outside began to swell fast, fed by streams of people arriving from all directions. William Calcraft, London's shabby executioner, unhurriedly began to check the rope, the bolts supporting the trap door on which the prisoner would stand and the lever that would send his body down at the appointed hour. At ten minutes to seven the governor of the gaol, Mr Jones, made a short visit to Müller's cell. He would return in less than an hour. As Jones left, the convicted man momentarily collapsed, clinging to Dr Cappel and begging him to stay by his side.

At twenty past seven, in the cold grey of pre-dawn, carriages carrying the aldermen and sheriffs from the London Coffee House in Ludgate Hill appeared at the end of the Old Bailey. Once at the Sessions House they would send up the order for Müller to be released to them. Twenty minutes later, as the first cold flicker of sunlight rose over the rooftops of the East End, they moved through the passage between the courthouse and the gaol, making for the chapel yard. Simultaneously, Governor Jones returned to the condemned cell and commended Müller and his conscience to God. Shaking his hand, Müller thanked him for his kindness. Then, pale and trembling, he followed the governor with a swift step, emerging into the courtyard to meet the sheriffs. Crossing the yard, they all entered the long, sombre press room.

By a quarter to eight the waiting mob in the streets had risen to fifty thousand, more than twice the number that had gathered for James Mullins' execution in 1860, more than had waited for the notorious hangings of Courvoisier or the Mannings in the 1840s, and far outnumbering the police lines. Surging and lulling between the barriers like a swarm of bees, the mass of people obliterated the ground from view. Those who could afford it leaned from surrounding windows, dressed in their best holiday costume, smoking or playing cards to pass the time. People perched on roofs. The sellers of sandwiches, pies, fried fish and ginger beer called their wares. Around them, pickpockets, drunks and brawlers, the depraved and the innocent were crushed shoulder to shoulder, pushing, quarrelling and joking. The judicially sanctioned killing of a murderer was providing an *entertainment* that unleashed and legitimised the mob so feared by politicians and the middle classes. *Populus*, as Thackeray had feared when he watched the hanging of Courvoisier in 1840, had *been growing and coming of age.*

At ten minutes to eight the bell of St Sepulchre's Church began to toll, its knell heard only momentarily within the gaol before it was drowned out by the thunderous yells that rose from the crowd into the rain-sodden air. When Calcraft's white head briefly appeared again on the scaffold at nine minutes to eight, the crowd went wild, shrieking with delight before he dipped back out of sight.

At six minutes to eight the prison bell began to ring. Down in the press room, the Reverend Ordinary Dr Davis began to intone the words from the burial service as Calcraft removed Müller's shirt collar and neckerchief then pinioned his arms with a leather strap of his own invention. Passing around the prisoner's waist, it held his elbows firmly by his sides and secured his wrists behind his back.

The prison bell tolled with increasing rapidity as, at four minutes to the hour, Calcraft said, *follow me*, and the group of chaplains, the convict and the executioner moved towards the stairs on one side of the room, led by the chief warder and with the governor and sheriffs bringing up the rear. It reached the scaffold as the sun broke through the clouds for the first time that day. To eager cries from the crowd of *Hats off!* and *Down at the front!*, Müller mounted the steps accompanied only by Dr Cappel. Standing on the platform, he looked up at the chain hanging from the beam and moved to position himself more directly under it. The condemned on the scaffold were not allowed to make a public speech. Müller's lips quivered as

Calcraft strapped his ankles and placed the rope around his neck. Ignoring the animal force of the crowd and the savage yells that lashed the air around them, Cappel took one of his hands, touched *the stripling* tenderly on the breast and broke from his prayers to engage in urgent conversation with the young German. Calcraft pulled a hood from his pocket and fitted it tightly over Müller's face. Seconds later the hangman shuffled off to pull the lever as the booming bell of St Paul's Cathedral began to toll the hour. Standing behind the sawdust line, Dr Cappel was leaning forward with his arms outstretched as Müller's body fell.

The bells were still. The multitude momentarily fell silent, before erupting into a deafening roar.

\*

Even before *the slight, slow vibrations of the body had ended,* wrote *The Times, there was robbery and violence, loud laughing and oaths, and fighting around the gallows far and near.* The roiling mass of people soon began to disperse down wide streets and through narrow courts, swarming south in a noisy surge down Ludgate Hill, north-east to Bow and east along Cheapside and into the City. They pulled out west towards the shops and theatres or pressed along Lombard Street, passing Thomas Briggs' bank and the clerks of the Royal Exchange with their black bags and silk toppers, heading towards the Fenchurch Street terminus and the pulsing docks beyond.

Müller was dead before the majority of the country even read the news of the Home Secretary's refusal to commute his sentence in their Monday morning papers. His body was left to hang for an hour before Calcraft cut it down. Then it was pronounced dead by Mr Gibson the prison surgeon and its clothes were removed and burnt. A cast or death mask was made of Müller's head and face before his body was put in a rough deal box and scattered with wood shavings and quicklime. During the afternoon it would swiftly be interred in the presence of the governor

and undersheriffs beneath the flagstones of the corridor joining
Newgate to the Sessions House – the passage through which he
had walked at the start and end of each day of his trial.

The final columns in Müller's entry in the great leather-bound
Newgate register were completed:

> *Verdict: Guilty.*
> *Sentence: Death.*
> *How disposed of: 14th Nov. Executed.*

Most of the papers that day, their reports filed and printed hours
before the execution took place, held the view that the country
should now allow its excitement to subside and – as the *Daily
News* put it – *rest calmly in well-warranted confidence in the
established administration of justice.* By the early afternoon,
though, the second editions were enlivened by unsubstantiated
reports that Müller had, at the very last moment, confessed his
guilt.

Minutes after the drop, they wrote, Dr Cappel had retired to
the press room, where he reported to the undersheriffs the details
of the urgent conversation he had shared with Müller before
Calcraft threw the bolt. Speaking in German, Cappel had said,
*Muller, in a few moments you will stand before God. I ask you
again and for the last time, are you guilty or not guilty?*

*Not guilty.*

*You are not guilty?*

Through his white hood, Müller replied, *God knows what I
have done.*

*Does he also know that you have committed this crime?*

As Calcraft descended towards the lever, Müller spoke his last
words.

*Ja. Ich habe es gethan.* Yes. I did it.

According to Cappel, the confession so fervently desired by a
religious society who feared the damnation of eternity and who

hungered for truth had been made in the very last seconds of Müller's life. With some satisfaction, the sheriffs immediately relayed the news to Sir George Grey in Whitehall, and to Sir Richard Mayne at Scotland Yard. Returning to Müller's cell, they read through the papers he had left, expecting to find a written confession. All they found, though, were repetitions of the statements he had already made about his innocence and justifications for his possession of the watch, chain and hat. Confounded, they decided to seal up the papers and withhold their contents from the public.

Over the next few days Dr Cappel was asked repeatedly to confirm Müller's scaffold confession and did so in a letter sent to Dr Juch – the editor of the German paper the *Hermann* – that was quickly reprinted in every newspaper. It astonished readers that Müller had been able to fence with words right up to the last and some remained unconvinced, writing impassioned letters to the Home Office for governmental confirmation of Müller's exact statement.

Dr Cappel's story appeared to confirm that the right man had been killed, weakening – Grey hoped – arguments for the abolition of capital punishment. The circus of the past four months had concluded in the satisfactory manner of the sensation novels, restoring order and promising, as *Lady Audley's Secret* had done, to leave *the good people all happy and at peace.*

Franz Müller's execution certainly demonstrated that justice was guaranteed by the rule of law. The country had needed to believe that the authorities had acted swiftly and effectively in the wider interests of society. Yet when reports of the baying crowd were read to Parliament the following day, MPs angrily raised questions about the deterrent effect of hanging. Did not such devilish, barbarous scenes – such saturnalia – undermine the foundations of a tolerant and civilised society? Did execution deter, completing the inexorable cycle of crime and punishment? Did it, through violence, turn violence into order? Two men were now dead: in this cold-blooded public strangulation MPs wondered whether the State was not setting an example of the very act it abhorred. Following their lead, the *Daily Telegraph* wrote of the general *uneasiness which arises from the necessity of taking a life for a life.* The *Times* anticipated a day when some other sentence might be substituted for the crime of murder. The *Daily News* thought it a lesson to philanthropists who felt tenderness for an assassin more keenly than the victim. Over the following weekend the penny press would divide sharply into those for and against capital punishment.

Unlike the neat endings of popular novels it was apparent that retribution would never quite cauterise the fear surrounding this crime. As the *Telegraph* had put it, *this sudden and effectual attack on what had been thought an almost inviolable security of life in the midst of bustle and public companionship* continued to poison tranquillity. It powerfully suggested that evil could filter into diurnal reality as unstoppably as the evening fogs.

# AFTERWORD

## *Certainty*

Müller's trial and execution took place on the cusp of legal change. The freedom of papers to comment on pending cases continued to be bitterly resented, although, after 1865, *The Times* followed the example of the *Daily Telegraph* in making efforts to avoid pre-judgement. Judge Pollock's controversial habit of diminishing the standards of proof in his advice to juries did not survive his retirement in 1866 and the manner in which judges could advise the jury became increasingly codified, ultimately proscribing the inclusion of personal opinion.

The furore surrounding the execution played out in the press and Parliament throughout the remainder of 1864. The Royal Commission inquiring into the issues surrounding capital punishment was still sitting and, giving evidence before it, even Sir George Grey admitted that there was a growing feeling against public hanging. Müller's sentencing judge, Samuel Martin, held fervently that murder was a crime of the lower classes and he was convinced of the deterrent power of the scaffold. Müller's barrister John Humffreys Parry, on the other hand, argued strongly that convicted murderers should be imprisoned for life with hard labour and without hope of reprieve. Parry believed emphatically that this would strengthen both the State's belief in the sacredness of human life and the operation of the law. Rejecting the idea that the prospect of execution exerted a silent influence over the minds of criminals, he was convinced that by removing the revulsion that sometimes led jurors to acquit, there would be greater certainty of conviction.

When the Royal Commission reported two years later they focused on the degrading spectacle of capital punishment. Newspaper reports of Müller's execution in 1864 were re-read to Parliament along with the Commission's majority recommendation to abolish public hanging. A bill was introduced but failed. The following year, when Gathorne Hardy became Home Secretary, it was reintroduced. J. S. Mill's widely reported, scathing argument that the success of the bill would lead to the feminisation of the mind of the country assisted in its defeat, but detractors were losing ground. Twelve months later, having passed its third reading and been approved by the Lords, it was given Royal Assent on 29 May 1868. The last public hanging in Britain had taken place just days earlier: after being respited twice to afford his defence extra time to establish his alibi, Michael Barrett was hanged at Newgate on 26 May for the Fenian bombing at Clerkenwell in which seven people were killed. His hanging took place before *a wild, rough crowd* [yet] *not so numerous nor nearly so violent as that which thronged to see Müller die.*

The first hanging to take place behind prison walls was that of Thomas Wells later that same year. The executioner was Calcraft. Private execution endorsed the belief that the convicts were individuals rather than simply emblems of corruption and it had another advantage: it sanitised the mob, removing the opportunity for worryingly large, politically motivated crowds to congregate. But though *the tide of ever-advancing civilisation* encouraged the total abolition of capital punishment in Portugal in 1867, Holland and Belgium in 1870, Italy in 1872, Finland in 1874 (though the last Finnish execution had taken place in 1826) and Switzerland in 1874, British governments remained unmoved. Capital punishment was not abolished in Britain until 1964, one hundred years after Müller's death.

Further legal changes following Müller's trial included the introduction in 1865 of the first bill to grant defendants the right to testify under oath, though the principle remained unpopular in Parliament until the Criminal Evidence Act of 1898. The process of appeal for convicted prisoners was enshrined in the Criminal Appeal Act of 1907. A century would elapse before the defence were given the last word, summing up their case after the prosecution's closing argument. After various debates during the twentieth century, the duty of the Crown to disclose material in their possession that might be helpful to the defence was not made law until 1981.

Had such disclosure been a legal duty in 1864, Beard and Parry might have made more of the various statements supporting Thomas Lee's evidence that he saw two men in Briggs' carriage on the night of 9 July. Had the men seen by Lee simply changed carriages before the train pulled away from Bow? Were the corroborating statements merely phantom sightings? Would Müller have shielded an accomplice when his own life was at stake? If someone else had been involved, would Müller have fled on his own to America? The two-man theory was never taken seriously by Inspector Tanner's investigation but, because it was never satisfactorily explained, it continued to highlight the potential dangers of passengers being able to pass in and out of confined railway carriages without being noticed.

Thomas Briggs' murder contained mysteries. Nothing had struck fellow travellers as out of place in the minutes either before or during the attack. The concept of the locked-room murder would emerge regularly in the detective fiction that developed during the following decade; public outrage at the dangerous isolation of the train compartment – what the American press called *those cramped-up boxes which pass for railway carriages* – would continue to grow. Anger at government obfuscation also raged in reaction to the increasing numbers of railway accidents. Two years after the murder, in February 1866, a bill was finally presented *to compel the directors of Railway Companies to provide efficient means of communication,* but it was not until 1868 that the Regulation of Railways Act finally enforced the rule on all non-stop trains travelling more than twenty miles.

Train companies now installed a cord that ran along the outside of the train under the roof gutter, attached to a bell in the guard's van. The 'solution' was both erratic and unstable. To operate it, the passenger had to open the window (which would probably stick) and grope about to find the cord while asking a fellow passenger to take hold of his legs to prevent him falling out. If he escaped decapitation by a bridge or passing train then the cord often broke or its signal went unheard above the noise of the engine. Some companies introduced small paned windows – quickly labelled 'Müller's Lights' – into the bulkheads dividing separate carriages but they were removed just as fast when passengers quixotically complained at the lack of privacy. Not until the 1890s did the South Eastern Railway run the first corridor train *of the American pattern,* an innovation quickly imitated on the Great Western line from Paddington to Birkenhead. Even then, as the railway historian Pendleton would note, passengers were locked within their own carriage *lest the third-class passenger should take a walking tour to the first class carriage and recline on its morocco and broadcloth.* By 1899, over three decades after Thomas Briggs' death, internal wires which gradually applied the brake were adopted on the majority of the country's lines.

*

On the day of Müller's execution, the *Telegraph* wrote that *respectability demanded not a victim but the victim for this violation of its safety ... We are bound therefore to be satisfied with*

*the awful scene of this morning ... We must still think that with
the brief agony of to-day a great crime was legally expiated.*

But the murder of Thomas Briggs unleashed a fear that would
not entirely evaporate. Müller's confession only partly calmed
public anxiety for, convicted on a balance of probability, too
much remained unexplained. He had never been positively placed
at the scene of crime. The murder weapon had neither been
established nor tied to him (though, very oddly given that it had
not formed a part of his evidence in court, the Briggs' family
doctor wrote to *The Times* in the days after the execution to suggest that he thought the injuries to his patient's crown were
caused by the handles of heavy tailors' shears *held by the blades*
[to] *become a very formidable weapon*).

Although the accumulation of circumstantial evidence pointed
to no one else, the trial still drew censure. Matthews' innocence
had always been assumed and there had been no attempt to conceal his identity until he could be placed in a line-up alongside
Müller. Thomas Lee had been ignored as had new evidence in
support of an alibi. The Blyths were not asked to identify the
crushed hat and questions remained about how Müller had managed to enter a first-class carriage without remark or hindrance.
Why, too, had Parry failed to ask any of the jury before the trial
whether they had already formed an opinion of Müller's guilt?

The fact that Müller had been given the benefit of eminent
legal counsel did not stop these questions being asked nor a fes-
tering uncertainty to linger even in those who, as one
correspondent to the *Daily News* put it, had *entered into the
chase after him as eagerly as the rest and ... rejoiced as grimly as
any when he was hunted down.* Concern also centred on the
GLPS's unswerving belief in his innocence. Was it not possible
that Müller had been present in the railway carriage and that he –
alone or with another – had bungled an attempted robbery? If so,
it was possible that he was neither a murderer in cold blood nor
an innocent. Briggs may have reacted arrogantly to a poor man

entering a first-class train compartment and may thus have been an involuntary agent in his own death. The argument ran that both the defence and the prosecution had failed to differentiate between murder and manslaughter, thereby possibly depriving Müller of the only defence that might have saved his life.

Several facts support the notion that Müller did not set out to murder. Thomas Briggs' shirt was ruffled but his dress was not extremely disordered or bloodied. Müller's crushed hat suggested that the German had received at least one blow during a struggle. It is possible that, faced with being robbed, Briggs had tried to make a voluntary and hasty escape from the carriage in the hope that he could move along the footboard and get into another compartment, but that he fell and was struck by the train, accounting for the blood found on its footboard and rear wheel.

There were those who believed, as one correspondent to the *Daily News* did, *that* [Müller] *had not done a wilful murder ... for I doubt whether he ever meant to kill Mr Briggs or that he did kill him. And this I take it is the meaning of his protest after the verdict was given. He felt he was innocent in one sense.* If the hypothesis were true, and if Müller did not – at the time – realise that the old man had died, it might account for his reckless disposal of Briggs' chain at Death's in Cheapside and his cavalier wearing of the dead man's hat. It could explain his actions during the week after the murder as guileless rather than indifferent. It would also make sense of his statement that he had not been convicted on a *true statement of the facts* and would support Dr Cappel's conviction that Briggs' death was not the result of premeditated murder but rather the unhappy result of a sudden temptation to rob.

Denied the opportunity to speak in his own defence, Müller was properly protected from incriminating himself under cross-examination but he was allowed no public opportunity to explain himself. His enforced silence ensured that many crucial questions were left unanswered. Had Müller been permitted to take the stand, he might have clarified his actions and proved that the actual cause of Briggs' death was his fall from the train. It is possible that the ambiguous feelings surrounding the case were rooted in something true – that Müller was both a murderer and a victim, and that Thomas Briggs' death was manslaughter rather than murder. If so, it would mean that a defence constructed on the supposition of Müller's total innocence was, as Dr Cappel put it in his letter to *The Times*, a *frightful mistake*, since it allowed no real room for mitigating evidence to be presented.

If Müller's intention had been only to rob, rather than murder, did this account for his last-minute confession? If – like the Blyths and the Matthews – he had been unaware of the furore over Briggs' death during the six days before it hit the weekend penny newspapers, then he might have embarked for America genuinely unaware that he had killed a man. This would certainly account for his surprise when arrested and, even once the cold horror of the truth had sunk in, it might also explain his ability so right-eously to maintain his own belief in his innocence to the very last moment.

Müller may thus have deluded himself into believing that his only crime was one of theft and his sangfroid may simply have been consistent with the fact that he had not killed Thomas Briggs in cold blood. Did Dr Cappel's words on the scaffold spark a sudden, visceral fear of imminent godly retribution that allowed him, finally, to accept the truth of what he had done? Or was Müller's apparently unfathomable silence about the events a cynical attempt to escape punishment for his crime?

Müller's refusal to account for himself puzzled both the press and public and, for some, it compounded their belief that an injustice had been done. His earnest gentleness and dignity, so at odds with the audacity of the attack, was endlessly curious. Even Parry, in his evidence to the Capital Punishment Commission of 1866, said that Müller bore the disposition of being *one of the most inoffensive and harmless persons possible.* Parry went on to say that in his experience *the great majority of murders are committed by persons who were never criminals before and ... who undoubtedly have not been educated in crime.*

There were, of course, those who were unshakeably convinced of Müller's guilt, including contemporary exponents of phrenology. This 'pseudo-science' sought to prove that intellectual ability and moral character were revealed in the shape of the human skull. Frederick Bridges, a phrenologist in Liverpool, believed that the peculiar characteristics of murderers were *very remarkable and can at once be detected by any novice in phrenology.* Examining the heads of more than three hundred murderers he found that all of them, for example, had their ears very low set.

Those who flocked to see the model of Müller in Madame Tussaud's Chamber of Horrors might have noticed that the German tailor's ears were indeed set rather low. Using the death mask made by the famous phrenologist Cornelius Donovan, Frederick Bridges measured Müller's skull and features and published his own findings. He considered that *Müller's head was of the true type of the murderer and robber ... Therefore if he had not confessed to the murder it would not have had the least weight with me.* The width of his head indicated *large destructiveness, combativeness ... and secretiveness.* His *artful lying, cunning and double dealing are in keeping with the excessive development of the organ of secretiveness.* Donovan agreed: he believed that the shape of Müller's head indicated *deep craftiness ... also much covetousness of property.*

The novelist Conan Doyle also found phrenology intriguing: in the opening chapter of *The Hound of the Baskervilles* (1901–2) Dr James Mortimer admits, *you interest me very much, Mr Holmes. I had hardly expected so dolichocephalic a skull or such well-marked supra-orbital development. Would you have any objection to my running my finger along your parietal fissure? A cast of your skull, sir, until the original is available, would be an ornament to any anthropological museum. It is not my intention to be fulsome, but I confess that I covet your skull.* This fashion for a quack 'science' accounts partly, at least, for the obsessive reporting of Müller's physical appearance. When the Liverpool phrenologist Dr Bridges reported that *the head of Müller is not of the lowest criminal class and had he been placed in favourable circumstances he might never have been tempted to commit such a crime*, desperate for anything that 'explained' the Müller conundrum, the public lapped it up.

*

When it learned of Müller's arrest in New York, *The Times* had comforted its readers that the modern technologies of steampower, photography and the electric cable had each played a triumphant part in the detection of crime. Countering fears that invention and progress were – as so many people feared – undermining civilisation, the paper suggested that – on the contrary – they made the world a safer place. No community could now feel itself to be isolated; the very speed of communication would conquer crime.

Over the ensuing decades, tests would be developed accurately to identify human blood (and, later, to 'type' it), fingerprints would point to the identity of criminals, and forensic pathologists would begin to piece together the truth from the microscopic clues found at crime scenes, from blood-spatter patterns, drug traces, footprints and the absolute angle of wounds. The wireless cable would ultimately halt the flight of the murderous Dr Hawley Harvey Crippen and his lover Ethel Neave in 1910 by allowing their ship's captain to telegraph his suspicions about the couple to the detectives on dry land. Well before that, by the end of the 1860s the vogue for sensation novels would develop into a passion for literary detection. These professional sleuths would harness scientific advance to sharp cunning and logical deduction, holding out the promise of solid 'proof' and observable, rigorous truth.

*

As to the reward, Jonathan Matthews' creditors learned that he was likely to receive the entire three hundred pounds and contrived to have him confined to Horsemonger Lane debtors' gaol. In the spring of 1865, after months of legal consideration by Treasury counsel, it was judged that John Death's evidence was given before the reward was offered and that the Blyths had answered police questions rather than come forward voluntarily. As a result, Matthews did receive the full three hundred pounds reward but, as he had once publicly speculated, most of it was swallowed up by debts and he enjoyed only fifty pounds of it. In an odd twist of fate, it so happened that Matthews' creditors were legally represented by Müller's solicitor, Thomas Beard.

In 1865 Müller's friend John Hoffa married Jane, a general servant in Threadneedle Street. He remained a tailor all his life.

Although it was said that Müller wrote to his father from Newgate and received replies from him, their contents were never made public and nothing more was ever discovered about the tailor's family in Germany nor of their reaction to his conviction. In April 1865 Müller's father was still quietly petitioning the Home Office for the return of the statement written by his son on the Saturday before his execution. The sister Müller claimed to have in New York never appeared and the woman in London who claimed to be a sister, Sophia Pearson, disappeared from record in the years following his execution. A man supposed to be a younger brother, Ferdinand, about whom nothing was heard at the time of the trial, died in March 1905: his body was found in the garden of his lodging house at 6 Park Terrace, East Finchley, London – an address remarkably similar and not so far away from where Franz once lodged with the Blyths. All in all, the Müller family remained as unknown to the British public as the Briggs family in suburban Hackney.

Particular in his own dress, it might have appealed to Müller's vanity that the low-crowned topper – also known as the Müller cut-down – became a popular style with young men throughout the 1870s, lasting well into the twentieth century. It was most notably favoured by the future Prime Minister, Winston Churchill.

*

The promising career of Inspector Richard Tanner, whose name after Müller's arrest become a byword for a new breed of detective, was cut prematurely short. In 1866 he investigated the famous Duddlewick Murder, in which John Meredith was acquitted at trial of murdering his nephew Edward. It was Tanner's last major case. Within three years, aged just thirty-seven, he was forced to retire from the Metropolitan Police with crippling rheumatism. He died of a stroke in 1873, not quite forty-two years old.

*

Does technological progress come at a price? How should a nation priding itself on its morality and civilisation deal with threats to the safety of its citizens? How can it best assimilate and behave towards foreign nationals drawn by the opportunities vested in its advanced wealth and liberal values? These were all questions loosed from the Pandora's Box of the British psyche by the train murder of 1864 and they accounted, in part, for the overwhelming public reaction to the crime.

The problem with the murder of Thomas Briggs was that no one would ever know the truth about what happened between Briggs and Müller on the night of 9 July. The struggle between a poor German artisan and a silk-hatted English banker bound preconceptions about the poor to a fear of foreigners in an incendiary combination. More to the point, the crime burst out of the usual backstreet or domestic loci to strike at all the middle classes held dear, temporarily, changing everything and everyone, trouncing peace of mind.

Though no further killing would occur on a British train until 27 June 1881, the bludgeoning of Thomas Briggs in his first-class train compartment appeared symptomatic of a world spinning out of control. It seemed to prove the ability of the disenchanted individual to wreak havoc on the national sense of security and to signify that danger was random. The fact that the attack occurred on a railway train emphasised a terrifying new reality: that technological cleverness had spawned progress and wealth, but at a cost. It suggested that the price to be paid for modernity was, even for the most privileged in society, vulnerability and death.

# *People*

| | |
|---|---|
| Adams, Charles | American Minister at the Court of St James's, London |
| Ames, Benjamin | Train guard, North London Railway |
| | |
| Ballantine, Serjeant William | Prosecution Barrister |
| Battiscombe, Reverend | Prison visitor |
| Beard, Thomas | Solicitor to the German Legal Protection Society, London |
| Blankman, Edmond | Co-Counsel for the Defence in the American extradition hearing |
| Blyth, Ellen | Landlady, 16 Park Terrace, Old Ford, Bow |
| Blyth, George | Husband of Ellen Blyth, City messenger |
| Brereton, Dr Alfred | Bow Road doctor |
| Briggs, Thomas | Chief Bank Clerk, Robarts, Curtis & Co., of Clapton Square, Hackney |
| Briggs, Thomas James | Second son of the above |
| Buchan, Caroline | Thomas Briggs' niece, of Peckham |
| Buchan, David | Husband of Caroline Buchan, warehouseman |

| | |
|---|---|
| Calcraft, William | London's public executioner |
| Cappel, Dr Louis | Minister of the German Lutheran Church, Alie Street |
| Clarke, George | Police sergeant, Metropolitan Police, Scotland Yard |
| Collier, Sir Robert | Solicitor General |
| Davis, Reverend | Newgate prison Ordinary |
| Death, John | Jeweller, 55 Cheapside |
| Death, Robert | Brother of the above, and his assistant |
| Digance, Daniel | Briggs' hatter, Royal Exchange |
| Dougan, Edward | Police constable, Metropolitan Police, K Division |
| Edwards, Pierrepont | Acting British consul, New York |
| Ekin, Alfred | Engine driver, North London Railway |
| Eldred, Mary Anne | Prostitute, Camberwell |
| Fishbourne, Thomas | Ticket collector, Fenchurch Street Station |
| Flowers, Mr | Magistrate, Bow Street Court |
| Foreman, Charles | Omnibus conductor |
| Giffard, Hardinge | Junior member of the prosecution team |
| Gifford, James | Shipping agent, London docks |
| Glass, John Henry | Journeyman tailor at Hodgkinson's, City |
| Greenwood, George | Superintendent, Chalk Farm Station |
| Grey, Sir George | Home Secretary |
| Henry, Thomas | Chief magistrate, Bow Street Police Court |

| | |
|---|---|
| Hoffa, John | Journeyman tailor at Hodgkinson's, City; friend of Müller |
| Howie, Daniel | Superintendent, Metropolitan Police, K Division |
| Humphreys, John | Coroner for East Middlesex |
| Jones, Elizabeth | Brothel keeper |
| Jones, Sydney | Bank clerk, Robarts, Curtis & Co., City |
| Judd, Charles | Suspect in the Briggs case |
| Kennedy, John | Chief of the New York Metropolitan Police |
| Kerressey, Walter | Detective Inspector, Metropolitan Police, K Division |
| Lambert, Lewis | Policeman K311, Metropolitan Police, K Division |
| Lee, Thomas | Acquaintance of Thomas Briggs; key witness at trial |
| Letheby, Dr Henry | Professor of Chemistry, London |
| Marbury, Francis | Counsel to the British Consulate, New York |
| Martin, Samuel | Trial judge |
| Matthews, Eliza | Wife of Jonathan Matthews |
| Matthews, Jonathan | London cab driver |
| Mayne, Sir Richard | Commissioner of the Metropolitan Police |
| Müller, Franz | German tailor |
| Murray, Robert | US Marshal |
| Newton, Chas | United States Commissioner, New York |

Parry, Serjeant John Humffreys    Defence Barrister
Pearson, Sophia                   Franz Müller's sister in London
Pollock, Frederick                Lord Chief Baron; trial judge

Repsch, Elizabeth                 Wife of Godfrey Repsch
Repsch, Godfrey                   Tailor, Old Jewry, City

Shaffer, Chauncey                 Counsel for the Defence,
                                  American extradition hearing
Steer, Thomas                     Detective Inspector, Metropolitan
                                  Police, D Division

Tanner, Richard                   Detective Inspector, Metropolitan
                                  Police, Scotland Yard
Taylor, Professor Alfred          Professor of Chemistry, Guy's
                                  Hospital, London
Thorne, Frederick                 Daniel Digance's hatmaker
Tiddey, William Ninnis            Superintendent, Metropolitan
                                  Police, D Division
Tieman, John Charles              Officer, New York Police
                                  Department
Timms, William                    Train guard, North London
                                  Railway
Toulmin, Dr Francis               Thomas Briggs' doctor

Vernez, Harry                     Bank clerk, Robarts, Curtis & Co.,
                                  City

Weist, Jacob                      Porter, London docks
Williamson, Frederick             Detective Inspector, Metropolitan
                                  Police, Scotland Yard
Woodward, Alfred                  Clerk, Electric and International
                                  Telegraph Company

# Select Bibliography

## ARCHIVES

*The National Archives, Kew*

CRIM 4/681
CRIM 5/4
CRIM 6/11
CRIM 10/53
HO 12/152/63401
HO 13/108
HO 14/24
HO 14/25
HO 45/681
HO 45/7078
HO 46/32
HO 46/33
HO 65/25
MEPO 3/75
MEPO 3/76
MEPO 7/25
PCOM 2/215
RAIL 529/113

*London Metropolitan Archives*: 1862 Weekly Dispatch Map
*London Transport Museum*: The Reinhohl Collection, Album 2
*American National Archives, College Park, Maryland*: US extradition file. Record Group 59: General Records of the Department of State 1789–2002, American National Archives, Franz Müller 1864, Loc. 250/48/9/7, Box 2
*The Metropolitan Police Historic Store*: Richard Tanner's notebook, 'Prisoners apprehended July 1856 to 1867'


WEBSITES

www.archive.org/details/trialoffranzmull025046mbp
http://hansard.millbanksystems.com/
http://archivemaps.com/mapco/london.htm
www.british-history.ac.uk
www.eh.net
http://newspapers.bl.uk/blcs/

## NEWSPAPERS, MAGAZINES AND JOURNALS

*Annual Register*, 1864
*Blackwood's Edinburgh Magazine*
*Cornhill Magazine*
*Daily Telegraph*
*The Era*
*Fraser's Magazine*
*Illustrated London News*
*Lloyd's Weekly Newspaper*
*New York Herald*
*New York Times*
*Phrenological Journal*
*Quarterly Review*
*Reynolds's Weekly Newspaper*
*The Times*
*The Spectator*
Other UK national and regional newspapers: British Library
   Newspaper Store, Colindale

## PUBLISHED BOOKS AND ARTICLES

Execution broadside: *Müller's Hanging* (London: Catnach Press,
   1864)
*Bradshaw's Railway Guide* (1864)
*The Post Office London Directory* (London: Kelly & Co., 1864)
*The Queen's London, A Pictorial and Descriptive Record of the
   Streets, Buildings, Parks and Scenery of the Great Metropolis*
   (London: Cassell, 1896)
*Report of the Royal Commission on Capital Punishment, Together
   with the Minutes of Evidence and Appendix* (London: Her
   Majesty's Stationery Office, 1866)
Abrahamsen, David, *The Murdering Mind* (London: HarperCollins,
   1973)

Alderman, Geoffrey and Colin Holmes (ed.), *Outsiders and Outcasts: Essays in Honour of William J. Fishman* (London: Duckworth, 1993)

Altick, Richard D., *Evil Encounters: Two Victorian Sensations* (London: John Murray, 1987)

——————, *Victorian Studies in Scarlet* (London: Dent, 1972)

Anonymous, 'Our Female Sensation Novelists', *Christian Remembrancer*, 46, 1864, 209–36

Ashton, Rosemary, *Little Germany: Exile and Asylum in Victorian Britain* (Oxford: Oxford University Press, 1986)

Aspland, Robert, *An Oration Delivered on Monday, October 16, on Laying the First Stone of the New Gravel-Pit Meeting-House in Paradise Field, Hackney* (Harlow: Longman, Hurst et al, 1809)

Ballantine, William, *Some Experiences of a Barrister's Life* (London: R. Bentley & Son, 1882)

Bartlett, David W., *London by Day and Night; or, Men and Things in the Great Metropolis* (London: n.p., 1852)

Begg, Paul and Keith Skinner, *The Scotland Yard Files: 150 Years of the CID* (London: Headline, 1992)

Bentley, David, *English Criminal Justice in the Nineteenth Century* (London: Hambledon, 1998)

Best, William Mawdesley, *A Treatise on Presumptions of Law and Fact* (London: Sweet, 1844)

Bleackley, Horace, *The Hangmen of England: How They Hanged and Whom They Hanged – The Life Story of 'Jack Ketch' Through Two Centuries* (London: Chapman & Hall, 1929)

Block, Brian P. and John Hostettler, *Hanging in the Balance: A History of the Abolition of Capital Punishment in Britain* (Winchester, Waterside Press, 1997)

Booth, Charles (ed.), *Life and Labour of the People* (London: Macmillan, 1889)

Boyle, Thomas, *Black Swine in the Sewers of Hampstead: Beneath the Surface of Victorian Sensationalism* (New York: Viking, 1988)

Braddon, Mary Elizabeth, *Aurora Floyd* (1863; Oxford: Oxford University Press, 1996)

——————, *Lady Audley's Secret* (1862; London: Wordsworth Editions, 1995)

Brantlinger, Patrick, 'What is "Sensational" about the "Sensation Novel"?', *Nineteenth Century Fiction*, 37, 1982, 1–28.

Browne, Douglas G., *The Rise of Scotland Yard: A History of the Metropolitan Police* (London: Harrap, 1956)

Cavanagh, Timothy, *Scotland Yard Past and Present* (London: Chatto, 1893)

Cobb, Belton, *Critical Years at the Yard: The Career of Frederick Williamson of the Detective Department and the CID* (London: Faber & Faber, 1956)

Collins, Philip, *Dickens and Crime* (London: Macmillan, 1962)

Collins, Wilkie, *The Woman in White* (1860; Oxford: Oxford University Press, 1996)

Cook, Tony and Andy Tattersall, *Blackstone's Senior Investigating Officers' Handbook* (Oxford: Oxford University Press, 2008)

Costello, Augustine E., *Our Police Protectors: History of the New York Police from the Earliest Period to the Present Time* (1885; Montclair: Patterson Smith, 1972)

Cunningham, Peter, *A Hand-book of London: Past and Present* (London: John Murray, 1849)

Cunnington, C. Willet and Phillis, *Handbook of English Costume in the Nineteenth Century* (London: Faber & Faber, third edition, 1970)

Dickens, Charles, *American Notes* (London: Chapman & Hall, 1842)

——————, 'Cab', *All the Year Round*, 25 February 1860, 414–16

——————, *David Copperfield* (1849–50; Oxford: Oxford University Press, 2000)

——————, *Dickens' London: An Imaginative Vision*, ed. Peter Ackroyd (London: Headline, 1987)

——————, *Dombey and Son* (1846–8)

————, *The Letters of Charles Dickens*, gen. ed. Madeline House and Graham Storey, 12 vols (Oxford: Oxford University Press, 1965–2002)

————, *The Pickwick Papers* (1836–7; Oxford: Oxford University Press, 1961)

————, *Selected Letters*, ed. David Paroissien (Oxford: Clarendon Press, 1981)

————, *Sketches by 'Boz'* (London: Chapman & Hall, 1836)

Dickens, Charles, Jr., *Dickens' Dictionary of London: An Unconventional Handbook* (London: Charles Dickens and Evans, 1897)

Donovan, C., *A Handbook of Phrenology* (London: Longmans, Green, Reader and Dyer, 1870)

Du Cane, Sir Edmund, *The Punishment and Prevention of Crime* (London: Macmillan, 1885)

Evans, Colin, *The Father of Forensics: How Sir Bernard Spilsbury Invented Modern CSI* (Thriplow: Icon, 2007)

Faust, Drew Gilpin, *The Republic of Suffering: Death and the American Civil War* (New York: Knopf, 2008)

Flanders, Judith, *Consuming Passions: Leisure and Pleasure in Victorian Britain* (London: HarperPress, 2006)

————, *The Victorian House: Domestic Life from Childbirth to Deathbed* (London: HarperCollins, 2003)

Frank, Lawrence, *Victorian Detective Fiction and the Nature of Evidence: The Scientific Investigations of Poe, Dickens and Doyle* (Basingstoke: Palgrave Macmillan, 2003)

Gatrell, V. A. C., *The Hanging Tree: Execution and the English People, 1770–1868* (Oxford: Oxford University Press, 1994)

Griffiths, Arthur, *The Chronicles of Newgate* (London: Chapman & Hall, 1884)

————, *Mysteries of Police and Crime: A General Survey of Wrongdoing and its Pursuit* (London: Cassell, 1898)

Hansard, *Report: Select Committee (Guards and Passengers Communication)* (1867)

Hamilton, Nicholas et al., *National Gazetteer of Great Britain and Ireland* (Virtue & Co., 1868)

Harrington, Ralph, 'The Neuroses of the Railway', *History Today*, vol. 44, no. 7, July 1994, 15–21

Hill, Frederic, *The Substitute for Capital Punishment* (London, 1886)

Hindley, Charles, *The History of the Catnach Press: At Berwick-upon-Tweed, Alnwick and Newcastle-upon-Tyne in Northumberland, and Seven Dials, London* (London: Catnach Press, 1886)

Holt Hutton, Richard, Review of *East Lynne*, *Spectator*, 28 September 1861, 1068–9

Hooper, William, *Central Criminal Court of London* (London: Spottiswoode, 1909)

Hughes, Winifred, *The Maniac in the Cellar: Sensation Novels of the 1860s* (Princeton: Princeton University Press, 1980)

Irving, H. B. (ed.), *The Trial of Franz Müller* (London: W. Hodge, 1911)

Irving, Joseph, *The Annals of Our Time* (London: n.p., 1869)

James, Henry, 'Miss Braddon', *The Nation*, 9 November 1865, 59

Kingston, Charles, *Famous Judges and Famous Trials* (London: Paul & Co., 1923)

Lankevich, George J., *American Metropolis: A History of New York City* (New York: New York University Press, 1998)

Lattek, Christine, *Revolutionary Refugees: German Socialism in Britain, 1840–1860* (London: Routledge, 2006)

Laurence, John, *A History of Capital Punishment: With Special Reference to Capital Punishment in Great Britain* (London: Sampson Low, Marston & Co., 1932)

Lock, Joan, *Dreadful Deeds and Awful Murders: Scotland Yard's First Detectives 1829–1878* (Taunton: Barn Owl Books, 1990)

Mansel, Henry, 'Sensation Novels', *Quarterly Review*, 113, April 1863, 482–502

Maunder, Andrew (ed.), *Varieties of Women's Sensation Fiction 1855–1890*, 6 vols (London: Pickering & Chatto, vol. 1, 2004)

May, Allyson N., *The Bar and the Old Bailey 1750–1850* (Chapel Hill: University of North Carolina Press, 2003)

Mayhew, Henry, *London Labour and the London Poor* (London: n.p., 1851, vols 1 and 3)

———— and John Binny, *The Criminal Prisons of London and Scenes of Prison Life* (London: Griffin, Bohn & Co., 1862)

Miller, James, *Miller's New York As It Is, or Stranger's Guide-Book to the Cities of New York, Brooklyn, and Adjacent Places* (London: n.p., 1862)

Miller, Thomas, *Picturesque Sketches of London: Past and Present* (London: Office of the National Illustrated Library, 1852)

Miller, Wilbur R., *Cops and Bobbies: Police Authority in New York and London 1830–1870* (Chicago: University of Chicago Press, 1977)

Mogg, Edward, *Mogg's Handbook for Railway Travellers* (London: Spottiswoode, 1846)

Oliphant, Margaret, 'Sensation Novels', *Blackwood's Edinburgh Magazine*, 1, May 1862, 567

Panayi, Panikos (ed.), *Germans in Britain since 1500* (London: Hambledon, 1996)

Pendleton, John, *Our Railways* (London: Cassell, 1894)

Pykett, Lyn, *The Sensation Novel: From The Woman in White to The Moonstone* (Plymouth: Northcote House, 1994)

Rae, W. Fraser, 'Sensation Novelists: Mrs Braddon', *North British Review*, 43, 1865, pp. 180–204

Ransom, P. J. G., *The Victorian Railway and How it Evolved* (London: Heinemann, 1990)

Richardson, James (gen. ed.), *Archbold: Criminal Pleading, Evidence and Practice in Criminal Cases* (London: Sweet & Maxwell, 1991)

Robbins, Michael, *The North London Railway* (Chislehurst: Oakwood Press, 1946)

Ruston, Alan R., *Unitarianism and Early Presbyterianism in Hackney* (Watford: Oxhay, 1980)

Schivelbusch, Wolfgang, *The Railway Journey: The Industrialization of Time and Space in the Nineteenth Century* (Berkeley: University of California Press, 1986)

Schlesinger, Max, *Saunterings In and About London* (London: Nathaniel Cooke, 1853)

Schmiechen, James A., *Sweated Industries and Sweated Labor: The London Clothing Trades 1860–1914* (London: Croom Helm, 1984)

Sims, G. R. (ed.), *Living London, Its Work and Its Play, Its Humour and Its Pathos* (London: Cassell, 1901–3)

Smith, Roger, *Trial by Medicine: Insanity and Responsibility in Victorian Trials* (Edinburgh: Edinburgh University Press, 1981)

Smullen, Ivor, *Taken for a Ride: A Distressing Account of the Misfortunes and Misbehaviour of the Early British Railway Traveller* (London: Barrie & Jenkins, 1968)

Spence, Jeoffry, *Victorian and Edwardian Railway Travel from Old Photographs* (London: Fitzhouse, 1977)

Stephen, James Fitzjames, *A History of the Criminal Law of England* (London: Macmillan, 1883)

———, *A General View of the Criminal Law in England* (London: Macmillan, 1863)

Sweet, Matthew, *Inventing the Victorians* (London: Faber, 2001)

Thackeray, William Makepeace, *The Paris Sketch Book* (London: Smith, Elder & Co., 1879)

———, 'Going to see a Man Hanged', *Complete Works*, vol. 3, 1898

Thesing, William (ed.), *Executions and the British Experience from the Seventeenth to the Twentieth Century: A Collection of Essays* (London: McFarland, 1990)

Tidy, Charles Meymott, *Legal Medicine*, 2 vols (New York: William Wood, 1882)

Wagner, E. J., *The Science of Sherlock Holmes: From Baskerville Hall to the Valley of Fear, The Real Forensics Behind the Great Detective's Greatest Cases* (London: Wiley & Sons, 2006)

'Waters' (William Russell), *Recollections of a Detective Police-Officer* (London: J. C. Brown & Co., 1856)

Wiener, Martin J., 'The Sad Story of George Hall: Adultery, Murder and the Politics of Mercy in Mid-Victorian England', *Social History Journal*, vol. 24, issue 2, May 1999

White, Jerry, *London in the Nineteenth Century: 'A Human Awful Wonder of God'* (London: Jonathan Cape, 2007)

Whitehead, James, *Historical Sketch of the Congregation of New Gravel Pit Church* (London, 1909)

Wilson, A. N., *The Victorians* (London: Hutchinson, 2002)

Wood, Ellen, *East Lynne*, ed. Andrew Maunder (1861; Toronto: Broadview Editions, 2000)

# Acknowledgements

Without access to and the help of staff at the British Library in St Pancras, the British Library Newspaper Reading Room in Colindale and the National Archives in Kew, this book could not have been written. Additionally, I have been generously helped by, and would like to thank: Professor Michael Lobban at the School of Law, Queen Mary, University of London; Richard Ireland, Senior Lecturer, Department of Law and Criminology, University of Aberystwyth; Professor Martin Wiener, Chair of History, Rice University, Houston, USA; Chief Superintendent Hamish Campbell and Detective Inspector Nick Sumner of the Metropolitan Police at New Scotland Yard; Alan McCormick, Curator of the Police ('Black') Museum at New Scotland Yard; Paul Dew, Metropolitan Police Historic Store; Julianne Young, Property Services Department at the Metropolitan Police; Sally England at Hackney Archives; Bridget Howlett, Senior Archivist and Doug Bertram, Image and Design at the London Metropolitan Archives; Glyn Hughes at the Meteorological Archives in Exeter; Julia Collins at Madame Tussaud's Archive; Margaret Donnelly, owner of the Top o' the Morning Pub (formerly the Mitford Castle); Sue Hill and John Beasley of the Peckham Society; Beth Spinelli at the New York City Police

Museum; Alan Moss at historybytheyard.co.uk; The London Theatre Museum enquiries service; the Guildhall Library; Judith Flanders; Peter Thorpe at the National Railway Museum, York; Caroline Warhurst at the London Transport Museum; Stephen Grosz for sharing his insights into the criminal mind.

Hackney-born Colin Mansel, erstwhile chairman of the North London Railway Society, was my guide as we retraced Thomas Briggs' railway journeys and explored Hackney and Old Ford. He has helped to make these places come alive while sharing his own research, unpicking genealogical conundrums and checking facts. I could not be more grateful for his immeasurable generosity.

Thank you to my friends: Peter Straus who suggested I look at the story; Andrea Wulf for helping with German; Joel Rose for his advice on aspects of New York history; Paul Sidey for reading the manuscript in its earliest stages, and David Miller, Lawrence Norfolk, Kate Summerscale and Frank Wynne for so incisively commenting on the first completed draft.

My inestimable agent, Caroline Dawnay at United Agents, my publisher David Shelley and his team at Little, Brown – including the perspicacious Zoe Gullen – and Aaron Schlechter, at The Overlook Press in New York, have all been endlessly clever as well as companionable supports.

Finally, as always, to two fantastic boys and one admirable man – Freddie, Bill and David – my thanks and love.

# Notes

## PROLOGUE: AN EMPTY RAILWAY CARRIAGE

1 **suburb of Chalk Farm:** Now Primrose Hill Station (renamed September 1950).

1 **speeds of 25 mph:** *Liverpool Mercury*, 12 July 1864, p. 7 col. e.

1 **exact time they pulled out of each station:** For stations on the line and the times between them, see also Bradshaw's timetables for 1864.

2 **The first thing he saw:** The description of the carriage is taken from Ames' first and second Bow Street warrants (copies in extradition proceedings), from the court transcript of the Central Criminal Court and from *The Times*, 12 July 1864, p. 11 col. c.

## CHAPTER 1: ALL HUMAN LIFE IS HERE

9 **a madman's toy:** Pendleton, *Our Railways*, p. 7.

9 **broadened the horizons:** As H. G. Wells later remarked, the steam engine on its tracks was the most iconic symbol of Victoria's reign.

9 **Tracks ran over rivers:** Pendleton, op. cit., p. 15.

10 **250 million passenger journeys:** Flanders, *Consuming Passions*, p. 187 ff.

10 **speed as the new principle:** Schivelbusch, *The Railway Journey*, foreword.

10 *the scorn of the punctual*: Pendleton, op. cit., introduction, p. viii.

10 *indispensable agent*: Ibid.

11 **fragility and helplessness of human life:** Harrington, 'The Neuroses of the Railway', *History Today*, vol. 44, no. 7, 1994.

11 *uneasiness ... amounting to actual fear*: Schivelbusch, op. cit. Also Harrington, op. cit.

12 *the triumphant monster, Death*: Dickens, *Dombey and Son*, chapter 20. The train as a visible expression of destruction and trauma was beginning to pervade the work of writers across the developed world – think, too, of Tolstoy's *Anna Karenina* (1873–7) where it partly symbolises all that is new and damaging, the sweeping away of an old order and, ultimately, of Anna's life.

12 **legally responsible for the safety**: Hansard, 12 March 1861. Mr Haliburton to Milner Gibson.

12 **Victorian trains were fairly safe and reliable**: <www.york.ac.uk/inst/irs/irshome/papers/rlyacc.htm>

## CHAPTER 2: SATURDAY 9 JULY 1864

13 **five feet nine**: Some reports from doctors say 5' 8". David Buchan at trial says 5' 9". A later letter (8 October 1864) in *Jackson's Oxford Journal* states that Briggs was under 11 stone.

14 **a decade old**: The East and West India Docks and Birmingham Junction Railway received Royal Assent in August 1846 and opened for passenger traffic in September 1850. It became the NLR at the start of 1853.

14 **first-class ticket**: NLR had no third class until the mid-1870s. Briggs was regularly described as a season-ticket holder which would have cost ten guineas a year. See Robbins, *The North London Railway*.

14 **soot that streamed from its chimneys**: Advice to passengers in *Mogg's Handbook for Railway Travellers*, 1846.

14 **watercress fields receded**: *National Gazetteer*, 1863.

14 **Bryant & May match factory**: The factory at which Annie Besant sparked the match-girls' strike of 1888, protesting against the use of toxic yellow phosphorus in matches.

15 **fog of industrial smoke**: Mayhew and Binny, *The Criminal Prisons of London*, pp. 3–8.

16 **Cheapside ... St Paul's**: Mayhew and Binny wrote in 1862 *of the incessant strugglings and chafings of the distant tides ... all the petty jealousies, and heart-burnings, small ambitions and vain parade of 'polite society' ... a strange incongruous chaos of the most astounding riches and prodigious poverty, of feverish ambition and apathetic despair, of the brightest charity and the darkest crime ... the scene of countless daily struggles, failures and successes.* The *Criminal Prisons of London*, pp. 9 and 18. Contemporary descriptions of St Paul's and the city are partly informed by Miller's

*Picturesque Sketches*. See also Mayhew, *London Labour and the London Poor*.

16  **horse-drawn omnibuses:** These packed public London 'buses carried an estimated one million passengers a day to and from the suburbs for the single fixed fare of sixpence. 'Outsides' would climb up an iron ladder to the roof, and women, children and the elderly crammed inside on five-a-side seats, jolted together, watchful for fleas in the straw-covered floor, amused or intimidated by the busy top-hatted conductor who touted energetically for business.

16  **King William Street:** Briggs' omnibus route from David Buchan's trial testimony. General omnibus routes: see the Reinhohl Collection at the London Transport Museum, particularly album 2, pp. 41–4, for records of horse-drawn routes from Dulwich to the City via Camberwell, and Peckham to the City via Gracechurch Street. For descriptions and numbers of cabs, see Mayhew, op. cit., p. 353 ff.

16  **He paid sixpence:** Flanders, *The Victorian House*, p. 361, also White, *London in the Nineteenth Century*, p. 76 ff.

16  **almost exactly at five o'clock:** Details from David Buchan's testimony at trial.

17  **said goodnight:** *The Times*, 19 July 1864, p. 7 col. c.

17  **a few minutes behind time:** Ibid.

17  **cane and bag on the seat beside him:** According to evidence of Thomas Lee given at Bow, 22 July 1864 (US extradition papers).

## CHAPTER 3: THE DUCKETT'S CANAL BRIDGE

18  **Edward Dougan, Policeman 71:** Number from trial transcript, Central Criminal Court.

18  **Mitford Castle:** Now the Top o' the Morning, in renamed Cadogan Terrace, Victoria Park.

19  **The dark-suited body was twisted:** Inquest report, *The Times*, 19 July 1864, p. 7 col. c.

20  **William Timms at his side:** Ordinarily Timms would have been expected to rejoin his train but it was widely reported that he stayed by Briggs' side.

21  **half a first-class return train ticket:** It is odd that half a ticket was found on Briggs as he was widely reported as holding a season ticket. It is possible that paper tickets were also issued in order to count passenger numbers in the Victorian bureaucratic system but it has proved impossible to substantiate this.

21  **a diamond ring:** Description of what Dougan found on the body from Bow warrants.

22 **Passing behind the pub:** All the early reports record that carriage 69 was locked at Bow. Later reports in September (e.g. *The Times*, 25 September 1864, p. 7 col. f) contradict this, stating that the carriage was kept at Chalk Farm at the other end of the line, though it seems clear that this was a mistake.

21 **uncoupled from the rest of the train:** Ames' testimony, also Kerressey and the Solicitor General. See also *The Times*, 11 July 1864, p. 9 col. a. Some reports suggest that the carriage was uncoupled at Bow, having been sent down the line attached to the rest of its empty train. Most, however, state that it was uncoupled at Chalk Farm.

22 **staying well past the time:** Although it was well past closing time, all local reports agree that the crowd at the pub refused to leave until the early hours of 10 July.

23 **head-first:** *Liverpool Mercury*, 13 July 1864, p. 7 col. d.

24 **Bow Division:** Bow, or K Division. When the Metropolitan Police were formed there were originally six separate divisions, soon enlarged to seventeen and then, in the mid-1860s, to twenty. They were identified by alphabetical numbers so that A, closest to Scotland Yard, was the Whitehall Division and Y was Highgate. See Browne, *The Rise of Scotland Yard*.

24 **over three hundred police constables:** MEPO, Police Order Books for the end of 1864, showing the numbers of police in divisions across London. Totals were: 130 first-class sergeants, 500 first-class constables, 2700 second-class constables and 700 third-class.

24 **no blood on Briggs' bruised hands:** *Daily Telegraph*, 25 September 1864, p. 5 col. e.

## CHAPTER 4: FERRETING FOR DETAIL

27 **he was dictatorial:** Cavanagh, *Scotland Yard Past and Present*, p. 74 ff. See also Browne, *The Rise of Scotland Yard*, p. 130 ff.

27 **fanatical about minutiae:** MEPO 7/25, Police Order Books.

27 **'brilliant':** Browne, op. cit., p. 166.

27 **Five foot seven:** Extradition proceedings evidence.

27 **the Chief Office:** Right in the heart of government at Whitehall, Scotland Yard took its popular name from this rear entry used initially only by visitors to the Commissioners.

29 **1434 yards:** Trial evidence of Edward Dougan.

29 **three and a half minutes:** Times from Ames' deposition at Bow.

29 **almost five pounds:** Dougan had found: in the man's left-hand trouser pocket, four sovereigns. In his right pocket, eight shillings and sixpence in silver and copper. In the left-hand pocket of his waistcoat was a florin (a two-shilling piece).

30 **cross to the opposite track:** Report on inquest, *The Times*, 19 July 1864, p. 7 col. c.

30 **Henry Lubbock ... visited:** MEPO 3/75.


CHAPTER 5: MORBID, HIDEOUS AND DELICIOUS

32 *Atrocious Murder*: *Daily News*, 11 July 1864, p. 4 col. a.

33 **Some wondered:** *Observer*, e.g. 17 July 1864, p. 7. Also the *Hull Packet and East Riding Times*, 22 July 1864, p. 3 col. e.

33 **a robbery on the same spot:** For example, *Daily Telegraph*, 15 July 1864, p. 6 col. a.

33 *instituting every possible inquiry*: *The Times*, 11 July 1864, p. 9 col. a.

33 *Mr Briggs' hat in mistake*: *Daily News*, 11 July 1864, p. 4 col. a.

34 *morbid, hideous and delicious*: Braddon, *Aurora Floyd*, p. 52, and *Lady Audley's Secret*, p. 319.

34 **cracks within the Victorian ideal:** Pykett, *The Sensation Novel*, p. 69.

34 *drug our thought and reason*: 'Our Female Sensation Novelists', *Christian Remembrancer*, 46, 1864.

34 *abominations of the age*: W. Fraser Rae, 'Sensation Novelists: Miss Braddon', *North British Review*, 43, 1865, pp. 180–204. Oliphant, 'Sensation Novels', *Blackwood's Edinburgh Magazine*, 1, May 1862.

35 *wander further afield*: *Spectator*, 28 September 1861, pp. 1068–9.

36 *the sense of insecurity evidently felt*: Hansard, 9 May 1865.


CHAPTER 6: THE SMILING FACE OF A MURDERER

37 **One delivered to Scotland Yard:** MEPO 3/75.

37 *known to be guilty of the darkest deeds*: Ibid.

39 **avoiding the light from the windows:** For example, *Observer*, 17 July 1864, p. 7.

39 **able to give a detailed description:** Robert Death's deposition, second Bow warrants.

40 **It appeared even to be smiling:** *Shoreditch Advertiser*, 16 July 1864, p. 2 col. f.

40 **thirteen local men:** The final inquest certificate (CRIM 41/681) lists the jurors' names: James Whelan, William Thomas Dennis, Thomas Grills, Charles William Felgate, William Dunk, Benjamin Franklin, Thomas Hudson, Alphonso Ker, Edwin William Woods, James Osborne, Charles King, James Lee and Henry Benjamin Savage.

40 *great surprise has been expressed*: *The Times*, 12 July 1864, p. 11 col. c.

40 **Briggs' black bag:** Ibid.

40 *something like those worn by foreigners*: Liverpool Mercury, 12 July 1864, p. 7 col. f.

41 *we may walk unconsciously*: Braddon, *Lady Audley's Secret*, p. 113.

41 the *Daily Telegraph*: The paper first appeared 1856 and within three years was outselling *The Times*, with a circulation of over 141,000 against its rival's 65,000. See Boyle, *Black Swine in the Sewers of Hampstead*, p. 41.

41 *If we can be murdered thus*: Daily Telegraph, 13 July 1864, p. 5 col. a.

41 **Five doctors**: *The Times*, 13 July 1864, p. 11 col. e. Post-mortem results taken mostly from the CCC trial transcripts, particularly the testimony of Francis Toulmin.

42 **deep, jagged wound**: *The Times*, 13 July 1864, p. 11 col. e.

42 *a great quantity of effused blood*: All descriptions from the second Bow warrants, testimony of Alfred Henry Brereton, 22 July 1864.

42 **sub-cranial haemorrhage**: *The Times*, 19 July 1864, p. 7 col. c.

## CHAPTER 7: SOMETHING TO ASTONISH THE PUBLIC

44 *one of the foulest murders*: The Times, editorial, 13 July 1864, p. 10.

45 **Mary Anne Moody**: *The Times*, 16 July 1864, p. 7 col. c.

45 *daintily murdered him*: Quoted in Altick, *Victorian Studies in Scarlet*, p. 199.

45 *swallowed up by the roar*: The Globe, 1863, quoted in Smullen, *Taken for a Ride*, p. 131.

46 *no man is safe*: The Times, editorial, 13 July 1864, p. 10.

46 the look of a foreigner: Ibid.

46 *the horrid consciousness*: Glasgow Herald, 27 August 1864, p. 3 col. d.

46 One correspondent hinted: MEPO 3/75.

47 height of the assassin: Ibid.

47 the legal establishment was sceptical: Evans, *The Father of Forensics*, p. 3.

48 reports of suspicious hats: For example, *The Times*, 13 July 1864, p. 11 col. e.

49 put under surveillance: MEPO 3/75: letter to Richard Mayne from the Liverpool Constabulary Force, 19 July 1864, confirming receipt of printed bills: *instructions have been given to the police of this borough to make every search as stopping offices and on board outward vessels also in the town.* See also *Reynolds's Weekly Newspaper*, 17 July 1864, p. 8 col. a.

50 these huge new posters screamed horrid murder: In the words of the *Daily Telegraph, all men knew that the death-hunt was afoot; that society, shocked by a hideous crime, was alert and eager to avenge it . . .* 13 July 1864, no page, clip in MEPO 3/75.

50  **equivalent to several years' pay:** A skilled City tailor would earn on average fifty pounds a year, a cabman on the other hand might earn far more – variously reported at between eighty and several hundred pounds a year. See Booth's 1889 report of the weekly average earnings of a hackney cabman as thirty shillings a week (*Life and Labour of the People*; Dickens' *All the Year Round* interview with a cabman corroborates this). But Mayhew (*London Labour and the London Poor*, 1864, p. 347 *passim*) estimated it at ten pounds a week, and up to eighteen pounds a week in summer.

## CHAPTER 8: IMPROBABLE HYPOTHESES

53  **Somer's Town:** White, *London in the Nineteenth Century*, p. 115.

53  **this was not the customer:** 'The Atrocious Murder', *Belfast Newsletter*, 15 July 1864, no page.

53  *The London detectives are ... upon their trial:* *Daily Telegraph*, 13 July 1864, p. 4 col. f.

54  **thrumming to** *the eternal tread:* Dickens, *David Copperfield*, chapter 32.

54  **There were the Irish:** White, op. cit., p. 148.

54  **Wealthy Germans:** Ibid., p. 145.

55  **half of all Germans in the country:** Sims (ed.), *Living London*, 1901.

55  **the support system of 'Little Germany':** For more on Germans in mid-Victorian Britain, see Panayi (ed.), *Germans in Britain since 1500*, and Ashton, *Little Germany*.

57  **etiquette manuals were divided:** Flanders, *The Victorian House*, p. 333.

58  **a hoax:** *The Times*, 11 July 1864, p. 11 col. f.

58  *foul and brutal crime:* Ibid.

59  **combined daily circulation:** Flanders, *Consuming Passions*, p. 147 ff.

59  **details of the brief:** For example, HO 65/25, letter, 10 November 1864.

59  **driving the general increase of literacy:** Altick, *Victorian Studies in Scarlet*, pp. 282 and 288, and Flanders, *Consuming Passions*, p. 164.

59  *The public mind:* *Lloyd's Weekly Newspaper*, 17 July 1864, p. 6 col. c.

60  **Tomkins reported:** CCC transcript, evidence of Thomas Lee under cross-examination by the Solicitor General.

60  **Thomas Lee admitted:** MEPO 3/75, Howie's note.

61  *sitting with his back to the engine:* Bow warrants, 22 July 1864.

CHAPTER 9: SOMETHING TO TELL

63  **a tall, dark man getting in and out of carriages:** Inquest report, *The Times*, 19 July 1864, p. 7 col. d.

64  **the post-mortem results:** *The Times*, 19 July 1864, p. 7 col. c.

64  **threats … her uncle had received:** Full details of this inquest reported in e.g. *The Times*, 19 July 1864, p. 7 col. c and d.

65  **five thousand metropolitan drivers:** Mayhew, *London Labour and the London Poor*, p. 347, though in Dickens' interview with a cabman, published in *All the Year Round* in 1860, the driver believes there are eleven thousand drivers, three thousand of them of hansoms and the rest of hackney cabs.

65  **was aiming to call it a day:** Charles Dickens, 'Cab!', *All the Year Round*, 25 February 1860, pp. 414–16

66  **Turning to the police waterman:** CCC transcript, evidence of Jonathan Matthews.

67  **a young German tailor from Chemnitz:** *The Times*, 21 July 1864, p. 11 col. f . Also 20 July 1864, p. 9.

67  **cramped rented rooms:** Inquest evidence reported in *The Times*, 9 August 1864, p. 7 col. c, and census information on the address at 68 Earl Street, 1861.

68  *not wearing so greasy as the nap:* CCC transcript evidence.

68  **a mark on the inside brim:** See report of Matthews' evidence, *Daily News*, 20 July 1864, p. 5 col. a.

68  **He had replaced it:** CCC transcript, Matthews' cross-examination by Parry.

69  **twenty-five shillings a week:** Müller's pay: CCC transcript. Another co-worker at Hodgkinson's, John Henry Glass, told the court that he earned between thirty and thirty-six shillings a week. In 1858 *The Times* argued that a middle-class household cost three hundred pounds a year (Maunder, *Varieties of Women's Sensation Fiction*, p. 42 note 4). At around a pound a week, these tailors earned around a fifth of that, insufficient for much more than the outlay for food, board and clothing.

69  **set out for the home:** *The Times*, 21 July 1864, p. 11 col. f.


CHAPTER 10: THE WIND BLOWS FAIR

71  **penny-gaffs:** Three-penny amusement galleries.

71  **Occasionally they passed dustmen:** Descriptions of London night-workers are taken from Mayhew, *London Labour and the London Poor*.

71 **hammered on the door of number 55:** Death's residential address is not substantiated. In the 1861 census he lived with his brother and spinster sister in nearby St Luke's and in 1871 in Bishopsgate, also in the City. Additionally, the 1861 census shows a silversmith shopman and his family living above the shop at 55 Cheapside. This shopman is not mentioned in any police statements or court testimony (by comparison to Mr Digance's employee). Given Parry's later attempts at trial to establish Müller's presence at the shop prior to 11 July, it seems unlikely that this shopman worked for the Deaths and more likely that he was employed by a neighbouring jeweller in Cheapside. In the absence of a specific City address for the Deaths in July 1864 I have made a decision to locate the events of 19 July at 55 Cheapside. It does not materially alter either Tanner's journey (both St Luke's and Bishopsgate are a matter of minutes further on from Cheapside) or the reaction of John Death to the photograph he is shown by the inspector.

72 **large groups of ... immigrants:** For more on outsiders in the East End see Alderman and Holmes (ed.), *Outsiders and Outcasts*.

72 **Old Ford:** Area descriptions from Hamilton et al., *National Gazetteer*.

73 **omnibus passing the end of Park Terrace:** See *Liverpool Mercury*, 23 July 1864, p. 5 col. c.

73 **sweated labour:** Booth, *Life and Labour of the People*, also Schmiechen, *Sweated Industries and Sweated Labor*.

73 **Seventy-two-hour working weeks:** Lattek, *Revolutionary Refugees*, p. 220 ff.

73 **twenty thousand stitches:** Schmiechen, op. cit., p. 24 ff.

74 **At six o'clock:** Some reports state 7 a.m., but police expenses in the MEPO file show that they had left Old Ford by that time.

74 **two small upstairs rooms were generally let:** *Manchester Guardian*, reprinted *New York Times*, 28 August 1864, report of testimony at the inquest on 22 August. The Blyths rented to Müller and another man, called Goodwin.

74 **paying four shillings a week:** 'The Murder of Mr Briggs', *Manchester Guardian*, 10 September 1864, p. 5, no column given.

74 **Müller had given proper notice:** Blyth's testimony taken primarily from the CCC transcript, supplemented by his statement of 8 November in Home Office files, the Bow warrants and Tanner's closing report in the MEPO files.

74 *a quiet, inoffensive, well-behaved young man:* CCC transcript, evidence of Ellen Blyth.

76 *Dear Friends:* CCC transcript. Later newspaper reports would occasionally state that the letter was sent to Goodwin, another German lodger at the Blyths', and that Goodwin gave evidence to Müller returning at 11 p.m. on Saturday 9 July, appearing much confused and having

hurt his ankle, e.g. *Leeds Mercury*, 21 July 1864, p. 2 col. e. No police statements were taken from Goodwin, however, and he was not called to give evidence during the trial held later that year.

## CHAPTER 11: TUESDAY 19 JULY 1864

78  **an omnibus over London Bridge:** See CCC evidence of Charles Foreman, omnibus conductor.

80  **Close to seven hundred pawn shops:** Sims (ed.), *Living London*, p. 36.

81  **a magistrate stood ready:** *The Times*, 23 July 1864, p. 7 col. a.

83  *a plain black beaver:* CCC transcript and Irving (ed.), *The Trial of Franz Müller*, p. 35.

83  *I went on board the* Victoria: Widely reported, e.g. *Jackson's Oxford Journal*, 23 July 1864, p. 3 col. d.

84  **the silversmith was ready to swear:** *Lloyd's Weekly Newspaper*, 24 July 1864, p. 7 col. b.

84  *dingy, fetid, close smelling rooms:* *Illustrated London News*, 22 August 1846, p. 125. See also Miller, *Cops and Bobbies*, p. x.

85  **collect government dispatches:** MEPO 3/75, letter from Sir George Grey to Sir Richard Mayne, 19 July 1864. See also 'The Murder of Mr Briggs', *Caledonian Mercury*, 20 July 1864, no page col. g.

85  **create a line of communication:** A transatlantic cable that sent messages via Newfoundland to London from New York in ten hours had been established in 1858 but its success was short-lived. Attempting to raise the volume, a New York operator blew the voltage of the system and it was not effectively replaced for another eight years.

85  **an effective cable:** The notorious fugitive Dr Crippen was caught in 1910, his arrest facilitated by wireless communication. It made the case the greatest cliffhanger in newspaper history, a blow-by-blow account of the case afforded by the Atlantic cable telegraph (see Evans, *The Father of Forensics*, p. 3).

85  **Tanner was caught off guard:** MEPO 3/75, Tanner's final report, 2 January 1865.

## CHAPTER 12: FLYING FROM JUSTICE

89  **four-pound ticket:** Advertisement for tickets on the *Victoria*: see *The Times*, 4 July 1864. Estimated journey time, see *The Times*, 20 July 1864, p. 9.

89  **Basic weekly provisions:** For details of the food given to each passenger for them to cook for themselves, and of the fights over the limited supply

of pork in the stews they made, see *Daily Telegraph*, second edition, 17 September 1864, p. 3 col. e.

90  *Manchester*: Information from *Illustrated London News*, 19 July 1851. Fare details from advertisement in *The Times*, 15 July 1864, reprinted 19 and 22 July.

91  **132,000 emigrants:** Details about emigration to the USA: see *Liverpool Mercury*, 25 July 1864, p. 6 col. d (reprinting an article in the *New York Times*, 9 July). Immigration figures also from *The Times*, 9 September 1864, p. 7 col. d. German immigration statistics from <www.archaeolink.com>.

91  **Frederick Adolphus Williamson:** See Cavanagh, *Scotland Yard Past and Present*, p. 62.

91  **In case the *Victoria* should dock in Ireland:** MEPO 3/75. Queenstown, named after a visit by Queen Victoria in 1849, was renamed Cobh in 1922.

92  **When Townsend saw Müller's photograph:** HO 12/152/63401. From the Memorial presented to Sir George Grey in Müller's defence before the execution.

92  **16 Park Terrace:** MEPO 3/75, Superintendent Tiddey's expenses, dated 23 July 1864.

92  **torn sleeve lining:** Report of the discovery of the sleeve lining from *Morning Star*, 22 July 1864, p. 5 col. b. See also *The Times*, 23 July 1864, p. 7 col. b.

92  **jigsaw of the pawnshop transactions:** MEPO 3/75, Tiddey's expense claims, particularly 20 July 1864.

93  **Glass told Tiddey:** CCC transcript, evidence of John Henry Glass.

94  **It was a good deal for both men:** Details of transactions from evidence given at the trial. See CCC transcript, evidence of John Henry Glass, Henry Smith and Alfred Wey. There are some discrepancies and contradictions in the evidence in relation to the exact amounts the items were pledged and redeemed for but they all agree about the actual items and the rough amounts they were thought to be worth. Since the discrepancies are tiny, I have here used Glass's evidence as to the amounts.

94  **alarmed its readers:** *The Times*, 19 July 1864, p. 7 col. d and e.

94  ***The Discovery of the Murderer*:** For example, *The Times*, *Daily News*.

94  ***London and all the world*:** *The Times*, 20 July 1864, p. 9.

CHAPTER 13: A FABRIC BUILT OF STRAWS

95  *the actual murderer*: *Morning Star*, 21 July 1864, p. 5 col. b.

95  *barring accidents*: *The Times*, 20 July 1864, p. 9.

95 **a truce:** Within a fortnight, on 1 August 1864, in talks preceding the eventual Treaty of Vienna, Denmark agreed to accede the disputed Duchies coveted by Prussia and Austria and lost around 40 per cent of its total landmass. The Treaty of Peace would not be concluded, however, until 30 October.

95 **a Cologne family of gun-makers:** *Morning Star*, 21 July 1864, p. 5 col. b.

96 *According to ... Matthews' friends*: *Daily Telegraph*, reprinted *Manchester Guardian*, 22 July 1864, p. 3.

96 *murderer in intention*: *Liverpool Mercury*, 21 July 1864, p. 7 col. c.

96 *great resolution*: Ibid.

96 **links** *in the chain of circumstantial evidence*: *Daily News*, 20 July 1864, p. 5 col. a.

96 *that wonderful fabric ... built of straws*: Braddon, *Lady Audley's Secret*, p. 97.

97 *the individual alluded to*: Reported widely in regional papers, but see e.g. *Leeds Mercury*, 20 July 1864, p. 4 col. a.

97 **another worrying detail:** Ibid.

99 **Mr Knox of Camberwell:** MEPO 3/75, date unknown, letter from William [?] Knox stored in July date order with other letters from members of the public.

99 **his daughter was able to confirm three things:** Atkinson's evidence that he carried around twenty-six letters, Hackney inquest 22 August, reported *The Times*, 22 August 1864, p. 8 col. f. Information also from Howie's reports, MEPO 3/74, 20–22 July 1864. Forename from Hackney inquest, reported *The Times*, 22 August 1864, p. 8 col. f.

99 **Professor Taylor's scrutiny:** MEPO 3/75, Tiddey's expenses between 18 and 26 July 1864.

99 **a respected warder:** MEPO 3/75, Detective Police Special Reports, 19 July 1864.


CHAPTER 14: NINETY IN THE SHADE

Information for this chapter is informed by the copies of the second Bow warrants, 22 July 1864, contained in the US extradition papers.

101 **several instances of oneupmanship:** Walter Fifield, *A History of the Extradition Treaties of the United States*, University of Southern California, Ph.D. thesis, 1936, p. 31.

102 **ninety degrees in the shade:** *Illustrated London News*, vol. xlv, no. 1270, 23 July 1864, p. 87 col. a.

103 *extremely temperate habits*: Report of the taking of warrants: *The Times*, 23 July 1864, p. 7 col. a.

104   **a bundle of new documents:** Evidence of Walter Kerressey, extradition papers.

104   **He also carried:** Extradition evidence. The crumpled hat and battered cardboard box remained in England, required as evidence in the ongoing Hackney inquest.

104   *City of Cork:* The *Manchester* was a comparatively slow steamer. See *Liverpool Mercury*, 21 July 1864, p. 7 col. c, and *The Times*, 23 July 1864, p. 7 col. a

105   *man in custody:* MEPO 3/75, telegraph to Sir Richard Mayne, 22 July 1864.

105   **Summoned by a concerned Mr Henry to Bow Street:** *The Times*, 25 July 1864, p. 12 col. c.

105   *ferocious* **in appearance:** MEPO 3/75, report, Paris, 23 July 1864.


## CHAPTER 15: WHO BUT A MADMAN?

107   *The assassin:* 'Crime and Detection', *Liverpool Mercury*, 12 July 1864, no page.

107   **little heed to prohibitions:** Bentley, *English Criminal Justice in the Nineteenth Century*, p. 43 ff.

107   **a frisson of unease:** Looking back, the eminent barrister William Ballantine would write in his memoirs that the 'new' breed of detectives might have behaved better had they followed the example of their predecessors, the Bow Street Runners, who never broadcast their plans but worked out their cases instead in silence and secrecy. Ballantine, *A Barrister's Life*, 1882. See also Bentley, op. cit., p. 43 ff.

108   *good and even gentlemanly:* *Daily News*, 22 July 1864, p. 5 col. e. *Shoreditch Advertiser*, 22 July 1864, p. 3 col. e.

108   **the importance of self-control:** Martin J. Wiener, 'The Sad Story of George Hall: Adultery, Murder and the Politics of Mercy in Mid-Victorian England', *Social History Journal*, vol. 24, issue 2, May 1999.

108   **a noble wretch or an underhand fraud:** *Daily News*, 21 July 1864, p. 5 col. b.

108   **prone to paying** *particular notice:* *The Times*, 23 July 1864, p. 7 col. a.

109   *We hear it complained:* Ibid.

109   *Neither Sir Richard Mayne nor his men:* *Reynolds's Weekly Newspaper*, 24 July 1864, p. 1 col. a.

109   *glaring incapacity:* Ibid.

110   **anxieties about the dangers of modernity:** For more on this, see Boyle, *Black Swine in the Sewers of Hampstead*, p. 78 ff.

110   **not turning the excitement of the present moment:** Letter to the editor from 'BN', *Daily News*, 21 July 1864, p. 5 col. b.

110   **Suggestions ... came from every quarter:** For example, *Daily Telegraph*, 14 July 1864, p. 4, col. e, and 15 July 1864, p. 5 col. f.

110   **an estimated ten thousand men:** Reprising *The Times*, 'The Situation in America', *Freeman's Journal*, 26 July 1864, no page col. h. *Jackson's Oxford Journal*, 23 July 1864, p. 3 col. e.

111   **letter ... from Worthing:** *The Times*, 23 July 1864, p. 7 col. c, and *Preston Guardian*, 23 July 1864, p. 8 col. f.

111   **the reopening of the inquest in Hackney:** Description from notes at inquest reported in *The Times*, 9 August 1864, p. 7 col. c.

111   **findings were inconclusive:** Reported in *The Times*, 26 July 1864, p. 12 col. d.

112   *it was the lamp:* *Daily Telegraph*, 26 July 1864, p. 6 col. b.

113   **on the off-chance that it might fit:** MEPO 3/75, letter dated 25 July from W. C. Rubidge, Oxford Street, and John Coles, Berkeley Square.

113   **Do Justice:** *Daily Telegraph*, 25 July 1864, p. 3 col. e.

113   **collection of crochets:** Braddon, *Lady Audley's Secret*, p. 202.

113   *the species of argument:* Braddon, *Aurora Floyd*, p. 314.

114   **A Barrister from Lincoln's Inn:** *Daily Telegraph*, 25 July 1864, p. 3 col. d.

114   **In an editorial:** *Daily Telegraph*, 25 July 1864, p. 4 col. d.

115   **truth had not been established:** Ibid. The view of the *Daily Telegraph* would be repeated only in the *Penny Illustrated Paper*, 13 August 1864, p. 1 col. a.


## CHAPTER 16: CITY OF STRANGERS

116   **begun to confess:** For example, *The Times*, 20 August 1864, p. 11 col. b; 4 August 1864, p. 11 col. e; 30 July 1864, p. 10 col. f.

116   **Sick with fear:** 'Alarming Incident in a Railway Carriage', *Liverpool Mercury*, 29 June 1864, p. 3 col. g.

117   **the *Victoria*, was making little headway:** *The Times*, 29 July 1864, p. 9 col. b.

117   **flung, in a matter of minutes:** 'News from Europe', *New York Times*, 25 July 1864, p. 8.

117   **in severe pain:** MEPO 3/75, reports to Mayne. See also *Daily Telegraph*, 7 September 1864, p. 3 col. f.

118   **quadrupled in the three decades:** Lankevich, *American Metropolis*, p. 91.

118   *Everything is done in a hurry:* Miller, *Miller's New York*, p. 23. See also Dickens, *American Notes*, chapter 6.

119   **Broadway was bewildering:** An estimated eighteen thousand vehicles a day: Miller, op. cit., p. 23 ff.

119 **Everett House Hotel:** Ibid., p. 62.

119 *English railcars*: 'Francis Müller the Murderer', *Harper's Weekly*, 10 September 1864, no page.

119 **witnesses were also expected:** 'Great Britain: Mysterious Murder', *New York Times*, 4 August 1864, p. 2.

120 **fifteen daily papers:** Miller, op. cit., p. 53 ff.

120 **remorseless lists:** For the scale of this war, see e.g. *New York Times*, 26 August 1864, which reports General Grant's Sunday losses of 4255 and rebel claims that they have taken 3000 prisoners.

120 **Pierrepont Edwards:** Edward Mortimer Archibald, who held the post for twenty-five years from 1857, was on leave. See Edwards' obituary, *New York Times*, 1971.

120 **Francis Marbury:** Obituary, *New York Times*, 19 March 1895.

120 **United States Marshal:** The head of the state law enforcement with a responsibility to ensure the effective operation of the judicial system and locally to represent national government.

121 **New York Police Headquarters:** The new building was occupied on 23 February 1863. For its history, see *New York Times*, 17 August 1891, p. 8.

121 **inefficient and corrupt:** Miller, *Cops and Bobbies*, p. 29 ff.

121 **proposed a plan:** *New York Times*, 7 August 1864, p. 6. See also: *New York Times*, 17 August 1891, p. 8; *New York Tribune*, 29 August 1864, reprinted *Leeds Mercury*, 10 September 1864, p. 12 col. a.

121 **arrest Müller and hold him:** MEPO 3/75, Tanner's second report to Sir Richard Mayne (the first lost), dated 9 August 1864.

122 **placed at the detective's disposal:** *New York Times*, 7 August 1864, p. 6.

122 *proofs of his stupidity*: 'News from Great Britain', *New York Times*, 7 August 1864, p. 3.

## CHAPTER 17: THE LAST PERSON IN THE WORLD

123 **Quackembos:** *Daily Telegraph*, second edition, 17 September 1864, p. 3 col. d.

123 *a possibility of Müller escaping*: MEPO 3/75, report dated 9 August 1864.

124 **sixty-dollar ... reward:** *The Times*, 8 September 1864, p. 7 col. a. Also MEPO 3/75, Tanner's reports back to Mayne. $60: see 'The Murder of Mr Briggs', *Manchester Guardian*, 19 September 1864, p. 3.

124 **a plan to intercept the *Victoria*:** MEPO 3/75, clip in Mayne's file from the *Courrier des Etats-Unis*, also a handwritten note with reference to Tanner's report.

124 *cracked vases, bird cages*: *New York Times*, 29 September 1864.

125 the *James Funk*: 'The Murder of Mr Briggs', *Manchester Guardian*, 19 September 1864, p. 3.

125 **Deutscher Rechtsschutz Verein:** *The Times*, 11 November 1864, p. 5 col. c.

126 **73 Moorgate Street:** *Leeds Mercury*, 7 September 1864, p. 3 col. b.

126 **earnestly inviting** *any person*: *The Times*, 9 August 1864; *Morning Advertiser*, 10 August 1864. Both clipped and located in MEPO 3/75.

126 **The German authorities wrote:** MEPO 3/75, reports dated 18 August (Munich) and 27 August (Cologne).

127 **Two armed crewmen:** 'Arrest of Franz Müller', *New York Times*, 26 August 1864.

128 **his arms grasped firmly:** For details of the arrest see 'Arrival of Müller the English Murderer', *New York Times*, 25 August 1864. See also *The Times*, 9 September 1864, p. 7 col. a and b.

128 *What is the matter?*: CCC transcript, evidence of George Clarke.

129 *I never was on the line*: US extradition file. Record Group 59: General Records of the Department of State 1789–2002, American National Archives, Franz Müller 1864, Loc. 250/48/9/7, Box 2: evidence of George Clarke.

129 **a large black trunk:** Irving (ed.), *The Trial of Franz Müller*, p. 67.

129 **answered all his questions:** CCC transcript, evidence of George Clarke and Richard Tanner. See also Tanner's interview with the *Daily Telegraph*, second edition, 17 September 1864, p. 3 col. e.

130 **a crowd of thousands:** MEPO 3/75, Kerressey letter to Daniel Howie, 26 August 1864.

130 **he disappeared below:** US extradition file, op. cit., evidence of Richard Tanner and John Death.

130 *was it a red stone?*: CCC transcript, evidence of Richard Tanner.

131 **photographed for police files:** Müller was photographed at the famous photographic gallery owned by Matthew Brady. Brady (1822–96) was a renowned photographer of celebrities and his assistants made graphic records of the battles of the American Civil War. He was credited with being the father of American photojournalism. As well as photographing the famous and the dead, his gallery took the likenesses of prisoners for police files and provided photographic cartes-de-visite, or albumen prints fixed to small pieces of card, for the middle classes.

131 **the office of Marshal Robert Murray:** *New York Herald*, 26 August 1864, p. 1 col. a.

131 *cowering wretch*: Ibid.

131 *To look at him*: 'Arrest of Franz Müller', *New York Times*, 26 August 1864.

132 *decidedly repulsive*: *New York Tribune*, 29 August 1864, reprinted *Leeds Mercury*, 10 September 1864, p. 12 col. a.

## CHAPTER 18: NO SLIPSHOD EXAMINATION

133 **The extradition hearing opened:** The detail of the extradition hearing is taken from the original US extradition papers held in the American National Archives (ARC Identifier 1229762 / MLR Number A1 857, series from Record Group 59: General Records of the Department of State 1789–2002). See also *New York Times*: 'The Müller Extradition Case', 27 August 1864; 'Law Reports', 28 August 1864; 'Local Intelligence', 29 August 1864. Richard Mayne's own copy of the printed proceedings of the hearing has also survived in the files of the North London Railway: RAIL529/113 [Old ref. NL4/13 (3)].

133 **ex-judge Beebe:** *New York Herald*, 26 August 1864, p. 1 col. a.

133 **small and stupefied:** 'The London Railway Murder', *New York Herald*, 27 August 1864, p. 4.

133 *diabolical* **locus:** *New York Herald*, 26 August 1864, p. 1 col. a.

134 **The agent apparently employed:** The *Leeds Mercury* of 7 September named him as Mr Edwards but there is no substantiating proof of this.

134 **to write with breathless lack of punctuation:** MEPO 3/75, letter from Kerressey to Howie, 26 August 1864.

134 **appearance rather more gentlemanly:** See also *New York Tribune*, 29 August 1864, reprinted *Leeds Mercury*, 10 September 1864, p. 12 col. a.

134 **a short, triumphant telegraph:** MEPO 3/75.

135 **The United States Circuit Court house:** Restaurant owner Ferdinand Palmo built the original opera house in 1844. William Evans, the English actor, founded Burton's Chambers Street Theatre there in 1848 and the company survived at that location until 1856.

135 **Nassau Street:** 139 Nassau Street. See *New York Times*, 27 August 1864, p. 8 col. b.

135 **Shaffer:** Also spelled Schaffer. The lawyer would become New York's district attorney.

136 **British–American extradition treaty:** The Webster–Ashburton Treaty, signed August 1842, followed by legislation in 1843 (6 & 7 Vict c 76).

137 **not admissible in New York:** *New York Times*, 27 August 1864, p. 8 col. b.

## CHAPTER 19: GATHERING CLOUDS

Material in this chapter is taken from the same sources as the previous chapter, specifically using the *New York Times* law reports of 28 August 1864, the printed proceedings of the extradition, op. cit., and the original transcripts of the hearing, op. cit.

141 **a negro slave called Anderson:** See Hansard, 25 July 1864, House of Commons. During the debate over the new Prussian extradition treaty the Anderson case is referred to: Britain refused on the grounds *that he could not be delivered up for this reason – that a man who killed another while defending his own liberty could not be guilty of murder according to the laws of this country.*

142 *I do not claim:* Law reports, *New York Times*, 28 August 1864.

142 **The court erupted into applause:** MEPO 3/75, Tanner's report to Richard Mayne, 28 August 1864.

143 *something of sublimity:* Printed extradition proceedings, op. cit., p. 17.

144 **Grotius:** Hugo Grotius (1583–1645) was a jurist in the Dutch Republic. With Francisco de Vitoria and Alberico Gentili he laid many of the foundations for international law.

147 **the Tombs:** Information on the Tombs is taken from Miller, *Miller's New York*, p. 31 ff, and Dickens, *American Notes*, chapter 6.

149 **Tanner managed:** Widely reported. See e.g. 'The Murder of Mr Briggs', *Manchester Guardian*, 19 September 1864, p. 3.

149 **Tanner was worn out:** Begg quotes Tanner, but unattributed: *I was 20 days and nights in the Harbour of New York during which time I do not think I ever went to sleep waiting for that ship.*

149 *Extraordinary as it may seem:* MEPO 3/75, Tanner's report to Richard Mayne, dated 28 August 1864.


CHAPTER 20: TURNING BACK

150 **to look for missing kin:** Faust, *The Republic of Suffering*, p. 127.

150 **New York *Morning Star*:** New York *Morning Star*, reprinted *Birmingham Daily Post*, 14 September 1864, p. 3 col. e.

152 **visited Francis Marbury:** MEPO 3/76, dated 3 September 1864.

152 **who delivered a letter:** 'The Murder of Mr Briggs', letter, *Manchester Guardian*, 22 September 1864, p. 3. Confirmation that the letter was delivered from marginalia to the Memorial on behalf of Müller in the Home Office Files HO 12/152/63401, first bundle. See also *Daily Telegraph*, second edition, 17 September 1864, p. 3 col. e.

153 **The law of England:** Miller, *Cops and Bobbies*, p. 74 ff, and Bentley, *English Criminal Justice in the Nineteenth Century*, p. 230. Also *Daily Telegraph*, 17 September 1864, p. 3 col. f.

153 **wearing anxiety:** From Begg, *The Scotland Yard Files*, p. 54 (no attribution for Tanner's report). It may have been some consolation to Tanner that, during his time away from England, he was on double pay: MEPO 3/76, Tanner's pay and reward note.

154 **sessions were repeatedly rescheduled:** The inquest was adjourned until

8 September but reopened then only in order to re-adjourn until the 19th.

154 **Rumours began to circulate:** *Liverpool Mercury*, 6 September 1864, p. 7 col. f.

154 **the country awoke to news:** *The Times*, 7 September 1864, p. 9 col. a.

155 *Müller may be innocent:* Reprinted *Leeds Mercury*, 7 September 1864, p. 2 col. e.

155 *the contagion of his example:* *The Times*, 7 September 1864, p. 8 col. a.

155 *It is a strange story:* Ibid.

155 **perfect scale model:** MEPO 3/76, letter dated 12 September 1864, also report by Daniel Howie dated 17 September 1864.

156 *being a married man:* MEPO 3/75, undated: c. 10 September 1864.

157 *we were hard up:* 'The Murder of Mr Briggs, a Curious Episode', *London Star*, 9 September 1864, reprinted *New York Times*, 25 September 1864.

157 **seen drinking:** *The Times*, 8 September 1864, p. 9 col. d.

## CHAPTER 21: THE APPEARANCE OF GUILT

158 **signalled her approach:** Description of the arrival of the boat at Queenstown from *Daily Telegraph*, second edition, 17 September 1864, p. 3 col. c.

158 **Within twenty minutes:** *Daily Telegraph*, 16 September 1864, p. 3 col. f.

159 **Müller changed:** Description of landing in Liverpool from *Daily Telegraph*, second edition, 17 September 1864, p. 3 col. c. Hat from Kerressey: 'The Murder of Mr Briggs', *Manchester Guardian*, 19 September 1864, p. 3.

159 *Fury:* 'The Arrival of Müller at Liverpool', *The Times*, 17 September 1864, p. 9.

159 **Prince's Pier:** *Daily News*, 17 September 1864, p. 5 col. f. See also *Lloyd's Weekly Newspaper*, 18 September 1864, p. 12 col. b.

160 **A ramshackle bed:** *Lloyd's Weekly Newspaper*, 18 September 1864, p. 12 col. b. Folding his clothes: 'The Murder of Mr Briggs', *Manchester Guardian*, 19 September 1864, p. 3.

161 **Much depended:** *Daily News*, 15 September 1864, p. 7 col. c. Also *Reynolds's Weekly Newspaper*, 18 September 1864, p. 1 col. f.

161 *if he had been an innocent man:* 'The Capture of Müller', *Observer*, 11 September 1864, p. 5.

161 *Reynolds's* **agreed:** *Reynolds's Weekly Newspaper*, 18 September 1864, p. 4 col. c.

162 the recent case of a traveller: *Reynolds's Weekly Newspaper*, 11 September 1864, p. 4 col. b.

## CHAPTER 22: A VERY PUBLIC ORDEAL

164 *too late for a peaceful solution*: Friedrich Engels, *The Condition of the Working Class in England* (1903; Oxford: Oxford University Press, 1993), p. 281 ff.

166 efforts to spruce himself up: *Lloyd's Weekly Newspaper*, 18 September 1864, p. 12 col. d.

166 *The people seemed surprised at the slight ... appearance*: 'The Murder of Mr Briggs', *Manchester Guardian*, 19 September 1864, p. 3.

166 Excitement quickly gave way: *Lloyd's Weekly Newspaper*, 18 September 1864, p. 12 col. d. Also 'Arrival of Müller in London', *The Times*, 19 September 1864, p. 7.

167 A German-speaking police officer: *The Times*, 19 September 1864, p.7 col. d and e.

168 *You are very kind*: Widely reported, e.g. 'The Murder of Mr Briggs', *Manchester Guardian*, 19 September 1864, p. 5.

168 the police were busy: MEPO 3/75. Tiddey's expenses from 18 to 23 September show he was away from home for six days, getting up the case for inquest and committal.

169 Daniel Howie: MEPO 3/76, Howie's reports from 17 September through to the following week.

169 *waif and stray of a foreign land*: *Daily Telegraph*, 19 September 1864, p. 4 col. e.

## CHAPTER 23: I'VE COME TO TELL THE TRUTH

174 hear the testimonies: MEPO 3/76, Thomas Durkin's report dated 19 September from Division F, Covent Garden.

174 The watch, chains, black bag: *Daily News*, 20 September 1864, p. 5 col. f.

175 *I could not positively identify*: All testimony in this chapter is taken from widespread reporting of the hearing on 20 September in *The Times*, *Daily Telegraph* and *Daily News*.

176 House of Detention in Clerkenwell: There had been prisons there since 1616 and in the Victorian period some ten thousand prisoners a year were incarcerated in Clerkenwell. Formerly known as the New Prison, it was rebuilt in 1847 and renamed.

176 **pillared portal:** Descriptions of the House of Detention taken from Mayhew and Binny, *The Criminal Prisons of London*, p. 611 ff.

177 *the question of the guilt or innocence:* Daily News, 20 September 1864, p. 5 col. f.

178 *Is that a hat to suit me?:* The Times, 21 September 1864, p. 10 col. c. Unless otherwise indicated, all details of statements given at the inquest that day are from this source.

179 *parramatta:* A light but coarse fabric with a weft of wool and a warp of cotton or silk.

179 *my father usually wore silk:* Daily News, 20 September 1864, p. 5 col. f.

## CHAPTER 24: FIRST JUDGEMENT

180 **Snippets of new information:** *The Times*, 23 September 1864, p. 10 col. c. See also e.g. *Jackson's Oxford Journal*, 24 September 1864, p. 3 col. d.

181 *The sale of the photograph:* The Times, 23 September 1864, p. 9 col. e. See also *The Times*, 30 September 1864, p. 9 col. e.

181 *Not even in the annals of crime:* Penny Illustrated Paper, 24 September 1864, p. 200.

181 **It was even reported:** *Reynolds's Weekly Newspaper*, 25 September 1864, p. 5 col. b.

182 *in possession of certain facts:* Ibid.

182 **removed from his cell:** Reports of the closing of the Hackney inquest and the Bow hearing are taken primarily from all three editions of the *Daily Telegraph*, 26 September 1864 (third edition, p. 5) and from *The Times*, 27 September 1864, p. 5. Police details are taken from orders and reports found in MEPO 3/76 from the week beginning 22 September.

184 **Thomas Müller:** CRIM 4/681, case no. 40/1, 24 October 1864.

185 **scribbling notes:** Widely noticed in the press; see e.g. *Reynolds's Weekly Newspaper*, 2 October 1864, p. 6 col. a.

## CHAPTER 25: A PINT OF MEAT AND VEGETABLE SOUP

188 **For more than a thousand years:** White, *London in the Nineteenth Century*, p. 407.

188 *mingled feelings of awe:* Dickens, 'Criminal Courts', *Sketches by 'Boz'* (1833–9).

189 **vellum-bound register:** Newgate Prisoner Entry Register, PCOM 2/215, 26 September 1864.

189 **several hundred prisoners:** Reports of numbers it could hold differ: five hundred in the *Illustrated London News* of 23 February 1850, fewer in other sources.

189 **flagged corridors:** Descriptions of the interior of Newgate are taken from a number of sources including: report of the Revd Ordinary J. Davis, *Illustrated London News*, 23 February 1850; Bartlett, *London by Day and Night*, 1852; Dickens, 'Visit to Newgate', *Sketches by 'Boz'*; and, particularly since it is the closest in date to 1864, Mayhew and Binny, *The Criminal Prisons of London*, 1862.

190 **Central Criminal Court:** Known as the Old Bailey after the street onto which it opened.

191 *exhibition*: Sims (ed.), *Living London*; Edward Mogg, *Mogg's New Picture of London: or, Strangers' Guide to the British Metropolis*, 1848; George Frederick Cruchley, *Cruchley's London in 1865: A Handbook for Strangers*.

192 *a disgrace to our nation*: *Spectator*, lix, 1861, p. 1397. See also Sweet, *Inventing the Victorians*, chapter 5.

192 **an excellent likeness:** *The Era*, 2 October 1864, p. 10 col. a.

192 *An argument has been founded*: *Jackson's Oxford Journal*, 8 October 1864, p. 6 col. c.

193 **Mr Flemming:** MEPO 3/76, report dated 13 October following statement made on 7 October 1864.

194 **substantial calendar:** *The Times*, 25 October 1864, p. 9 col. a.

194 **five ... rules of evidence:** Stephen, *A General View of the Criminal Law of England*, p. 302.

194 *reasonable doubt*: Stephen, *A History of the Criminal Law in England*, vol. 1, p. 437.

194 **reasonable hypothesis:** Stephen, *A General View of the Criminal Law of England*, p. 271.

195 **Charles Cottu:** Page 91 of Cottu's report, quoted in Stephen, *A History of the Criminal Law in England*, p. 439.

195 **evidence of character:** Clarification to the law on evidence of character, 1863, see Stephen, *A History of the Criminal Law in England*, p. 449.

195 **circumstantial evidence:** Stephen, *A General View of the Criminal Law of England*, p. 274.

## CHAPTER 26: THE GREAT MÜLLER CASE

197 **the start of the sessions:** Sessions at the Old Bailey took place eight times a year or, roughly, every six weeks.

197 **the grand jury:** For an explanation of how the grand jury worked in the

nineteenth century, see Bentley, *English Criminal Justice in the Nineteenth Century*, pp. 9 and 131.

197 *one trial for wilful murder*: *The Times*, 25 October 1864, p. 9 col. a.

198 *numerous and urgent*: *The Times*, 28 October 1864, p. 7 col. a.

198 **Pubs and taverns:** *Daily News*, 28 October 1864, p. 2 col. a.

198 **Old Court:** For descriptions of the Old Court at the Old Bailey Sessions House, see *The Times*, 22 October 1864, p. 11 col. a. See also Mayhew and Binny, *The Criminal Prisons of London*, 1862, p. 73 ff, and Hooper, *Central Criminal Court of London*, 1909.

199 **Allwood's coffee and dining rooms:** *Daily News*, 28 October 1864, p. 2 col. a.

199 **William Ballantine:** May, *The Bar and the Old Bailey*, p. 169.

200 **opposed to the death penalty:** *Oxford Dictionary of National Biography*. On capital punishment, see *Report of the Royal Commission on Capital Punishment 1864–66*.

201 **trial witnesses:** The Treasury list of witnesses: CRIM 4/681, item 40 (reverse). Also Irving (ed.), *The Trial of Franz Müller*, introductory material.

## CHAPTER 27: THE TRIAL: FIRST DAY

203 *guilty or not guilty?*: The trial chapters are based on four main sources: the Central Criminal Court trial transcripts, H. B. Irving's *Notable English Trials* series, and the court reports of *The Times* and the *Daily Telegraph* in their various editions between 28 and 31 October 1864.

## CHAPTER 28: THE TRIAL: SECOND DAY

220 **injured his standing:** *Daily Telegraph*, 29 October 1864, p. 2 col. a.

225 **summarise the defence's case:** Ewart's Act (The Prisoners' Counsel Act) of 1836 gave defence counsels the right to address juries for the first time but made no provision for them to sum up their argument once all witnesses had been called.

226 **apparently exhausted and depressed:** 'The Murder of Mr Briggs', *Freeman's Journal*, 29 October 1864, no page col. d.

## CHAPTER 29: THE TRIAL: THIRD DAY

230 *Stupid and confused*: *Daily Telegraph*, 31 October 1864, p. 2 col. a.

233 *massive, sinewy hands*: *The Times*, 31 October 1864, p. 7 col. a.

234 *the scene in court*: Daily Telegraph, 31 October 1864, p. 2 col. b.

234 **denied fire, food or refreshment**: Bentley, *English Criminal Justice in the Nineteenth Century*, p. 270 ff.

236 **black cloth over his wig**: The black cloth was traditionally donned by judges prior to delivering a sentence of death.

236 *Prisoner at the bar*: Irving (ed.), *The Trial of Franz Müller*, p. 147.

## CHAPTER 30: THE SHADOW OF DOUBT

238 **The new cell was long and narrow**: Mayhew and Binny, *The Criminal Prisons of London*, p. 601 ff.

238 **Müller turned twenty-four**: Müller was born 31 October 1840, according to the Home Office report from the consul in Cologne. MEO 3/75, dated 27 August 1864.

238 **rarely been** *equalled*: The Times, 31 October 1864, p. 6 col. b.

239 *there ought not to rest*: Ibid.

239 *a lurking doubt*: Daily Telegraph, 31 October 1864, p. 4 col. e.

240 **to appeal to the Queen's mercy**: Prior to Victoria's accession, appeals went directly to the monarch. See Gatrell, *The Hanging Tree*, p. 201.

240 **They were not unusual**: See Gatrell, op. cit., p. 207.

240 **Mary Hartley's death sentence**: The Times, 27 August 1864, p. 12 col. b.

240 **The consensus was that**: London correspondent, New York Times, 17 November 1864.

241 *effect was ... that of a slaughtering*: 'Execution of Bousfield', Morning Chronicle, 1 April 1856.

241 **did** *not answer their purpose*: Cooper, *Executions and the British Experience*, chapter 4, p. 78 ff.

241 **vigorously to be debated**: Today we are equally exercised by the question of how a civilised society is to behave and concerned about the example we sets to the rest of the world; particularly with regard to the justification of incarceration without trial (e.g. Guantanamo Bay), extraordinary rendition and the politically sanctioned yet secret torture of terrorist suspects.

241 *deterred, or frightened or moralised*: Thackeray, *The Paris Sketchbook*, p. 254.

242 *Where is the reason*: Thackeray, 'Going to see a Man Hanged', *Fraser's Magazine*, vol. 22, August 1840, p. 150.

242 *odious levity*: Collins, *Dickens and Crime*, 1962, p. 226. For more on Thackeray and Dickens' writing on capital punishment during the 1840s, see Wilson, *The Victorians*, p. 336 ff, and Barry Faulk's opening essay in *Executions and the British Experience*.

242 **abandoned his abolitionist stance:** *Daily News* (5 articles), 1846, three reprinted in editions of Dickens' *Miscellaneous Pieces*. *The Times* (2 letters), 1849, *Letters of Charles Dickens*, vol. 5, p. 642 ff. See also Schwarzbach's essay in *Executions and the British Experience*, p. 94.

242 **crowd of thirty thousand:** 'The Great Exhibition of Hanging', *Lloyd's Weekly Newspaper*, 28 February 1864.

243 **a perplexing inconsistency:** *Reynolds's Weekly Newspaper*, 6 November 1864, p. 1 col. a.

243 *a solid pyramid of facts*: *Daily News*, 5 November 1864, p. 4 col. b.

243 **letters in their hundreds:** Letters from Home Office file HO 12/152/63401 (first bundle).

245 **What he needed was new evidence:** *Daily News*, 4 November 1864, p. 3 col. d.

245 **Neither man was able to recognise the other:** *The Times*, 5 November 1864, p. 9 col. e.

246 *small token of our appreciation*: MEPO 3/76, 8 November 1864.

246 *his help in this case*: MEPO 3/76, letter from Greenwood at the Treasury to Mayne dated 2 November 1864.

246 **Jonathan Matthews wrote:** MEPO 3/76, 8 November 1864.


CHAPTER 31: CONDEMNED FOR A THUMBMARK

247 **sold in their hundreds of thousands:** Hindley, *A History of the Catnach Press*, pp. 65–8. A similar pamphlet on the Road House murders was said to have sold thirty thousand copies, while execution broadsides in the 1840s regularly sold between 1.5 and 2.5 million copies. Copies of pamphlets relating to Müller are found in MEPO 3/76 and also, annotated by George Grey, in HO 12/152/63401.

248 *Digance and HIS hat*: MEPO 3/76, pamphlet 'Has Müller been tried?'

248 **James Walter Smith:** *Daily News*, 11 November 1864, p. 2 col. e.

248 *this kind of new evidence would demand a new trial*: MEPO 3/76, 10 November 1864.

248 **W. F. Finlason:** HO 12/152/63401 (first bundle), 11 November 1864.

249 **most judges remained unconvinced:** The M'Naghten Rule, languishing behind science, was superseded by the Durham Rule in 1954 which set a precedent for diminished responsibility. I am grateful for the advice of Professor Ireland from Aberystwyth on the nineteenth-century legal attitude to the plea of insanity. See also Smith, *Trial by Medicine*, p. 107 ff.

250 *any one of three verdicts*: Stephen, *A History of the Criminal Law of England*, p. 175.

251  **Ellen Blyth answered the question:** Müller's Memorial. Also reported *The Times*, 9 November 1864, p. 10 col. d.

251  **inveterate publicity-seeker and reputed fraud:** For example, newspaper clips from the *Norwich Argus*, February and March 1864, filed in HO 12/152/63401 (second bundle).

251  **the chemist had made a statement:** *Glasgow Herald*, 7 November 1864, p. 3 col. c.

253  **decline to meet them:** Handwritten note on printed form of deposition in HO 12/152/63401 (first bundle, attached to Grey's notes considering each angle of the Memorial).

253  **sit *en permanence*:** For example, *The Times*, 11 November 1864, p. 5 col. c.

253  **his warders ... certain:** *Daily Telegraph*, 12 November 1864, p. 3 col. c.

253  *worthy of most serious consideration:* *Evening Star*, 10 November 1864.

254  **obtained permission to visit Newgate:** A claim made by Donald Shaw in *London in the Sixties, with a Few Digressions, by One of the Old Brigade* (London: Everett, 1908).

254  *no one has more strongly felt:* HO 12/152/36401, Battiscombe's letter, dated 10 November 1864.

255  **sold for up to four pounds:** Preparations for the execution were widely reported. See e.g. *Observer*, 13 November 1864, p. 6.

255  **a treaty of peace:** In 1866 Prussia went to war with Austria, establishing a swift victory. The Franco-Prussian War of 1870–1 resulted in the French conceding Alsace-Lorraine. Germany was united into a federal system in 1871 with the king now becoming Emperor (or Kaiser).

255  **a Continental rival:** Wilson, *The Victorians*, pp. 350–1.

255  **Opinion was growing in Germany:** Browne, *The Rise of Scotland Yard*, p. 167.


## CHAPTER 32: CITY OF DEVILS

257  **pea soupers:** See e.g. Miller, *Picturesque Sketches of London*, p. 243 ff.

257  **Sir George Grey wrote that:** HO 13/108, dated 12 November 1864.

257  **made his peace with God:** *Daily Telegraph*, 14 November 1864, p. 3 col. b.

258  **A private draft statement:** HO 12/152/63401, Grey's handwritten statement, dated 10 November 1864.

259  **Mullins stood on the scaffold:** *The Times*, 20 November 1861, p. 4 col. g.

261  *a great change has come over the public opinion:* *Manchester Guardian*, 9 August 1864, p. 4.

CHAPTER 33: ST SEPULCHRE'S BELL

262 **amazement at the appeals:** HO 12/152/36401 (second bundle), 13 November 1864.

263 **Richard Stevens:** Ibid.

263 **Briggs family gave vent:** *The Times*, 17 November 1864, p. 10 col. f. See GLPS reply and editorial, *The Times*, 23 November 1864, p. 12 col. e and p. 8 col. f.

264 **strong force of police:** MEPO 7/25, Police Orders Book 'Directions for Policing the Execution'. Taverns: *Daily Telegraph*, 14 November 1864, p. 5 col. c.

264 **a network of bones:** *The Times*, 15 November 1864, p. 9.

264 **the full moon:** A penumbral lunar eclipse, which would be difficult to see even on a clear night.

265 **the aldermen and sheriffs:** 'The Briggs Murder Case', *Brisbane Courier*, 25 January 1865.

265 **Crossing the yard:** Dickens, 'A Visit to Newgate', *Sketches by 'Boz'*.

266 *Populus*: Thackeray, 'Going to see a Man Hanged', *Fraser's Magazine*, vol. 22, August 1840, p. 150. Also Miller, *Picturesque Sketches of London*, p. 185 ff.

267 *the stripling*: *The Times*, 15 November 1864, p. 9 col. c.

267 *the slight, slow vibrations of the body*: *The Times*, 15 November 1864, p. 9 col. b.

268 **beneath the flagstones:** Mayhew and Binny, *The Criminal Prisons of London*, p. 609 ff.

268 *rest calmly in well-warranted confidence*: *Daily News*, 14 November 1864, p. 4 col. b.

269 **sheriffs immediately relayed the news:** HO 12/152/63401 (second bundle), Newgate 14 November statement from Under Sheriff Septimus Davidson.

269 **decided to seal up the papers:** *The Times*, 15 November 1864, p. 9 col.d, reprised *The Times*, 16 November 1864, p. 10 col. d.

269 **a letter sent to Dr Juch:** The *Daily News* was one of the first to report Cappel's statement in its second edition, 14 November 1864, p. 5 col. e. The letter to the *Hermann* was printed in *The Times*, 22 November 1864, p. 5 col. e.

269 **fence with words:** Dr Cappel's letter to *The Times*, 16 November 1864, p. 10 col. d.

269 *the good people all happy*: Braddon, *Lady Audley's Secret*, p. 355.

269 **turn violence into order:** Beth Kalikoff, 'The Execution of Tess d'Urberville', Thesing (ed.), *Execution and the British Experience*, p. 111 ff.

270 **general *uneasiness***: *Daily Telegraph*, 15 November 1864, p. 2. col. a.

270 ***sudden and effectual attack***: *Daily Telegraph*, 15 November 1864, p. 2. col. a.


# AFTERWORD: CERTAINTY

271 ***The Times* followed the example of the *Daily Telegraph***: Bentley, *English Criminal Justice in the Nineteenth Century*, p. 46 ff.

271 **diminishing the standards of proof:** Ibid., p. 205.

271 **growing feeling against public hanging:** For the different contemporary arguments, see Hill, *The Substitute for Capital Punishment* and Block and Hostettler, *Hanging in the Balance*.

272 **Parry believed emphatically:** *Report of the Royal Commission on Capital Punishment 1864–66*.

272 **when Gathorne Hardy became Home Secretary:** Capital Punishment within Prisons Bill 1867.

272 **the feminisation of the mind of the country:** Hansard, House of Commons debate, 21 April 1868. Also Annual Register 1868, p. 17.

272 ***a wild, rough crowd***: Description of Barrett's hanging, *The Times*, 27 May 1864, p. 9.

272 **convicts were individuals:** Gatrell, *The Hanging Tree*, p. 590.

272 ***tide of ever-advancing civilisation***: Hansard, debate on abolition, 12 June 1877.

273 **the defence were given the last word:** Criminal Procedure (Right of Reply) Act 1964.

273 **duty of the Crown to disclose material:** Bentley, *English Criminal Justice in the Nineteenth Century*, p. 300.

274 ***those cramped-up boxes***: 'Müller, the Railway Murderer', *New York Times*, 3 December 1864.

274 **train *of the American pattern***: Pendleton, *Our Railways*, vol. 2, p. 210.

274 ***lest the third-class passenger should take a walking tour***: Ibid.

274 **internal wires which gradually applied the brake:** Spence, *Victorian and Edwardian Railway Travel*, introduction, p. iii.

274 ***respectability demanded not a victim but the victim***: *Daily Telegraph*, second edition, 14 November 1864, p. 4 col. c.

275 ***held by the blades***: *The Times*, 16 November 1864, p. 10 col. c.

275 **already formed an opinion of Müller's guilt:** This was questioned by the *New York Times* on 1 December as details of the trial reached America. 'The Müller Trial', no page.

275 ***as eagerly as the rest***: *Daily News*, 10 November 1864, p. 3 col. c.

276 ***had not done a wilful murder***: Ibid.

277 ***frightful mistake***: Cappel's letter to *The Times* was widely reprinted

and appears in full in the *New York Times* London report of 3 December 1864.

278 *one of the most inoffensive and harmless persons*: Capital Punishment Commission Report 1866, p. x.

278 *by any novice in phrenology*: HO 12/152/63401 (second bundle). Also *Liverpool Mercury*, 19 November 1864. Dr Donovan's report, 'Phrenological Examination of Müller's Head', *Caledonian Mercury*, 18 November 1864.

278 *the true type of the murderer*: Donovan's report, op. cit.

279 *I confess that I covet your skull*: Conan Doyle, *The Hound of the Baskervilles*, chapter 1.

280 **Horsemonger Lane debtors' gaol:** *Birmingham Daily Post*, 6 December 1864, p. 2 col. g.

280 **an odd twist of fate:** MEPO 3/76. See correspondence between 25 November 1864 and 28 March 1865.

280 **still quietly petitioning:** HO 13/108.

280 **an address remarkably similar:** *Observer*, 26 March 1905, p. 3.

281 **the Müller cut-down:** Cunnington, *Handbook of English Costume in the Nineteenth Century*, p. 282 ff.

# Index